A Place Called Chinese America

A Place Called
Chinese America

Diane Mei Lin Mark
and Ginger Chih

Cover photograph: Lee Toma family, circa 1895. Courtesy, Chong How Fo family

Frontispiece: Arizona Historical Society

Chapter opening photographs: Courtesy of:

1. Institute of Texas Cultures
2. Arizona Historical Society
3. Colorado Historical Society
4. Library of Congress
5. Arizona Historical Society
6. Kenneth and Ida Lim
7. National Archives
8. Hawaii State Archives
9. Yuri Kochiyama
10. Susan Cook
11. Ginger Chih

Cover and book design: Nancy Kirsch Sugihara

Printed in the United States of America

A 402632 01

Contents

Preface

Chinese America is a growing population of people, an articulation of experience, and a place of heart. It is the labor and achievement of 135 years in this country. It is the spirit which inspired the journey to Gold Mountain, and transformed struggle into dignity.

The main purpose of this book is to examine the dynamics of our history, culture, and community. We hope that our readers will gain a sense of the vitality of Chinese America through the many oral history excerpts and photographs, most of which are published here for the first time.

Our first chapters discuss the early contact between China and America, the conditions in mid-nineteenth century China which led tens of thousands of her people to emigrate for overseas work, and the early experience of Chinese in the United States. Although the Chinese were originally attracted to California by the Gold Rush, their presence in the United States coincided with the young nation's westward movement, and the need for a labor force to develop the frontier. The Chinese built railroads which linked the continent, transformed the barren land of California into a rich farming region, and performed factory work which strengthened a growing western economy.

But from their first days in America, the Chinese encountered racist hostility. The false accusations that they were taking jobs from whites and corrupting the moral fiber of the cities snowballed into a violent Anti-Chinese Movement in the 1870s and 1880s. Chinese immigration was restricted with the Chinese Exclusion Act of 1882, the first United States law to discriminate on the basis of race. Successive laws extended the inequities to other areas of Chinese American life as well.

In the midst of this social and legislative discrimination, the Chinese managed not only to survive, but to build a community and contribute significantly to American society. We examine the creation of the original Chinatown bachelor societies and a complex system of organizations to provide order, maintain the culture, and serve as surrogate families.

A special chapter discusses the wives of the pioneer immigrants, their traditional role in China, and how the arrival of women changed Chinatown society. In the first decades of the twentieth century, there was the beginning of a new generation born in the United States.

Chapter 6 is the midpoint of our chronicle. Although America's Chinese were elated by the founding of the Chinese Republic in 1911, China's regression into political and social unrest in the next decades made life in the United States a better alternative for the immigrants. The Chinese began to regard America as home, yet were not fully accepted.

But World War II presented an entirely new set of circumstances. China and the United States were allies, and Chinese Americans demonstrated their loyalty in both the military and the civilian war effort. The slow process of clearing legalized discrimination from the law books began with the repeal of the Chinese exclusion legislation in 1943. Both psychologically and politically, this period was a turning point in Chinese American history. For the first time, Chinese could apply for citizenship, own property, qualify for government employment, and live in areas other than Chinatown. The Chinese discovered that legal changes did not result in the immediate transformation of public attitudes, but they persisted in their entry into these new realms of American society. In their bid for mainstream acceptance, however, a culture was almost lost.

In the late 1960s, young Chinese Americans, inspired by the social movements of the period, began to seek out a lost identity. They found that the story of Chinese America, absent from their school books, was one in which they could take great pride. They discovered and gave new forms to a revitalized Chinese American culture. Chinese American political activists turned their attention to such growing Chinatown problems as housing, health, youth gangs, and employment.

The last chapters of the book highlight the events and issues of the recent past, and show that the concept of Chinese America is, most importantly, one of growth and diversity. Chinese America is composed of people from a wide range of geographical backgrounds, classes, generations, and political persuasions. Some Chinese Americans are from families which have been here for six or seven generations, while others are new immigrants who are still adjusting to this new land. Some Chinese Americans have been given widespread recognition for their achievements. Many others wage daily struggles to support themselves in Chinatown ghettos. It has been our intent to provide an overall perspective with regard to all these different elements in our community. We have also attempted to present Chinese American history in the contexts of domestic United States history and the relationship between the United States and China.

We express our sincere gratitude to the countless people who helped us bring this publication from concept to fruition. The Organization of Chinese Americans, Inc. (OCA), a national advocacy organization of concerned Chinese Americans, proposed and sponsored the project. The United States Department of Education supplied grant funding for its development. Special thanks to our Project Officer Catherine Z. Brown and Carl P. Epstein, former acting director of the Department's Ethnic Studies Program. Kung-Lee Wang, founder and first national president of OCA, served as the hardworking chairman of our advisory board, and also took responsibility for overall management and liason work among the many parties involved. Hayden Lee, OCA's former Executive Director, provided key support in research, budgeting, and administration.

Advisory Board members Irma Tam Soong, Dr. Stanley Sue, Dr. Samuel Chu, Beulah Kwoh, Dr. Ai-li Chin, Charles Moy, and Dr. Otis Shao offered constructive ideas and critiques at the first and final stages of the project. Wan-go and Virginia Weng lent their efforts to funding procurement and initial conceptualization.

In the course of research for this book, we travelled across the country, stopping in each region to interview people, collect photographs and observe Chinese American communities as they exist today. In each area there were OCA members and project supporters who provided invaluable research assistance and introductions. There were also a great many people who took time to share their life stories and family albums with us. The long list of these men and women is included in the Appendices. We extend our heartfelt thanks to each of them.

Teru Kanazawa transcribed a large volume of taped interviews. Liz Hohl, Laureen Wong, George Cooper, and Dr. Charles Lee gave us detailed readings of the manuscript. Him Mark Lai proffered research advice and shared a much-appreciated manuscript review. We are grateful to our editor Rosemary Eakins for her skilled assistance in the final polishing of the text and our designer Nancy Kirsh Sugihara and Kenzi Sugihara for their expert production advice and encouragement.

We thank our families and friends for their support throughout the project. And last but not least, we celebrate the Chinese American pioneers, past and present, who are the inspiration for this book.

The Organization of Chinese Americans

Founded in 1973, the Organization of Chinese Americans, Inc. (OCA) is a non-profit, non-partisan advocacy organization of concerned Chinese Americans. It operates a national office in Washington D.C. and has developed over twenty chapters throughout the United States. OCA is dedicated to securing the inherent rights of Chinese American citizens and permanent residents and lobbies on Capitol Hill in their interests.

The primary objectives of OCA include: upholding the Constitution of the United States; fostering democracy; promoting active participation of Chinese Americans in civic and national life; securing justice, equal opportunity and equal treatment of Chinese Americans; eliminating prejudices and ignorance and enhancing the image of Chinese in America; promoting the cultural heritage of Chinese and other Asians.

OCA's Political Education Committee identifies and builds support around issues affecting Chinese Americans. OCA takes no collective position on the politics of any foreign country, but concentrates instead on the political status of Chinese in America. OCA's Business Advisory Council directs its attention to the fields of American business and industry. The Organization of Chinese American Women articulates the particular concerns of women. The local chapters foster leadership and membership participation, and sponsor special projects. OCA's national newsletter, *Image*, is distributed bi-monthly to members and other community organizations. It communicates information regarding federal programs and legislation as well as OCA concerns and chapter activities throughout the country. Every two years, the organization holds a national convention with an educational symposium which addresses areas of concern to Chinese and other Asian Americans. Public participation is welcomed.

In the 1980s, OCA will work towards:

*liberalization of immigration quota policies for Chinese applicants;

*expansion of bilingual and bicultural educational programs;

*initiation of bilingual vocational training for new immigrants, refugees, school dropouts, and former youth gang members;

*improvement of resettlement programs for refugees from China, Southeast Asia, and Hong Kong;

*resolution of economic development issues such as Small Business Administration assistance for qualified Asian Americans;

*declaration of an annual Asian and Pacific American Heritage Week by Executive Order;

*support of equal opportunity employment, including upward mobility management training for Asian Americans and assessment of government and foundation programs for minorities.

A Place Called Chinese America

1 Beginnings

In the fifth-century pages of Chinese history, the explorer-priest Hui Shen announced the discovery of a distant kingdom called Fusang. The foreign land was peaceful and civilized, he reported, and shared its name with a tree from which natives stripped bark for clothing and paper. A written language was in use. In marriage the woman chose the man. But perhaps even more surprising than this social custom was the absence of two others: wars and taxes.[1]

If Fusang, 7,000 miles east of Tahan, was indeed the west coast of North America, as some historians have contended, then this Buddhist priest and his fellow missionaries were the first Chinese to see America, nearly 1,000 years before Columbus.

The earliest Chinese in North America mentioned in Western records, however, were several crewmen, craftsmen, and domestic servants who arrived on Spanish galleons in the sixteenth century. Beginning in 1565, the vessels sailed annually between Mexico and the Philippines, where many Chinese traders had settled in years previous. A number of Chinese journeyed eastward from there to Baja California and Acapulco, Mexico.

United States-China Clipper Trade

In the late 1770s the newly-formed United States of America, seeking to strengthen its economic base, turned to the wealth of China, following the example of many European nations. Americans had shown a growing interest in purchasing silk, porcelain, tea, lacquer ware, furniture, and other Chinese goods.

In 1784 the *Empress of China*, the first American ship to travel the trade route to China, set sail with a cargo of thirty tons of ginseng, in addition to pig lead, pepper, woolen clothing and skins. Interested merchants saw that upon her return to New York, laden with Chinese goods, the *Empress of China* realized a twenty-five percent profit on an original investment of $120,000. Other American vessels soon followed her example, and the China Trade became a lucrative enterprise. Between 1794 and 1812, American ships made 400 voyages to China.[2]

European and American vessels docking at Guangzhou (Canton) hired Chinese crewmen for the return voyage. In 1785, the *Pallas* sailed into Baltimore harbor, and among its crew members were three Chinese: Ashing, Achun, and Accun. The men lived in Maryland and Philadelphia under the sponsorship of Levi Hollingsworth, a merchant, for almost a year. They were the first Chinese known to have lived in the United States.

Trading ships also took Chinese to various ports on the Pacific coast of North America. Several Chinese carpenters and smiths were with English Captain John Meares when he established a settlement at Nootka Sound on Vancouver Island in 1788.

Captain James Cook's "discovery" of the Hawaiian Islands in 1778 established Hawaii as a key stopping point on the trade route between China and the Pacific coast of the Americas. In 1789, Captain Simon Metcalf sailed the schooner *Eleanora* from Macao to the Pacific Northwest, with a stopover in Hawaii. His crew was composed of ten Americans and forty-five Chinese. The islands became even more important to traders when it was discovered that sandalwood, cherished in China for its use in incense, fans, and carved art, flourished in the Hawaiian mountains. Soon Hawaii became known to the Chinese as Tan Heong San, or the "Sandalwood Mountains." Between 1790 and 1840, thirty-six-million pounds of the wood were exported to China.[3]

In Monterey, records indicate that Chinese were confirmed in Christian churches possibly as early as 1793. José Augustin de los Reyes of Macao, conceivably a Chinese who had adopted a Western name, is the first mentioned. The second, listed in 1815, is Ah Nam of Chinsam, who was employed as a cook for Governor de Sóla.

The initial maritime trading voyages established ocean connections between China and countless ports in the West. Although Chinese continued to arrive in America as seamen, craftsmen, domestics, students, and merchants during the first half of the nineteenth century, immigration was limited and privately-funded. Immigration records from 1820 to 1849 list only forty-three Chinese in the United States.

The Opening of China

For 4,000 years, China had been a self-contained nation which maintained minimal contact with the outside world. She called herself Zhong Guo, the Middle Kingdom—center of the world's civilization. Although treaty ports were established in the

A 1780 painting of the "Thirteen Factories" in Guangzhou, by an unidentified Chinese artist. (Peabody Museum of Salem)

sixteenth century to allow some foreign access to the country, the Chinese government enforced many restrictions. Transactions could only be made with the Hongs, Chinese merchant guilds which were given monopolies to act as brokers. All business was conducted in the waterfront area outside Guangzhou known as the Thirteen Factories. Periodically, the Manchu emperor insisted that all foreign traders and diplomats kowtow in tribute to him. But the China enterprise was so profitable that foreign traders restrained protest and acquiesced to the Chinese rules.

In the mid-nineteenth century, a series of events culminating in China's defeat in the Opium War forced the Empire to abandon its isolationist policies. Although opium had been imported into China since the seventeenth century, in the nineteenth century, the British used opium to offset a trade imbalance which had developed to their disadvantage. To regain the silver she was transferring into the Chinese economy, Britain increased Chinese import of the habit-forming drug, accepting only silver as payment. Opium traders made huge profits and eventually Britian's commercial expansion came to depend on the sale of opium. Although Chinese government edicts prohibited the selling and smoking of opium, the trade flourished. While 4,500 chests were imported annually from 1800–1821, by 1838, the average volume imported had increased to 40,000 chests a year.[4]

In an attempt to control drug sales, Commissioner Lin Tse-hsu was sent to Guangzhou in 1839 to eradicate the opium trade. Lin confined the British to the Thirteen Factories for six weeks, confiscated 20,000 chests of the drug and burned six-million dollars' worth.

Britain responded with the cry of battle, and the first shots of the Opium War were fired. From 1839 to 1842, the Chinese navy, equipped only with wooden war junks and archaic weapons, battled the modern British navy along the Chinese coast and was beaten at almost every turn. Finally the Chinese government saw no choice but to sign the Nanjin (Nanking) Treaty, on Britain's terms. The treaty abolished the old trade system and opened Guangzhou, Shanghai, Xiamen (Amoy), Ningbo (Ningpo) and Fuzhou (Foochow) to foreign residents and trade under the protection of foreign councils. It also ceded Hong Kong to England. The United States and France quickly took advantage

Wooden junks maintained by the Qing government were no match for the iron steamers of the British navy.
(New York Public Library)

of the new political situation and were awarded similar privileges. This agreement became known as the first of the Unequal Treaties.

The Opium War and subsequent diplomatic dealings with China revealed to the West the declining power of the Qing (Ch'ing) Dynasty's Manchu rulers, who had controlled China since 1644. China's humiliating loss in the Opium War and her own internal turmoil received full and sensational coverage in the American press. This early, negative, image would later affect American attitudes towards Chinese immigrants.

In addition to the expansion of trade, the Nanjin Treaty brought more Christian missionaries to China. European and American missionaries established churches and mission schools throughout

China. In later years, a sizeable number of their converts emigrated to America as workers, students,[5] and even missionaries to Chinese communities. But often the Chinese saw the Western missionary in China as a foreign element bent on disrupting the Confucian order of their society. For example, the Chinese felt that the education of women, proposed by the missionaries, was bound to disrupt the male-dominated marriage relationship.

Decline of the Qing Dynasty

In Chinese legend, the decay of a dynasty and its loss of Heavenly Mandate was portended by mass famine, flooding, peasant revolts, and official corruption. In the 1840s, China suffered all of these crises. Staple crops were ruined by drought and floods in 1846 and 1848, and the people suffered massive starvation and poverty. Rather than assisting its subjects, the Manchu court sent its militia to challenge precious land ownership in besieged areas. The heightened differences between the rulers and those chafing under their rule caused peasant revolts throughout the land. Secret societies such as the Hung Men, or Heaven and Earth Society, resumed active operations.

Perhaps the most famous of these mass revolts was the Taiping Rebellion. Its leader, Hung Hsiuch'uan, was a Hakka clansman who felt divinely inspired to lead a fight for the *Taiping Tienguo* or Heavenly Kingdom of Great Peace. His gospel combined Chinese tradition with a unique interpretation of Christianity. Rallying points were human equality, women's rights, land reform, and even simplification of the Chinese language. Hung's army of converts numbered half a million, and for thirteen years battled the Imperial forces through the Yangtze Valley, leaving heavy destruction in its wake. Between 1851 and 1864, some twenty-million Chinese were killed. In the duration and force of the Taiping Rebellion and other peasant revolts was demonstrated the disillusionment and frustration of the Chinese people and their willingness to fight for radical changes in their living conditions.

Mass Emigration for Overseas Work

Struggling for survival during this troubled period, many villages sent their most able-bodied males to the cities and ports to find employment. Once there, thousands of men enlisted for work as unskilled laborers and were sent abroad to Peru, Cuba, Mexico, Southeast Asia, Canada, Hawaii and California.

A massive emigration of Chinese laborers was about to begin. It was the third largest wave of emigration in Chinese history. The first occurred in the seventh century, when groups sailed to Taiwan and the Pescadores for seasonal work in the agricultural fields. The second wave consisted of Chinese explorers, settlers and traders who journeyed to other lands after Macao was established

Studio portraits were sent back to China, furthering the myth that America's streets were indeed paved with gold. (Institute of Texan Cultures)

This is a translation of a circular distributed by a labor broker to Chinese in the port city of Guangzhou. It described the image of America believed by many Chinese as they sailed for her shores:

Americans are very rich people. They want the Chinaman to come and make him very welcome. There you will have great pay, large houses, and food and clothing of the finest description. You can write to your friends or send them money at any time and we will be responsible for the safe delivery. It is a nice country, without mandarins or soldiers. All alike; big man no larger than little man. There are a great many Chinamen there now, and it will not be a strange country. China god is there, and the agents of this house. Never fear, and you will be lucky. Come to Hong Kong, or to the sign of this house in Canton, and we will instruct you. Money is in great plenty and to spare in America. Such as wish to have wages and labor guaranteed can obtain the surety by application at this office."

as a trading post by the Portuguese in 1557. During the third wave in the mid-1800s, thousands from Guangdong Province felt compelled to leave China for work despite the Qing Dynasty law of 1712 which forbade emigration under penalty of death by beheading.

While some Chinese emigrants managed to pay for their passage by mortgaging farms or businesses, or borrowing money from relatives, most accepted one of two types of labor agreement. The first, and more oppressive, was the contract labor system. The Chinese agents who had contact with foreign merchants in the treaty ports shipped indentured laborers under contract to nations in need of cheap labor. Many unfortunate laborers were kidnapped or tricked by mercenary brokers, and then sold into service. Accounts of their inhumane treatment in South and Central America are numerous and the system was called the "pig-selling business" by the Chinese. American dealers and ships played a large role in the coolie trade,[6] and were responsible for countless deaths. In 1855, for example, nearly 300 of the 450 coolies aboard the American ship *Waverly* traveling from Swatou to Callao, Peru, died by suffocation. On other ships coolies organized mutinies. Some men committed

suicide. But the majority of coolies felt compelled to labor in the mines and fields of these host countries.

The second labor arrangement, and the more popular among emigrants to California, Southeast Asia, and Australia, was that of the credit-ticket system. Under this arrangement, the emigrant's passage was advanced by a merchant or company and deducted from his pay in the ensuing months. The system was organized by Chinese entrepreneurs. It afforded the most personal freedom for the new immigrant, but there was no protection from sponsors who wished to take advantage of his initial dependency.

Joining the Gold Rush

The discovery of gold at John Sutter's Mill in 1848 precipitated a large migration of adventurous souls to California from all over the world. By 1850, 500 Chinese had joined 58,000 other soldiers of fortune in the mines. In two years, the number of Chinese who had made their way to the gold fields had

An English-Chinese Phrase Book was compiled by Wong Sam and Assistants in San Francisco in 1875. It included sentences in English of practical value in matters of work, self-defense, recreation, and everyday survival. These are examples:

The men are striking for wages.
He assaulted me without provocation.
He claimed my mine.
I will expel him if he don't leave the place.
He tries to extort money from me.
He falsely accused me of stealing his watch.
You have violated the Constitution of this State.
He was choked to death with a lasso, by a robber.
Can I sleep here tonight?
Have you any food for me?
Have you any grass for my horse?
She is a good-for nothing huzzy [sic].
The passage money is $50 from Hong Kong to California.
Can all the people go to Heaven?
No one can go to Heaven without being a Christian.
The United States have many immigrants.
The immigration will soon stop.

increased to 25,000. The Chinese name for America, Gam San, or Mountain of Gold, was coined during this period.

One Chinese account of the early Gold Rush period tells the story of a man named Chang De-Ming, who used his ingenuity and skill to make a sizable profit panning gold in 1849. He wrote letters home to Guangzhou, urging his relative Chang Ren to come to America. Chang Ren, hearing the glowing tales of Gam San, was immediately inspired to make the Pacific journey. From brother to brother, villager to villager, word reached Guangzhou, and spread through the Pearl River Delta: in Gam San a man could strike it rich.[7]

Because of earlier contact with the West, the focal point for passage to America was Guangzhou.

At the docks, labor agents reinforced the emigrant's dreams of quick wealth to be had in hospitable foreign lands. With strong family and ancestral ties to the village, most of the emigrants considered that their journey would be merely a sojourn. The typical immigrant to Gam San was a young man from Guangdong Province who planned to spend his working years in the United States, and then return to his village and retire as a wealthy man.

"Gam San hak mo yut chin, yau bat bak!" was a popular saying of the period. It meant that if a California sojourner could not save a thousand dollars, he would surely obtain at least eight hundred.[8] California's fabled mountains of gold offered hope in troubled times.

A prelude to the hard times ahead was the long, two-month sea voyage to America during which the immigrant was crowded into the ship's hold with hundreds of others. Many were too seasick to leave their bunks. Those not sick from motion became sick from the stench. Fights broke out frequently between rival groups, such as the Hakka and Punti, or between passengers and crew. Fatalities were not uncommon.

Nearly all of the Chinese who migrated to California in the Gold Rush period disembarked at San Francisco, known to the Chinese as the Big City, or Dai Fow. In order of population size, Sacramento was called Second City, or Yee Fow, and Marysville was the Third City. Other large Chinese settlements formed at Auburn, Placerville, Nevada City, Coloma, Angels Camp, Chinese Camp, Coulterville and Hornitos. After purchasing their supplies in one of these towns, the immigrants travelled along the San Joaquin and Sacramento rivers towards the gold mines.

Chinese miners followed veins throughout the interior and crossed the California boundaries to Nevada, Oregon, British Columbia, Idaho, Montana, Colorado and South Dakota. The escapades of "John Chinaman" in the mountains of gold, complete with waist-length queue, blue pants and jacket, wide-brimmed straw hat and American boots, have won a permanent place in the folklore of the Old West.

As the Chinese miners increased in number, however, the whites became increasingly hostile to them. The Chinese were obliged to work leftover and undesirable claims from which white miners had already taken the most accessible ore. They were often beaten, robbed, and kicked off claims by other miners who considered them an economic threat. Many Chinese left the mines as a result and began cooking, washing laundry, selling supplies and providing other services for the mining communities.

By the 1860s the surface mines of California were exhausted and big corporations which could employ large-scale and modern techniques began to take control of the mining industry. Most of the white miners, too independent to work for the larger enterprises, left for gold rushes to the north and west of California. As a result, the Chinese

The rocker was a popular device used by the Chinese gold miners because it could be quickly dismantled and carried if a quick getaway was necessary.
(Nevada Historical Society)

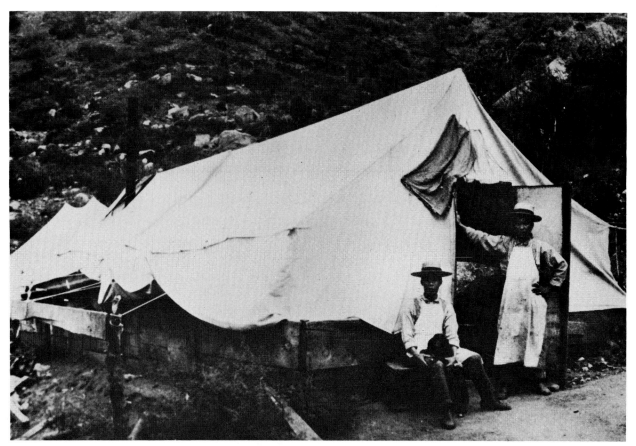

The Chinese operated the support system for many work camps. This restaurant, which was housed in a tent, served miners in Ryland mine.
(Arizona Historical Society)

were hired by the mining companies and were laboring in the mines a few years later when job-searching whites returned from exhausted veins upcountry.

With the mines well worked over by the mid-1860s, many Chinese began packing up their campsites and moving to the cities. Others moved to the coastal or agricultural areas in search of work. Some men returned to China to stay, but the vast majority saved their money for periodic visits, returning to the United States to continue their long distance support of their families. In America, they were reconciled to living in cramped, substandard quarters with other "single men," remitting the bulk of their earnings to their families in China. Their hopes of quick wealth were dimmed by the difficulties they faced in the new land, and they realized their sojourns would last many years.

Thousands of poignant separations of immigrant men and their wives are reflected in this folksong:

I beg of you, after you depart, to come back soon,
Our separation will only be a flash of time;
I only wish that you would have good fortune,
In three years you would be home again.

Also, I beg of you that your heart won't change,
That you keep your heart and mind on taking care
  of your family;
Each month or half a month send a letter home,
In two or three years my wish is to welcome you
  home.[9]

Chinese Build the Railroad

In 1864, the chairman of the Chinese Six Companies, a mutual aid organization, received a request for Chinese laborers to work on the construction of the Transcontinental Railroad. Two railroad companies were engaged by the Federal government, to be paid by the number of miles of track laid. The predominantly Irish crews of the Union Pacific were to build westward. And the Central Pacific, once it had recruited a sufficient number of workers from the sparsely-populated west coast,

was to build towards the east. The Civil War was raging and therefore there was a critical labor shortage. Unable to gather more than a few hundred white workers, Charles Crocker, the partner in charge of construction for Central Pacific, suggested to his superintendent, J. H. Strobridge,

Chinese railroad workers transported dirt by the cartload to fill in this Secrettown trestle in the Sierra Nevada Mountains.
(Southern Pacific Transportation Company)

Several snow storms in the winter of 1865–'66 piled forty-foot drifts in the Sierra Nevadas.
Workers built underground passageways and even living quarters beneath the snow.
(University of Washington Library)

that they hire Chinese workers. Strobridge argued that they were physically incapable of heavy manual work. But there was little alternative, and an initial experiment with fifty Chinese laborers led to the subsequent hiring of hundreds more after they had demonstrated their capacity for steady and excellent work. By the time of its completion, 12,000 Chinese workers had played a part in the construction of the Transcontinental Railroad.

Throughout the cruelly harsh winter of 1865–'66, the Chinese fought their way through the Sierra Nevada mountains. Successive storms piled snow into forty-foot drifts. The workers dug tunnels into an underground city below the surface and did not see the light of day for months as they traveled the underground passages from work to living quarters throughout the winter. Sometimes avalanches caused thunderous cave-ins and killed

untold numbers of men. In a few cases, whole camps hurtled down the mountainside.

In the summer of 1866 the workers were faced with the ominous task of chiseling and blasting a road through the granite walls of Cape Horn. They used picks, shovels, black powder and one-horse dump carts. Lowered in baskets, they drilled holes and placed and lit dynamite in the sides of sheer cliffs. Many were killed when they were not pulled up quickly enough, or when the ropes holding their baskets snapped—hence the origin of the expression "not a Chinaman's chance."

For their work from sunrise to sunset, six days a week, the Chinese initially received one dollar a day, or twenty-six and later thirty dollars a month. White workers received the same wages, but had their board paid as well. Groups of from twelve to twenty workers were organized among the Chinese, with a cook and a head man who purchased provisions for the men and distributed their pay, from which expenses were deducted. Their diet typically consisted of rice, salted cabbage, dried oysters, dried cuttlefish, dried fish, mushrooms, pork, poultry and boiled tea.

In protest over the adverse and inequitable working conditions, 2,000 Chinese tunnel workers in the high Sierras went on strike in June 1867. They asked for a pay raise to forty dollars a month, as well as the same eight-hour day which the white laborers were working. They also objected to being whipped or otherwise abused by company overseers. The strike startled management, but was unsuccessful because of lack of support from other workers. Wages were increased, however, to thirty-five dollars a month.

Competition between the Union Pacific and Central Pacific crews heightened as the two sets of tracks drew closer to each other. Animosity between Irish and Chinese which had developed years earlier in the gold mines sharpened the rivalry. When the Union Pacific boasted that it had laid six miles of track in one day, the Central Pacific answered with seven. The Union Pacific responded with seven and a half miles, and claimed it could do eight. Charles Crocker claimed that the Central Pacific could lay ten miles in a day—on the day before the last sixteen miles were laid, the Chinese workers laid ten miles, and added an extra 1,800 feet. In comparison to the arduous Sierra Nevada experience, laying track on flat ground was relatively quick work, the hot desert sun notwithstanding.

After six years of tremendous toil, the railroad which joined one coast of the nation to the other was completed in 1869 when the rails were joined at Promontory Point, Nevada. The joyous, back-slapping celebrations excluded the Chinese, and throughout the official ceremony, just one brief mention was made of their labor.

In search of new jobs, the Chinese dispersed and moved on. Some headed east; others returned to towns they had seen during construction of the railway; some signed up for more railroad work, such as extending the Transcontinental to the Northwest Territory. Many headed back to California, where they found jobs in rural areas or in the cities. A number returned to China.

In a Chinese-language account of the pioneer

Tea carriers kept a constant supply of hot boiled tea available for Chinese workers. This practice spared the Chinese from the dysentery which plagued other crews.
(Southern Pacific Transportation Company)

experience, an oldtimer sits back and expresses his disillusionment with the Gold Mountain dream:

> *'Let's go to America!*
> *Let's go to America!*
> *Let's go to America!'*
>
> *The cries were sung out loudly and exaltingly*
> *Thereupon America became the utopia of my grandfather's generation.*
>
> *Now here I am in this paradise.*
> *But where is it?*[10]

The early Chinese immigrant workers in America confronted grueling labor in the mines and railroads, racial hostility from others, and heartbreaking separations from loved ones. But the history of the Chinese in America, despite its bittersweet beginnings, is not a sad story. Rather, it is a story of struggle and inspiration—like a tree—the Fusang, perhaps—planted, suppressed, and blossoming again.

2 Nation Builders

In 1868, China lifted its ancient ban on emigration to foreign countries, and, because of continued strife in the villages, thousands of Guangdong Chinese set off to join their countrymen in Gam San. That same year, China and the United States signed the Burlingame Treaty, which outlined a reciprocity in trade, consuls, and immigration which had been lacking in earlier treaties between the two nations. Articles five and six extended mutual immigration privileges to their citizens:

The United States of America and the Emperor of China cordially recognize the inherent and inalienable right of man to change his home and allegiance, and also the mutual advantage of the free migration and emigration of their citizens and subjects respectively from one country to the other for the purpose of curiosity, of trade or as permanent residents.

Citizens of the United States visiting or residing in China shall enjoy the same privileges, immunities, or exemptions in respect to travel or residence as may there be enjoyed by the citizens or subjects of the most favored nation; and reciprocally, Chinese subjects visiting or residing in the United States shall enjoy the same privileges, immunities and exemptions in respect to travel or residence as may there be enjoyed by the citizens or subjects of the most favored nation. But nothing herein contained shall be held to confer naturalization upon citizens of the United States in China, nor upon the subjects of China in the United States.[1]

Although the Burlingame Treaty received immediate opposition from organized labor, American financial interests were enthralled by the potential expansion of trade and exploitation of Chinese labor. Envisioning wide expansion of American commerce, an American newspaper editor who had been accustomed to describe the Chinese as barbaric and treacherous was moved to write: "When the forefathers of our best Boston people were digging for roots in swamps and forests . . . the Chinese were rich, civilized, fertile in poets, philosophers, economists, moralists, and statesmen."[2]

For the Chinese immigrant, here was a guarantee of free immigration and a legally-defined standard of treatment in America.

Shortly after the signing of the treaty, however, the United States government, at the insistence of California, returned to the negotiation table with an ammendment which allowed the United States to regulate, limit, or suspend Chinese immigration, but "not absolutely prohibit it." Nevertheless, until the Chinese Exclusion Act of 1882, which was an outgrowth of this amendment, an average of 12,000 Chinese workers immigrated freely every year.

Despite the escalating controversy over the presence of the Chinese in California, Chinese labor was adrenalin to the western American economy. Chinese workers built the foundation for the transformation of California into one of the richest

Olives were among the many crops planted and harvested by Chinese farm workers who migrated up and down the Pacific Coast.

(Postcard, courtesy Daniel K. E. Ching)

farming regions in the United States and the world. Simultaneously, their labor in California's factories helped make possible rapid industrial development in the cities.

California

The potential for successful Gold Rush surface mining was largely exhausted by 1860, and frontiersmen and miners, many of whom were originally farmers from the Midwest and the east coast, began to turn to the land in California for work. As the settlers surveyed the region in search of farm sites, however, they were infuriated to dis-

cover that most of the State land had already been apportioned. Large grants of land had been acquired by individual speculators during the first decade of statehood. Moreover, the government had given the railroad companies ten square miles of land for each mile of track constructed. The railroad land amounted to more than 20,000,000 acres, or sixteen percent of the land formerly owned by California. By 1870, one five-hundredth of the California population monopolized one half or more of the State land available for farming use.[3]

As a result, subsistence farming, characteristic of other parts of the country, never developed in California. In 1860, the average size of a farm in California was 466 acres, in contrast to an average size of 199 acres in the rest of the country. At first, the basic California export crop was wheat, but by 1870, recession, drought and grain competition from Russia and the Mississippi Valley led to the serious consideration of other enterprises.

Growers began to consider the production of fruit and wine, for which there was a growing market. The completion of the Transcontinental Railroad in 1869 provided two major reasons for pursuing the idea. First, the railroad permitted the rapid export of crops to other states, replacing water routes which were fine for grain but impractical for perishable goods. Second, the completion of the railroad released 10,000 Chinese workers at a time when California growers were searching for a large source of labor to work the fields.

Reclamation

Much of the intended area of cultivation was located in the north central territory of the State, which was covered with swamp. These tule lands spread across the San Joaquin and Sacramento River deltas. Although delta landowners realized the rich agricultural potential of their land, it was not until the late 1860s, when the Chinese returned *en masse* from the mines and railroads, that the growers found their solution. Agricultural experience in the Pearl River Delta at home had provided the Chinese with the knowledge necessary for reclamation and irrigation work. Thousands were hired to prepare the land for use by constructing miles of levees, dikes, and ditches. Chinese skilled in hydraulic engineering directed the construction of these networks of irrigation channels. Once drained, the land was readied for crop production.

In the 1870s, the Chinese completed such ambitious projects as the reclamation of Sherman Island, which required the building of a six-foot levee around the entire island. From 1878 to 1884, Chinese workers constructed levees and drained Bouldin and Roberts Islands in preparation for planting. Chinese reclamation work was accomplished with the sole use of shovels, wheelbarrows, and the force of many workers. The men worked for days in water up to their waists, struggling to transform the marshlands into fields suitable for agriculture. Their reclamation work throughout

Vegetable peddlers walked daily from house to house, carrying fresh produce in baskets balanced on yo-yo poles.
(Nevada Historical Society)

California boosted the value of land from one to three dollars per acre to twenty to one hundred dollars per acre. This, coupled with railroad development in the State, greatly increased property value for landowners.

Agriculture

"It is quite apparent . . . that the transition from wheat to fruit acreage would have been delayed for a quarter of a century, had it not been for the presence of the Chinese in California," wrote historian Carey McWilliams. "They were a vital factor, one is inclined to state *the* vital factor, in making the transition possible."[4]

In the 1870s and 1880s, Chinese farming skill and labor developed the orchards, vineyards, farms, and hop yards which rescued the young state from industrial disaster. "The Chinese actually taught their overlords how to plant, cultivate, and harvest orchard and garden crops," wrote McWilliams. "Their skill in this work is acknowledged and it is difficult to believe that they became experts overnight. Most of their employers, moreover, were novices."[5] Fruit exports from California rose steadily, from 1,832,310 pounds in 1871 to 11,996,000 pounds in 1884.[6]

In time the growers came to regard the Chinese as the ideal workers, not only because they were reliable, but because as single men, they were easily housed in barely adequate quarters. Moreover, they were willing to migrate, leave for San Francisco or another farming region when the harvest was over, and return the next season. For the Chinese, there were few other employment options. For the growers, conditions for expanding the industry and increasing profits were excellent.

Migrant Farmwork

Chinese farmworkers were usually recruited by Chinese foremen who negotiated with the landowners, kept accounts, and paid the workers after deducting expenses. Migrant worker camps were constructed throughout the area for their use.

Throughout the 1870s and 1880s, Chinese workers moved up and down the Pacific Coast performing field labor which required constant stooping

Drying squid in the sun for shipment and sale in China. Monterey, California.
(California Historical Society)

in the hot sun. Drawing upon their own agricultural background in Guangdong, Chinese workers brought vast acreage to productivity, planting and harvesting strawberries, apples, olives, hops, sugar beets, peaches, cherries, pears, peanuts, cotton, wheat, cabbage, pumpkins and many other crops. Even during the anti-Chinese fervor of the 1880s, they made up an estimated seventy-five to eighty-five percent of the State's farmworkers.

The Chinese not only worked the land, but developed new agricultural methods and hybrid varieties of many plants. The Bing cherry was named after Ah Bing, a foreman working in Milwaukee, Oregon, in the 1870s. On the other side of the continent, in Massachusetts and later in Florida, Lue Gim Gong began in the 1880s to perfect by cross-pollenization a host of new fruits, including varieties of apples, currants, peaches, tomatoes, grapefruit and raspberries. He is best known for the orange which bears his name and for which he won the Wilder Medal from the U.S. Department of Agriculture in 1911.

By the 1900s the California fields were filled with Japanese, Filipino and Mexican laborers, but Chinese participation continued, although to a lesser degree. Into the first decades of the twentieth century, farmwork was one of the few occupations open to new Chinese immigrants. Jim and Lily Quock remember those days:

Lily: When he [Jim] first came from China, all they had was farmwork for the people who don't speak English and don't understand the language too much. That's why they sent them to the farm to work.

Interviewer: Who did you work for?

Jim: Two Chinese. They hire so many farmworkers, picking fruits, weeding.

Interviewer: Where did you live while you were working on the farm?

Jim: In a cottage.

Lily: On bunkbeds and all that, some sleep on the floor.

Interviewer: All Chinese people?

Lily: Yeah.

Interviewer: Were the people young people like you?

Jim: Old and young both.[7]

Tenant Farmers

As tenant farmers, the Chinese signed contracts to grow specified crops for landowners who often had little knowledge of farming. Various sharecropping agreements were made for furnishing equipment, marketing crops, and dividing proceeds. Chinese leased land in the California Delta, working orchards on the banks of the Sacramento River from Freeport to Isleton. Although the largest number of tenant farmers were Chinese, fields were also leased to other ethnic groups, such as the Portuguese and Italian farmers, second in number to the Chinese at this time. Each group was contracted to raise different crops, and within this division, the Chinese grew fruit, potatoes, and onions.

Sea Industries

In the 1870s, Chinese fishing communities dotted the Pacific shoreline, with a concentration situated between Monterey and Tomales Bay. Chinese junks built in California camps cruised the waters along the coast for abalone, shark, squid, sturgeon, and flounder, most of which were dried for consumption by the Chinese communities. A Chinese shrimp industry developed off Hunter's Point in the San Francisco Bay and at Point Pedro on the rim of San Pablo Bay.

The only surviving Chinese fishing village in California today is China Camp, built a century ago and located north of Point San Pedro. It was originally leased for $3,000 a year to Chinese fishermen by land owner Richard Bullis. In the days of strong anti-Chinese feeling, Bullis also became their front man and marketed the catch in San Francisco.[8] A portion of the shrimp was dried and sent to China, Japan and Hawaii. During the height of activity at China Camp, twenty to thirty tons of shrimp were caught and readied for sale each week.

Urban Factory Work

Small-scale manufacturing endeavors established by California businessmen as early as the 1850s experienced rapid growth in the 1860s, when the Civil War hindered the flow of manufactured prod-

Chinese-owned cigar companies chose English brand names to give their products an equal chance in a market hostile to the Chinese. To counter this, white cigar makers used labels to indicate that theirs were produced by white men only. (Library of Congress)

ucts from the east. Local factories prepared for increased production. Chinese workers recruited into these industries brought productivity to unprecedented levels as they had done in agriculture. After the Civil War, however, eastern factories were free to compete with the western firms, and the Chinese soon came under attack: white unions claimed that the Chinese were the cause of the decline in the economy. Through political agitation, the unions were able to drive many Chinese from the urban industries in the late 1870s and 1880s. Before this came about, however, Chinese workers had contributed substantially to the growth of those industries.

As early as 1859, Chinese workers were being hired by the cigar industry, the first manufacturing business to employ them. With Chinese labor, the production value of the California cigar industry increased from $2,000 in 1864 to $1,000,000 two years later.[9] By 1868, California had replaced Massachusetts as the fourth largest state in cigar productivity.

In 1870 ninety percent of the cigar makers in San Francisco were Chinese. George Lee of San Francisco recalls his family's involvement in the industry:

My grandparents worked in a cigar factory. This was in the 1850s. They came to the United States and they opened a cigar factory. Most of the Lees were making cigars. Right on Battery Street. Before the

CIGAR MAKERS' ASSOCIATION of the PACIFIC COAST, SAN FRANCISCO, CALIFORNIA.

The Cigars herein contained are made by

WHITE MEN.

This Label is issued by authority of the

Cigar Makers' Association of the Pacific Coast,

AND ADOPTED BY LAW.

This space is occupied by the SEAL of the CIGAR MAKERS' ASSOCIATION on genuine white label goods.

Imitations have in this place the name of the rascal who counterfeits it.

LABEL OF CIGAR MAKERS' ASSOCIATION OF THE PACIFIC COAST

Chinese-owned cigar companies chose English brand names to give their products an equal chance in a market hostile to the Chinese. To counter this, white cigar makers used labels to indicate that theirs were produced by white men only. (Library of Congress)

earthquake. Eighty to ninety workers in the factory. All Chinese.

After the earthquake, why, we moved to some place else. There was a cigar factory on Richmond Street and they stayed there for another 30, 40, 50 years. Then they stopped. There are no more hand-made cigars—all machine-made now. So, my grandfather and my father and my brothers all worked in a cigar factory.[10]

California shoe manufacturers, also competing with east coast industry, found Chinese workers to be the solution to their problems. By 1873, Chinese workers were responsible for half of the shoes and boots produced in California. Because of the quality and availability of Chinese labor, the industry grew from a $1.5 million business in 1870 to a $3 million enterprise in 1875.[11]

While the work in east coast garment factories was performed by European immigrant women, California factories primarily employed Chinese men. In crowded sweatshops, Chinese produced dresses, shirts, work clothes and undergarments for the San Francisco market, reducing the State's need to import east coast merchandise. Chinese were also recruited to work in the earliest woolen mills in California in the late 1850s, and they were the labor force which made possible the expansion of that industry through the 1860s and the 1870s. By 1873, they comprised eighty percent of the workers in the woolen industry.[12]

In each of these industries, factory owners tal-

lied handsome profits while shop conditions and wages became an increasing point of contention between workers and owners. Chinese workers, denied entry into white unions, organized themselves and voiced their grievances. In the cigar industry, for example, the Hall of Common Virtue, a Chinese guild, won pay increases by striking and forming closed shops.

The entry of Chinese workers into the manufacturing industries was prompted by the shortage of white labor in California. White men in the cities were in a position to seek more lucrative work and avoided the garment and other industries, which on the east coast employed women and children. By 1870, Chinese workers had developed the tobacco, shoe, and woolen industries to rank among the major enterprises of California. When white workers found themselves in need of work during the recession of the 1870s, they pressured factory owners to dismiss the Chinese, claiming that they were depriving white men of work. Having learned the trades, more Chinese organized their own shops, as they had begun to do in the 1860s. By the mid-1870s, Chinese boot and shoe workers were largely employed by their fellow Chinese. With the hiring of white labor in other industry shops, wages increased, so that the cost of labor was higher than it was for the east coast competition. This, coupled with the development of better equipment and production techniques in the east, forced the decline of most of the small manufacturing industries in California by the 1880s.

Other Regions

From the 1860s to the 1880s railroad work brought the Chinese to nearly every region under development in America. Thousands of laborers left California for work in the Pacific Northwest, the Southwest and the South. Veteran rail workers from the Transcontinental line were joined by more recently-arrived workers in the work force

of the Northern Pacific and Canadian Pacific railroads, which were both completed in the mid-1880s. The Northern Pacific Railroad, constructed across Washington, Idaho and Montana, employed 15,000 Chinese, who comprised two-thirds of its western division labor force. Upon its completion, they worked on other railroad projects which joined Portland to Puget Sound and Seattle and Tacoma to the eastern regions of Washington. They also completed a section of the Seattle-Walla Walla railway which transformed Seattle into the main coaling port on the west coast.[13]

In the Southwest, the Chinese built the Southern Pacific Railroad eastward across Arizona, New Mexico, and southward to San Antonio, Texas. In the South, Chinese workers were hired in the 1870s and 1880s to construct segments of the Alabama and Chattanooga Railroad, the Texas and Pacific Railway, and a line in Georgia. When the rail work was completed in these areas, many Chinese returned to California, but others settled in the South and Southwest, filling a variety of regional labor needs and forming small communities.

Pacific Northwest

Although the Chinese were excluded from salmon fishing, by the 1870s they had become the mainstay of the canneries along the Pacific Northwest waterways to British Columbia and Alaska. In the canneries, the Chinese worked eleven hours a day, gutting and preparing the fish, hammering the cans into shape over iron cylinders, cooking, testing, and completing the canning process. Employers could find few other workers with their willingness and stamina, largely because cannery work was one of the few fields open to them in the Pacific Northwest. For their work, the Chinese

Industry competition between east and west coast shoe manufacturers prompted heavy recruitment of Chinese labor in California.
(Library of Congress)

Although they were banned from salmon fishing, the Chinese were the mainstay of the industry's canneries.

(Oregon Historical Society)

were paid one dollar a day. Although they worked in the canneries until the 1930s, they were largely replaced by Japanese and Filipino workers who arrived towards the turn of the century. One observer in the 1870s described the efficiency of Chinese cannery work:

> *The salmon, when taken to the cannery, are placed on a long table, where the head, tail and fins are cut off, and the entrails removed by a few flashing strokes of a large knife, in the hands of an expert Chinaman, the average time for each of these large fish being less than half a minute. . . .*[14]

Hundreds of Chinese laborers were contracted directly from Hong Kong to work in vast devel-

opment projects in Oregon during the 1870s and 1880s. They constructed railroad lines, cleared wilderness land, ditched swamps, and developed major roads to bring Oregon to a comparable level of growth with other parts of the west coast.

Chinese also served as an integral part of the support system of the work camps. They cooked meals, washed clothes and supplied provisions in mining camps and small towns not only in the Pacific Northwest, but throughout the country. Individuals or small groups of Chinese men often left the company of their countrymen to set up small enterprises which served a predominantly white clientele. One such person was a man known as China Joe, who settled in southeastern Alaska during the gold strikes. After working his way up the coast from San Francisco, he settled in Alaska, where he opened a store and restaurant in Fort Wrangell. Later he bought an abandoned steamer, pulled it up onto the beach and transformed it into an off-season hotel for prospectors and trappers. He welcomed everyone during the winter months, regardless of ability to pay. And in the spring, he sent them off with provisions and renewed hope for the coming season, telling them to take care of the bill when they struck it rich.[15]

Southwest

By the 1890s, farms were being developed in the rural areas of Arizona by Chinese who saw promise in the Southwest. A popular site for farming was the Silver Lake district, where Chinese rented, leased, or sometimes settled in hopes of acquiring title, working the land to productivity. There were farms along the Santa Cruz River, through Oracle, bordering on Rillito; in Fairbanks; in San Pedro

A Chinese farmsite in Oregon, before 1909.
(Oregon Historical Society)

Ching Chong Wong Provision Store, Clifton, Arizona, early 1900s.
(Arizona Historical Society)

Valley; in the Patagonia areas; and elsewhere throughout the Territory. In the 1890s the draining of Silver Lake caused the loss of irrigation water for the farms, and most Chinese moved towards towns to enter the grocery business.

John Kai arrived in Arizona from Oakland, California in 1918. He made a living by hauling dynamite to the mines, running a boarding house and supplying lumber and other goods to the mining community. When the mines closed down, he decided to farm:

I never did like the restaurant business, never liked the laundry and I grew up in the grocery business, which I did not like because you work seven days a week, every day of the year. The farming business when it's small, you have to work, when it's big it's

mass production. I never farmed before. When I saw someone was farming, I asked for all kinds of information, so I ask the fellow, a white man. Of course, we are pretty good friends. One day he said, "John, why don't you develop a piece of land? There's a lot of land around here that you can develop." I said, "How much you making?" He said, "Oh, I make very good." I said, "How much money you pay for your lease?" And he said, "I pay $20,000 to $25,000 per year, never less than $20,000."

So that woke me up, and by golly, in the old days, $20,000 is a lot of money. So, I said to my brother Bing, "Let's go farming. You know farming is a great future. You don't want a grocery business. In the farming business, you can hire a foreman." So we got into farming.[16]

The South

Southern planters, deprived of Black slaves with passage of the Thirteenth Amendment, turned to Chinese workers to solve their labor needs. In June, 1869, the Arkansas River Valley Immigration Company began a program of recruitment of Chinese workers for the local plantations, planning to import one thousand laborers from China. With Arkansas leading the way, other Southern states began discussing the merits of Chinese labor. The Memphis *Alta*, in an article entitled, "Chinamen in the South," posed the question, "[Now that the Arkansas planters] have set the ball in motion, will the people of Tennessee, Mississippi, and Alabama be backwards?"[17]

The issue of maintaining the entrenched Southern plantation system by replacing Black labor with Chinese was deemed a serious one; a full-fledged convention to discuss the matter was convened in Memphis in July, 1869. Proponents of the idea argued that introducing the Chinese would motivate the emancipated Negroes to return to their former level of productivity. Convention delegates came from Tennessee, Mississippi, Louisiana, Alabama, Georgia, South Carolina, Kentucky, Missouri and California. They voted to raise one million dollars to develop plans for bringing Chinese to the South.[18] Beyond the Memphis Convention, however, a political storm was brewing. Southern and Western Democrats found themselves on opposite sides of the Chinese issue. Opposition was voiced by those who feared an invasion of "heathen Chinee." Due to a number of reasons, the large influx of Chinese workers dreamed about at the Memphis Convention never materialized.

Chinese contingents began arriving in the South in the 1870s, although not in the predicted numbers or for the specific purpose of plantation work. The majority came as workers for various railroad projects, and, following those involvements, found work throughout the Southern region. They worked as field hands and sharecroppers in Mississippi, where, like Blacks, they led lives marred by intense racism. From plantation work, they moved to the grocery business, opening small stores in Black communities throughout the South. Georgia planters hired Chinese to tend their rice fields. Several hundred laborers brought from China to Arkansas labored on the cotton plantations but many left when other opportunities arose. As early as 1866, Louisiana sugar cane fields were worked by Chinese hands who entered the country from Cuba. They were joined in later years by Chinese from the Philippines. Eventually, the men saved enough money to leave the plantations for lives as self-employed fishermen and truck farmers.[19]

During the period, the Chinese migrated throughout the Southern states whenever work was available. Some of the men who settled in the South arrived after traveling and working in other regions of the United States as well. Edward Wong and Mamie Wong Moy remember their father's early travels in search of work:

Wong: My father worked in Newcastle, California as a fruit picker and also a fruit crater.

Moy: Then somehow, someway, he was in upstate New York, in Buffalo, Albany, Niagara Falls, as a waiter. And then, because of friends and relatives, he came down to Texas. That was the result of friends of the family who were connected with Pershing's group. When General Pershing came from Mexico, he brought a lot of the Chinese immigrants with him.

Wong: Some were already in business, and said to my father, well, come to Texas. That's what he did. I expect that's what many people did. He was employed at a store for a while and shortly thereafter acquired his own store. It's still that way. In fact, one of the families in San Antonio is there as the result of our family, when we visited California.

As the Reconstruction Era neared its end, the demand for Chinese labor in the South declined. Southern capitalists no longer saw the need for the Chinese in their overall plans for the South as Blacks rejoined the labor force. Most of the Chinese who remained in the South after the 1880s dispersed and opened grocery stores or restaurants throughout the Sun Belt.

Hawaii

Chinese labor was crucial to the growth of the mid-nineteenth century Hawaiian economy. Sugar cane was growing wild in the Hawaiian Islands at the time of Captain Cook's arrival in 1778, and pioneer

Chinese had in the early 1800s attempted to establish mills on Lanai, Maui and Kauai. But it was not until 1850 that the Royal Hawaiian Agricultural Society was formed by *haole* (Caucasian) planters to develop the industry. If the sugar planters were to succeed, the work would require thousands of laborers. The native Hawaiian population had declined drastically as foreign disease and the spirit-crushing effect of western control took their toll. Their numbers dropped from 300,000 in 1778 to 107,000 in 1836[21] to 84,165 in 1850.[22] The remaining Hawaiians showed little desire to work in the sugar fields owned by *haole* companies.

The first group of 195 Chinese laborers was brought to Hawaii from Hong Kong in 1852. When they proved capable of the work, the planters requested further recruitment. Between 1852 and 1909, 45,000 of the 219,825 laborers brought to Hawaii were Chinese. In the early years the Chinese were contracted for five years at three dollars a month, plus passage, room and board.[23] In plantation camps their lives were strictly regi-

mented, the terms of their contracts were restrictive, and, in some cases, they were abused by the *lunas*, or overseers. Many left the plantations in search of other work as soon as their five-year contracts expired, but it was their initial labor which established the sugar industry as a key factor in Hawaii's rapid economic growth. Chinese field workers were initially important in the coffee and pineapple industries as well.

While some of these early immigrants returned to China, others used their savings to open small businesses in Honolulu Chinatown. Others became independent farmers. Their crops included potatoes, corn, wheat, cabbage, onions, taro, rice, pulu fiber, bananas and garden vegetables. They raised and marketed pigs, ducks and chickens. They played the dominant role in the rice industry of the Islands, building irrigation ditches, reclaiming swamp, and converting old Hawaiian taro patches to new use. As rice field owners and laborers, Chinese met the growing demands of both local and California markets, the latter increasing dur-

From the 1850s to the 1880s, thousands of Chinese were brought to Hawaii for field work on the sugar plantations.
(Hawaii State Archives)

Many plantation workers saved their earnings and initiated small businesses after the expiration of their five-year field contracts.

(Hawaii State Archives)

ing the Civil War years when Southern sources curtailed production. At its height in 1890, the Hawaiian industry exported over ten million pounds of rice.

Chinese also introduced numerous fruits, vegetables, trees and flowers to the Islands, including the lychee, longan, sa-li (Chinese pear), kumquat, loquat, persimmon, mandarin orange, pomelo, apple-banana, bamboo, beansprout, Chinese cabbage, lotus root, pea, soybean, and many others.

As the Chinese left the plantations to organize and manage farms or businesses of their own, they came into economic competition with others. Before the turn of the century Hawaii had witnessed their rapid advancement from field workers to entrepreneurs. *Haole* and native Hawaiian economic and political interests felt threatened by their suc-

cess, and began imposing sanctions to control it.

Throughout this short period of free immigration, Chinese laborers played a major role in the development of the American West. The Chinese were recruited to perform work which others refused to accept, or for which they lacked the expertise. Later, they found themselves in the middle of labor disputes between workers and employers. They were blamed for economic conditions which were actually created by market swings and magnate avidity for profit. They were limited by statute or societal pressure to a few industries such as small manufacturing, construction and agriculture. Yet within these narrow boundaries, Chinese labor played a major role in the creation and development of industries which enriched the lives of all Americans in the years to come.

Nation Builders   27

3 The Anti-Chinese Movement

The origins of anti-Chinese sentiment in America can be traced back decades before the arrival of the first Chinese immigrant workers. In the 1780s the notions derived from Marco Polo's tales of a Celestial Kingdom endowed with fragrant plum blossoms, fine silks, and venerable philosophers were supplanted by a more negative image of China. Although some profits were made in the clipper trade, the commercial bonanza American companies were led to expect from their successes in the first period of trading failed to materialize. China had outlined strict parameters for foreign traders, designating where they could dock their ships, with whom they could trade, and what items were acceptable for the transactions. To maintain the balance of trade, American skippers combed the New World for the few items China agreed to buy, such as sea otter pelts, sandalwood, and edible snails from deserted islets. Disgruntled by these restrictions and the inability to make their projected profits, American traders exaggerated their accounts of Chinese corruption and barbarism.

Some traders expressed their frustration by scoffing at Chinese food, dress, and customs: "The first impulse of an American, when he sees for the first time a Chinese, is to laugh at him. His dress, if judged by our standards, is ridiculous, and in a Mandarin, a stately gravity sets it off for a double derision. His trousers are a couple of meal bags . . . his shoes are huge machines, turned up at the toe, his cap is fantastic and his head is shaven except on the crown, whence there hangs down a tuft of hair as long as a spaniel's tail."[1] The comparison of the queue to a spaniel's tail and other references to animals seemed designed to demean Chinese people to a sub-human, and therefore inferior, status.

Writers as well-regarded as Ralph Waldo Emerson employed their literary skills to spread the pejorative image on the homefront:

"The closer contemplation we condescend to bestow, the more disgustful is that booby nation. The Chinese Empire enjoys precisely a Mummy's reputation, that of having preserved to a hair for 3 or 4,000 years the ugliest features in the world. I have no gift to see a meaning in the venerable vegetation of this extraordinary (nation) people. They are tools for other nations to use. Even miserable Africa can say I have hewn the wood and drawn the water to promote the civilization of other lands. But China, reverend dullness! hoary ideot! [sic], all she can say at the convocation of nations must be— "I made the tea."[2]

America's image of China was also influenced by reports from Western diplomats and missionaries in service there. In published memoirs, a number of diplomats questioned the level of Chinese civilization, reporting infanticide, violent crimes, and harsh treatment of women. The state of science and medicine was considered stagnant; the rulers of the country were as despotic as its military was archaic. Conversely, other diplomats praised China, claiming that she was as civilized as the West. But these authors were in the minority.[3]

The most prolific group writing about China during this period, however, were missionaries.

29

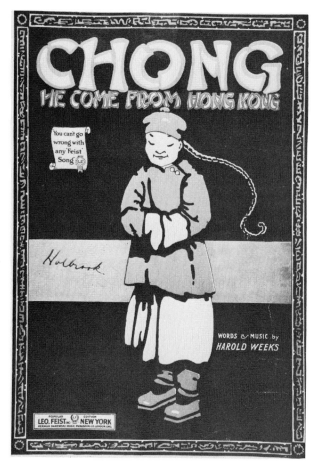

Song sheet cover. When not depicted as a threat to American society, the Chinese were subjected to comical caricatures.

(Courtesy, Daniel K. E. Ching)

Protestant missionaries began field work in China in 1807, with the arrival of the Reverend Robert Morrison, and they published quantities of books, reports, and journals during the following decades. Their concern for the salvation of souls prompted them to live closer to the Chinese than had the traders and government officials. They learned the language, founded schools, and established medical clinics. But as they made these positive efforts, their published commentaries reinforced the diminished standing of the Chinese in the eyes of the American public. The missionaries wrote that "the very name of our saviour is disapproved, if not hated by millions."[5] They referred to the Chinese as "children of darkness" who needed to be led out of heathenism and idolatry.

By 1820 an unflattering portrait of China had filtered into textbooks used in American schools.

Several authors joined in the popular derision of China, but perhaps the best known was Samuel Goodrich, who wrote under the name of Peter Parley. He penned countless gazetteers and histories for all age levels in a first person-present tense form which suggested an intimate knowledge of China. The image of China he presented in 1833 remained constant throughout his writings: "Few nations, it is now agreed, have so little honor, or feeling, or so much duplicity and mendacity. Their affected gravity is as far from wisdom, as their ceremonies are from politeness."[6]

American newspapers played a major role in forming a negative Chinese image for the American public. The penny press was born in the 1830s and by 1840 its rivalry with the more established Wall Street press fixed its battleground on the most colorful topic of the day, the China story. With sensationalized reports, the penny press stopped at nothing to out-scoop the infuriated Wall Street publishers, and gained more readers with each edition. American readers were fed a detailed account of China's crushing defeat in the Opium War (1839–'42), and even pro-Chinese publications like the *Niles National Register* conceded: "With every successful collision between the Chinese and their invaders, the imbecility of the former appears more and more manifest."[7]

In 1868, the signing of the Burlingame Treaty resulted in favorable news coverage for China because it opened the way for increased American commercial involvement. But a year later, the honeymoon between Burlingame's "New China" and the American press was over. Headlines of the Tianjin (Tientsin) Massacre of 1869, during which both Chinese and foreigners were killed, were splashed across front pages throughout the United States. The incident was just one of a series of clashes which were the result of mistrust between Chinese and foreigners. Editorials lashed out at the "pagan, almond-eyed heathens" and spoke afresh of a "yellow peril,"[8] a barbarous and uncontrollable horde.

Chinese immigrants who joined the search for California gold in the 1850s and 1860s were therefore preceded by a negative image of their motherland. Although scattered with favorable comments, the China field reports from traders, diplomats, and missionaries generally sought to prove that China did not deserve its reputation as a civilized

The anti-Chinese movement spread across the United States in the 1870s and 1880s.
(Library of Congress)

nation. Later, descriptions of Sino-Western conflicts in the popular press repeated the message of China's political and military debility.

Persecution in the Mines

Abuse of the Chinese began almost as soon as they arrived in California. Its cause was both economic and racist. Although the mines were filled with foreigners, the Chinese were visibly different because of their physical features. As the competition for the fabled ore increased, the Chinese were relegated to the ethnic floor. If they discovered a richly endowed site, they were soon driven out by other miners, for the motto in mining towns was "California for Americans!"

Antagonism towards the Chinese increased as the hills became more crowded and the gold veins were worked over. As early as 1852, the California Legislature reinstated the Foreign Miner's Tax,

which had earlier applied to Mexicans and now was aimed at the Chinese. The tax of three dollars per month was raised to four dollars in 1853 and six dollars in 1855. In 1856 the tax was reset at four dollars. From 1850 to 1870 half of the state's income came from this source.

In addition to the legitimate tax collectors, Chinese were frequently approached by "impostors" who traveled the diggings with blank licenses and fictitious receipts in hand. At the risk of being assaulted, stabbed or shot, Chinese were compelled to purchase miner's licenses, regardless of whether or not they were engaged in mining. Consequently, the Chinese miners evaded the collector whenever they could. A runner was dispatched to warn a nearby settlement when a collector was heading its way, and with this notice, the miners would break camp and retreat to the foothills for a few days. Because Chinese were not allowed to testify against whites in court, the abuse proceeded unchecked.

Gambling and opium were facets of Chinatown life which fell victim to a press eager to paint Chinatown as a hotbed of vice and degradation.
(New York Public Library)

Despite persecution, Chinese continued to seek out and work mines bearing any semblance of potential. With persistence, they were often successful with even the leanest claims already worked and abandoned by others. Infuriated by this ability, white miners began to make their own plans to dislodge their competition. In 1852, the Columbia mining district of Tuolumne County held a mass meeting during which various merchants, sponsors, and shipowners were assailed for their part in bringing Chinese to California. The miners resolved to deny district mining rights to all Asiatics and South Sea Islanders and subsequently informed other mining camps of their actions.

One mining camp after another followed suit.

Each passed general resolutions condemning Chinese and ordering them out of their districts. A notice posted in Mariposa in 1856 expressed the typical tact of intimidation:

> *Notice is hereby given to all Chinese in the Agua Fria and its tributaries, to leave within ten days of this date. Any failing to comply shall be subjected to thirty-nine lashes, and moved by force of arms.*[9]

Racist images of the Chinese were exaggerated beyond belief in town meetings, miners' conventions, and legislative assemblies. A minority report by a committee on Mines and Mining contained this statement:

> *"RESOLVED: That their [Chinese] presence here is a great moral and social evil—a disgusting scab upon the fair face of society—a putrefying sore upon the body politic—in short, a nuisance."*[10]

Chinese miners were served notice and escorted, sometimes violently, out of the mining areas. Vigilante gangs rode through the hills from the late 1850s, causing such unrest that the government sent aid to local sheriffs to stop the kidnapping and violence.

"The Chinese Must Go!"

Beyond the gold mines, anti-Chinese sentiment grew rapidly, finding fertile ground in the economic and social conditions of late nineteenth-century America. Anti-Chinese agitators complained loudest and longest about economic competition, claiming the Chinese took jobs from whites by working for low wages. Moreover, the nation was recovering from the bitterly fought Civil War, and the issue of slavery was a sensitive one. Anti-Chinese spokesmen compared Chinese laborers in the mines and railroads to Black slaves in the South. "The Chinaman is not chattel it is true," wrote Portland's *Daily Oregonian* in 1880, "but in some respects he answers the purpose of a chattel, and the social growth and development which is produced through his agency is little different from that which was fostered by southern slavery. The tendency in both cases must be to destroy the elements of white American labor; to concentrate power, wealth, and political influence in the hands of a minority, and to weaken the democratic spirit."[11]

Declining gold production in the 1870s and the completion of the Central Pacific Railroad in 1869 brought hundreds of unemployed white laborers into the western towns. Hard times had arrived. The stock market plummeted. Drought caused a decrease in farm production. The economy experienced a depression in 1873 and again in 1876. Labor unions fighting for white workers' rights in a climate of monopoly and exploitative business control misfocused their attention on the Chinese. In the ensuing anti-Chinese movement of the 1870s and 1880s Chinese were scapegoats for the frustrated anger of the white working class, while America's corporate barons generally escaped unscathed.

In August of 1870, an anti-Chinese convention held in California unified opposing elements, made much of the state's labor movement, and called for the support of east coast labor groups. Delegates passed a resolution urging the repeal of the Burlingame Treaty and a halt to Chinese immigration. Momentum was sustained by a series of mass meetings sponsored by labor unions in San Francisco. With the Republican and Democratic parties evenly matched for political control of California, the labor vote was of crucial importance to both. To win the support of labor, politicians adopted anti-Chinese platforms and drafted numerous local and state laws which attacked the customs and the means of livelihood of the Chinese:

*Sidewalk Ordinance, 1870: Prohibited persons from walking on the sidewalks while using poles to carry goods.

*Cubic Air Ordinance, 1870: Required every lodging house to have no less than 500 cubic feet of air space for each lodger. (In protest of the law, Chinese refused to pay the fines and went to jail, causing such a crowded situation that the City was in violation of its own law.)

*Queue Ordinance, 1873: Stated that every Chinese prisoner in jail should have his hair cut to one inch in length. (In China, all Chinese men were forced to wear their hair in queues to demonstrate their submission to Manchu rule. Without their queues, immigrants would not be able to re-

Anti-Chinese activists claimed that the Chinese were lowering California's standards of living by spreading disease, working for cheap wages and eating rats.
(New York Public Library)

turn home, for failure to comply with the edict was penalized by death.)

*Laundry Ordinance, 1873 and 1876: Required that every laundry employing a horse-drawn vehicle pay $2 per quarter, those with two vehicles $4 per quarter, and those with no vehicles, $15 per quarter. Most Chinese were in the third category.

Hostility towards the Chinese became so widespread among white workers that anti-Chinese agitators could arouse anti-Chinese demonstrations with minimal effort. At an 1877 San Francisco rally in support of striking east coast railroad workers, a group of agitators rallied the crowd and led them to Chinatown. Rampaging through the streets,

Denis Kearny delivered fiery sandlot speeches which attracted the support of large numbers of workingmen.
(New York Public Library)

Denis Kearney was an Irish sailor who had invested his money in mining stocks and lost it all when the market crashed. Embittered and vengeful, he took to the sandlot soapboxes to deliver fiery discourses on the evils of land and rail monopolies, and the Chinese. Through supportive publicity in the *San Francisco Chronicle,* he emerged a hero and champion of the white working class.

Kearney's *Manifesto* stated his goal and contained a sample of his racial tirades:

We have made no secret of our intentions. We make none. Before you and before the world we declare that the Chinaman must leave our shores. We declare that white men, and women, and boys, and girls, cannot live as the people of the great republic should and compete with the single Chinese coolie in the labor market. We declare that we cannot hope to drive the Chinaman away by working cheaper than he does. None but an enemy would expect it of us; none but an idiot could hope for success; none but a degraded coward and slave would make the effort. To an American, death is preferable to life on par with the Chinaman.[13]

In 1877, Kearney organized the Workingmen's Party of California, which brought the Chinese question to the national level. The party sponsored parades and conventions and agitated for legislative action. Kearney was jailed for inciting riots but upon his release found that he was even more popular with working men who shouted with him, "The Chinese Must Go!" Although the Workingmen's Party of California lasted just five years, the furor it aroused led to state and federal investigations of the Chinese question and to subsequent recommendations to end Chinese immigration.

they assaulted residents and destroyed everything in sight.

Throughout California, the slightest provocation often resulted in rioting, desecration of property, and even murder. The Los Angeles Riot of 1871 began with a fight between two feuding Chinese organizations. In the ruckus, two police officers were wounded and a civilian was killed. The news provoked a spontaneous riot. An incensed crowd charged into the Chinese quarter and, within four hours, killed eighteen Chinese and looted and burned several buildings. Protests were lodged in Washington, D.C. by the Chinese Six Companies and the Chinese government, and the United States agreed to pay indemnities to the families of victims. Arrested rioters, however, received only brief prison terms.[12]

Violence Across the Land

California labor unions, despite their noisy campaign to rid the State of the Chinese, were not making the progress they desired. Most of the state and local laws which had been passed to limit Chinese immigration and employment had been repealed. Some were found to be unconstitutional; others were impossible to enforce. Anti-Chinese forces began to realize that nothing short of an act

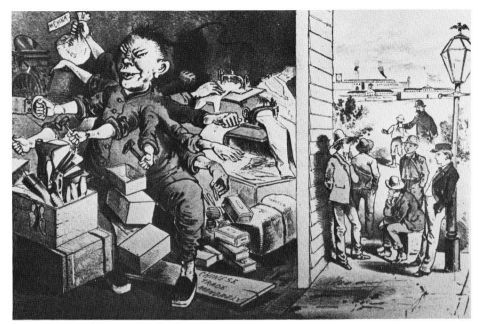

Anti-Chinese hysteria increased during the depression of the 1870s. The Chinese were scapegoats for western America's economic ills. (New York Public Library)

by the United States Congress would remove the Chinese. A nationwide appeal was instigated and by the late 1870s the anti-Chinese movement had spread to other states and territories with Chinese populations.

Although Chinese labor had built roads, mail routes, steamship lines and towns in Oregon, the Chinese were the victims of discriminatory laws and racial assaults. The most violent of these clashes was the Snake River Massacre of 1877. Ten Chinese miners who were working a claim on the Snake River in Wallowa County were attacked and murdered by seven white men, who then took flight with a reported $5,000 to $10,000 in gold dust. The three bandits who were brought to trial were acquitted.[14]

In October, 1880, a rioting mob in Denver chased the Chinese population out of Chinatown, gutted their quarters, and hanged one man. Earlier in the day, a crowd of 3,000 townspeople had gathered outside a pool hall where two whites had provoked a fight with two Chinese. The town's eight policemen on duty were joined by 125 special police and the fire department. When the Mayor failed to pacify the angry crowd he ordered the firemen to turn their hoses on the people, who responded by pelting the firemen with bricks. The Chinese scattered in all directions, many taking refuge in the wilderness. Some were protected by

sympathetic and courageous townspeople. One such person was Jim Moon, a gambler, who stood between the mob and a Chinese friend and shouted, "What in hell do you fellows want?" When he heard no response, he continued, "This Chinaman is an inoffensive man, and you shant touch him, not a—one of you!" Moon emphasized his sincerity "with the mute elegance of a leveled revolver, [and] the crowd turned abruptly away, being afraid, according to the slang phrase common in this country, 'to face the music,'" wrote an eyewitness London *Times* correspondent.[15]

In another part of the city, four Chinese were saved from the mob by Liz Preston, the madam of a local brothel. She was ably assisted, according to fireman William Roberts, by "ten Amazonian beauties" brandishing champagne bottles, stove pokers, and high-heeled shoes.

During the month preceding the attack on Chinatown, the *Rocky Mountain News* had stepped up its anti-Chinese campaign by heavily publicizing the opium overdose of a white youth on October 8. It was suggested that the Chinese be driven out of town because of their threat to white women, and to young boys who fell victim to opium dens and "Chinese harlots." The Democratic Party sponsored parades which popularized such slogans as, "Down with the Chinese; they are Robbing our Wives and Children of Bread!"[16]

By 1881, Chinese laborers had constructed the Southern Pacific Railroad to El Paso, Texas. Some 2,600 Chinese built the railroad east from El Paso to the Pecos River, where they met tracks built westward by Irish railroad workers. In addition to the driving exploitation of company foremen, Chinese laborers faced intense animosity from others, including Mexicans, Apache Indians, and whites. Numerous attacks and murders occurred. At the trial of an Irish laborer accused of murder, Judge Roy Bean ruled that there was no Texan law against "killing a Chinaman."[17]

Anti-Chinese sentiment was rife in all regions where substantial numbers of Chinese had immigrated to work. In Hawaii the *Honolulu Advertiser* published anti-Chinese editorials, pointing to problems in California, Southeast Asia, and Australia. Three main complaints against Chinese voiced in Hawaii were their failure to assimilate; the threat of their outnumbering the native Hawaiians; and the claim that they would lower the moral standards of the Islands.[18]

Although westerners had introduced numerous diseases which wreaked havoc on the local population, blame was shifted during this period to the Chinese. The Chinese were accused, for example, of bringing leprosy to Hawaii. In a short time the disease became known as *mai pake*, or Chinaman's disease. In 1878, King Kalakaua signed a law restricting the landing of ship passengers to protect public health. The law also reasserted the government's right to control immigration. Between 1878 and 1884, the Legislative Assembly heard twenty different anti-Chinese petitions. A struggle developed between sugar planters, whose measure of profit depended on Chinese labor, and the kingdom's anti-Chinese forces. At the end of the nineteenth century, Hawaii became a United States territory, subject to all American laws concerning the Chinese.

The Chinese Exclusion Act

On May 6, 1882, the Anti-Chinese movement, spearheaded by organized labor, won its first national legislative victory with the passage of the Chinese Exclusion Act. A number of factors led to its enactment. The major railways were built and the economic development of the west had been given its foundation. There was no longer a labor shortage. The use of Chinese as strikebreakers in North Adams, Massachusetts, Belleville, New Jersey, and Beaver Falls, Pennsylvania, brought the Chinese issue closer to home for east coast observers. Meanwhile, the Democratic and Republican forces, in a close battle for control of Congress, realized that to win the crucial western votes they had to support the anti-Chinese stand. With minimal opposition, the Exclusion Act passed easily through both houses. Under the law, the immigration of Chinese laborers was suspended for ten years, illegal entrants faced deportation, and Chinese were denied the right to become naturalized citizens. It was the first United States law to restrict immigration on the basis of race.

Three years earlier, President Rutherford B. Hayes had vetoed a congressional act calling for Chinese exclusion because it was in violation of the Burlingame Treaty. The next year, the United States negotiated with China and came to an agreement: in the Treaty of 1880, the United States was granted the right to regulate, limit or suspend immigration, but not to prohibit it. This treaty laid the basis for the 1882 Exclusion Act, and fourteen additional pieces of anti-Chinese legislation passed in the following decades.

Chinese in America protested the 1882 law, as they would the passage of subsequent laws in later years. The Six Companies voiced broad objections on behalf of the community, although many Chinese waged individual legal battles in the courts.

Exclusion Era Attacks

For the anti-Chinese forces, the 1882 suspension of immigration was only the first step towards total exclusion of the Chinese, and the movement gained momentum in the 1880s. One of the worst atrocities recorded was the Rock Springs Massacre in Wyoming. On September 2, 1885, a Welsh miner and two Chinese miners argued over who had been assigned to a certain chamber. A fight ensued, and one Chinese was killed by the blow of a shovel. By

Westshore riot, Seattle, 1886.
(University of Washington Library)

this time a crowd of white miners had gathered and it drove all the Chinese out of the mines and back to Rock Springs Chinatown. Later in the day, a mob of some 150 men and women, many of them drunk, headed for Chinatown. Shots were fired and, outnumbered, the Chinese fled to the hills.

"The Chinamen were fleeing like a herd of hunted antelopes, making no resistance," declared one eyewitness. "Volley upon volley was fired after the fugitives. In a few minutes the hill east of the town was literally blue with hunted Chinamen."[19] Those who were not quick enough perished in the flames which destroyed Chinatown. In all, twenty-eight Chinese were killed and fifteen were wounded. For a month, riots persisted throughout the State until federal troops were summoned by Governor Warren.

White miners had become completely frustrated in their attempts to protest exploitative treatment of the Union Pacific Coal Department. Their strikes were consistently unsuccessful because the Chinese refused to participate. Blame was shifted from the root cause of their problem, company policy, to a subsidiary element which was more easily attacked, the Chinese. This was a common scenario for attacks on the Chinese during the period.

The Rock Springs Massacre generated protest on the east coast by humanitarians, pacifists and Chinese supporters who requested government aid for the Chinese. Diplomatic protests were lodged by the Chinese government, after it conducted its own investigation at the massacre site. The United States government paid $150,000 in indemnities to families of the Rock Springs victims, but none of the white miners were indicted by the Sweetwater County grand jury which tried them.

An Anti-Chinese Congress was convened in Seattle on September 28, 1885, with delegates from all over the Territory. The body resolved that the Chinese should be expelled from Western Washington by November 1, 1885. They condemned the employment of Chinese in industry and homes, and moved that "ouster committees" oversee explusions in Tacoma and Seattle.[20]

On November 3, 1885, about 300 armed Tacoma citizens loaded 700 Chinese residents on wagons and drove them to the outskirts of town. The Chinese were forced to spend the night in the open, finding what shelter they could from the cold and drizzling rain. Two of them died of exposure. Chinatown was set aflame. Most of the homeless Chinese took the next trains to Portland.

In early 1886 the Washington Legislature passed

From the Business Directory of Seattle and Vancouver, 1879.
(University of Washington Library)

a bill which prohibited aliens from owning land. In addition to the Alien Land Law, Representative Charles Munday introduced three other anti-Chinese measures, but they were either tabled or defeated. A spokesman for the opposition was Representative Orange Jacobs, who argued that, as a free nation, America was just as much the home of the Asiatic race as of other races.

Incensed by the failure of the Legislature to compel Chinese expulsion, forces in Seattle took matters into their own hands. Anti-Chinese rallies aroused the populace, and on February 7 and 8, 1886, five- and six-person "committees" swept through Chinatown and demanded that the Chinese pack up and leave. Within hours, 350 Chinese were transported on wagons to the wharf. The Sheriff quickly summoned the militia and home guard after the police announced they would prevent abuse of the Chinese but would not halt their removal. The captain of the *Queen of the Pacific* agreed to take the Chinese to San Francisco for a fare of seven dollars per person. A collection was taken and the tickets were paid for by the agitators; eight Chinese paid for themselves. But before they could set sail, a writ of habeas corpus was served on the captain, requiring him to bring his passengers to court the next day.

In court, the judge told the Chinese that although the mood of the city was hostile, they could elect to remain in Seattle and receive all possible protection. Only sixteen accepted this offer.

The first shipload of Chinese sailed out of Seattle harbor, and as the remaining Chinese were escorted back to their homes by the militia, either to await the next ship or to begin rebuilding, the response was riotous. Governor Squire declared martial law and requested federal troops; National Guard troops remained stationed in the city for six months.[21]

In the years following the Exclusion Act, the Chinese in California continued to be restricted by discriminatory legislation. In countless towns, they were victims of hostility and were often expelled by angry mobs.[22] Every Chinese person was driven out of Humboldt County in 1885 when a Eureka councilman was accidentally killed by a stray bullet fired in a fight between two Chinese. A decade later, the Humboldt Chamber of Commerce claimed "That [expulsion] was in 1885, and since then Humboldt has had no Chinese. Even in far-off China, the coolies know that they are not permitted to come here and none ever attempt it."[23]

By 1886, almost every Arizona town had formed an Anti-Chinese League. Weekly meetings began with a procession through the streets; there was brass and choral music, and speeches by town leaders. Women were welcomed and given front row seats.

A burlesque play, *The Chinese Must Go*, ridiculed Chinese customs. It played to howling audiences at the Bird Cage Theatre in Tombstone. Citizens of that town developed the most rabid Anti-Chinese League in all of Arizona, adopting as its slogan, "Starve Them to Death!" Beginning in February, 1886, they organized for the expulsion of "the Pigtails" by boycotting the town's Chinese businesses. To get rid of the "problem" once and for all, a wealthy Tombstone businessman volunteered passage money for 100 Chinese to Boston, where he preferred they live. In Prescott, Arizona, white residents also resented the economic competition and refused to patronize Chinese enterprises. In 1887, a fire set by arsonists destroyed Sam Lee's restaurant on Railroad Avenue in Prescott, but was discovered in time to avert destruction of the entire Chinatown.[24]

Although the Chinese were by no means the only men engaged in gambling, opium smoking and the business of prostitution, they received all the blame for the presence of these and other vices in various cities. The press, finding the anti-Chinese stance popular, published "Chinese Must Go" headlines and stories with little concern for the truth. Sensitive to the mood in these towns, politicians delivered the speeches and passed the legislation which guaranteed votes for the next election.

Further attacks on Chinatowns continued through the early 1900s and, as Chinese migrated east to escape persecution, Midwest and east coast cities saw their share of anti-Chinese demonstrations. The North Atlantic region experienced the heaviest increase in Chinese during these years. Its population numbered 137 in 1870, 1,628 in 1880, and 61,707 in 1890. North Central states followed, with 9 Chinese in 1870, 813 in 1880, and 2,357 in 1890. The Chinese communities on the west coast saw an increase from 62,831 in 1870 to 102,102 in 1880, but declined to 96,844 in 1890.[25]

An etching from Helena's Social Supremacy *depicting the servile social position of the Chinese.*
(Montana Historical Society)

HELENA'S CORRECT STANDARDS OF LIVING.

The Geary Act of May 1892 required the Chinese to carry Certificates of Residence.
(Arizona Historical Society)

Further Federal Legislation

On October 1, 1888, the United States Congress passed the Scott Act, which prohibited Chinese laborers from returning to the United States even if they possessed a valid re-entry permit. Only five classes of individuals might be admitted under the act: officials, teachers, students, merchants, and travelers. Twenty-thousand laborers visiting their families in China were prevented from returning to work in the United States.

The Scott Act violated the Treaty of 1880, which stated that the United States could not prohibit immigration from China. But when laborer Chae Chan Ping challenged the act in court, the government claimed that Congress had the power to regulate immigration, and bar or deport any alien, regardless of treaties or constitutional rights.

Both Republicans and Democrats joined the anti-Chinese band wagon. The Exclusion Act, first enacted in 1882, was renewed every decade. It was not repealed until 1943. (Library of Congress)

The Geary Act of May 5, 1892 renewed for ten additional years laws restricting immigration. It required all Chinese to obtain certificates of residence within the year, and stripped them of protection in the courts. Illegal aliens would be sentenced to up to one year of hard labor in prison and deportation.

A massive protest was organized in Chinese communities throughout the country. The Chinese Consul and the Six Companies advised against registering, and pooled their money to hire lawyers to fight the Geary Act. As a result, just 13,242 of the 106,668 Chinese in the United States had registered by the end of the provided period. In a test case, Fong Yue Ting *vs.* the United States, the Supreme Court ruled that the registration requirement was constitutional. The Chinese government, in its weakened state, could do no more than protest. The Chinese legation lodged a series of objections beginning in 1889, but it was not until three years later that the United States government replied. The State Department rejected the protests and maintained that the Geary Act was aimed at protecting the rights of Chinese laborers who qualified for American residence, and further contended that those rights were superior to those enjoyed by Americans in China.

Among the few American groups who raised their voices to protest the anti-Chinese movement and subsequent government policies were the Protestant churches. Missionaries who had worked with Chinese people in China and the United States favored their immigration to America, viewing it as an extension of mission evangelism. The Reverend Wilbur Choy, the first Asian American bishop, says that the Church played a significant role during this intensely anti-Chinese period:

The churches of that period were very much interested in missionary work throughout the world and the very reason they went out, sending missionaries to China and other countries, made them feel that they needed to be the ones to speak up for and stand up for the Chinese who had been mistreated here. When the criticism of the Chinese was that they didn't understand English, that they spoke a foreign tongue, it was the churches that established English classes for them. When they were called heathens and idol worshipers, the churches not only had English classes but Bible classes as part of their evangelistic effort to convert Chinese to Christianity. Not just to win numbers, in that sense, but out of their understanding of what their faith means—God's love is expressed through Christ for all people, then must be made known to all people. We might question some of the methods that they used, but in general, it was a very

Honolulu Chinatown was set on fire by the Board of Health as a "remedy" to control bubonic plague when one man's death was so diagnosed. The fire of January 20, 1900 damaged 38 acres and rendered 4,000 people homeless. (Hawaii State Archives)

unselfish and courageous type of work with our present insight into psychology and even to theology.

At the time when anti-Chinese feelings were strongest, when there were all kinds of anti-Chinese legislation, almost the only ones to speak up in congressional committees for Chinese were the American missionaries. Among the Methodists who spoke up very strongly against that kind of legislation was Otis Gibson in San Francisco, our Methodist missionary, and his counterparts in the Presbyterian Church, the Baptist Church and other groups of that kind. After a congressional hearing where Gibson testified, they burned him in effigy in San Francisco.[26]

In Hawaii the Chinese community organized a campaign of agitation and information, passed resolutions at a mass meeting held on April 20, 1908, and voiced concerns to immigration officials, President Theodore Roosevelt and officials of the Chinese government in Washington D.C. The United Chinese Society of Hawaii sent a petition to Commissioner General of Immigration David J. Keefe protesting discriminatory treatment in immigration procedures. It concluded with an appeal to relax the exclusion laws in Hawaii's case, "in order that our people may not feel that they are the cursed of the earth."[27] The Hawaii Chinese, at first confident that given all the facts, the American government would revise the Hawaiian immigration rules, were granted no exception.

Meanwhile, to encourage revision of the exclusion laws, Chinese in America appealed to their compatriots at home to boycott American-made goods. The economic boycott of American goods took hold in Shanghai in 1905 and spread southward; merchants in Guangdong and Fujian, the home provinces of most Chinese in America, were its most staunch supporters. For one year, Chinese merchants, students and workers refused to buy American products, attend American schools, ship goods on American vessels, or work for American firms. The annual thirty to forty million dollar American trade with China was substantially affected and soon the United States government requested China to stop the boycott. An imperial edict and substantial financial loss among Chinese merchants resulted in its suppression.[28]

The anti-American boycott did not result in the repeal of the exclusion laws, as its most radical proponents had hoped, but it prompted some significant policy changes in America's consular service. Most importantly, the support of the boycott in China as well as in the overseas Chinese communities of Cuba, British Columbia, the Philippines, Sumatra, and Hawaii raised the issue of the racist exclusion laws to international proportions. The fact that the United States was enforcing legislation in direct contradiction to its touted democratic principles had been publicized widely.

Despite the hostile climate in the United States, the unchanged poor conditions in China continued to make Gam San a desirable alternative for many Chinese. If they could not qualify as members of one of the five categories exempt from exclusion, they sought entry into the United States by posing as members of exempt groups, by crossing the Canadian or Mexican borders illegally, or by claiming derivative citizenship as "paper sons."[29] Although the worst anti-Chinese violence in the United States was over, anti-Chinese sentiment continued to be expressed in many ways. It began with the Chinese immigrant's first encounter with America—Angel Island.

4 Birth of Chinatown

On April 28, 1979, hundreds of Chinese Americans gathered on a small island in San Francisco Bay. The group unveiled a 6,000-pound granite monument inscribed with a Chinese couplet, which in translation reads:

> Leaving their homes and villages, they crossed the ocean
> Only to endure confinement in these barracks;
> Conquering frontiers and barriers, they pioneered
> A new life by the Golden Gate.
>
> —Ngoot P. Chin, poet.[1]

Among the crowd were older Chinese who had been detained at the island immigration station for weeks, months, and even years in the first decades of the twentieth century. The day was filled with haunting memories for them. Second and third generation Chinese Americans came in tribute. The injustices of Angel Island were being acknowledged.

Although the barracks which once housed Chinese immigrants awaiting entry into the United States are now silent and abandoned, their walls literally tell the Angel Island story. Poetry written by anonymous detainees is carved into the wooden walls in Chinese calligraphy. Two examples from Building #317, the Chinese Detention Barracks, eloquently express the frustration and anger of immigrants who felt unjustifiably detained:

> There are tens of thousands of poems composed on these walls.
> They are all cries of complaint and sadness.
> The day I am rid of this prison and attain success,
> I must remember that this chapter once existed.
> In my daily needs, I must be frugal.
> Needless extravagance leads youth to ruin.
>
> All my compatriots should please be mindful.
> Once you have some small gains, return home early.[2]
>
> —By One from Xiangshan

> The building with three beams is just sufficient to cover my body.
> It would be unbearable to tell the truth about the happenings on these slopes.
> Wait until the day I am successful and can fulfill my wish;
> I will not be benevolent and will level and uproot the station.[3]
>
> —Anonymous

Angel Island: 1910–1940

The detention of Chinese on Angel Island was a deliberate part of the effort of the American government to enforce its anti-Chinese immigration policies. After the 1882 Exclusion Act, United States officials tightened entry procedures and sent Chinese arrivals through a series of hurdles to

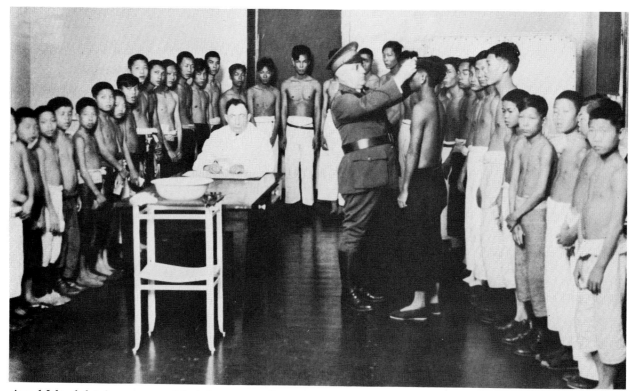

Angel Island detainees were subjected to unusually stringent medical examinations for the detection of contagious diseases. Chinese immigrants felt this was one more racist obstacle to their entry to the United States. (National Archives)

prove they were within the five exempted categories. Before 1910, the immigrants were detained at a wharf shed on the waterfront. From 1910 to 1940, most of the 175,000 Chinese immigrants to America entered through Angel Island. Other ethnic groups were processed through the Island, but the largest number and longest detained were the Chinese.

All Chinese immigrants were given physical examinations and closely interrogated for one or two hours. The same questions were then asked of the immigrant's close relatives. If the two sets of answers differed, the immigrant faced deportation. Sometimes the immigrant was questioned again, stretching the whole procedure to two or three days. Officials considered the Chinese to be guilty of carrying false entry papers unless proven innocent. Former detainees claim that the station was not without a few corrupt examiners who took advantage of their position to extort money from the immigrants. Those detainees who could not justify immigration were forced back onto ships returning to China.

Many Chinese survived the interrogations by arranging for coaching on the answers to questions so absurd that even legitimate immigrants could easily be stumped. It was a common opinion among Chinese that the discriminatory nature of the Exclusion laws justified their circumvention. Relatives in San Francisco paid workers on the Island to smuggle in "crib sheets" for the immigrants to study. Typical questions were: How many houses are there in your village? Where is your house located? Does your family have a clock? Which wall is it hung on? Does your front door face east or west? Which direction does the family altar face? Recite your family history. How many steps are there in your father's house?

One of the most widespread and successful methods of entering the country was playing the "paper son." The 1906 San Francisco earthquake and fire had destroyed the city's immigration records. With the loss of these documents, the Chinese were afforded the opportunity to claim American citizenship. In the following years, many immigrants reported several children in China, usually

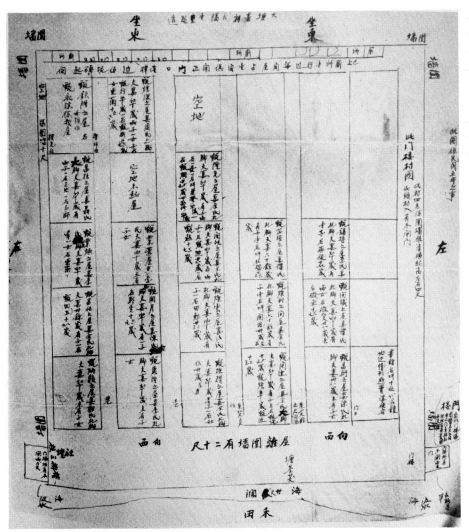

sons, who one by one would request entry, as off-spring of United States citizens. These "slots" were often given or sold to extended family or other villagers, or sometimes sold through brokers. The responsibility of the young immigrant, related only on paper, was to memorize the "paper father's" family history, village layout, and trivia such as the positions of wells and house windows. Alerted to the "paper son" arrangement, immigration officials intensified their interrogations of new arrivals. The immigrant needed to have precise answers to questions devised to outwit and trap him.

San Francisco resident Jim Quock remembers coming to America as a "paper son" and what it took to survive the interrogation:

(I came to America) because my grandfather was here during the Gold Rush times, the 1860s. Somebody robbed him and he got killed and they never found the body or anything. My grandmother told us that grandpa had got a lot of gold, made quite a bit of money, you know. So that's what got in my mind, "Oh, this is a fortune. I'm going over to America to make money." Only fifteen at that time. So the only way I could come is to buy a paper, buy a citizen paper. I paid quite a bit of money, too. I paid $102 gold! That's quite a bit of money at that time in China.

They give you a book of about 200 pages to study—all your life, your family, your brother's name, the whole village, almost. They ask you all kinds of questions when you get to the United States, the immi-

gration (station) at Angel Island. . . . I was there for three weeks. They ask you questions like how many steps in your house? Your house had a clock? Questions like that. You got to remember all this. They asked me, "Where do you sleep at your house?" I said, "I sleep with my grandmother and my brother." They say, "Okay, which position do you sleep?" All kinds of questions, you got to think. But, I'm pretty smart. I said, "Tonight I sleep over here, tomorrow maybe I sleep over there, it doesn't matter."[4]

In 1922 Angel Island detainees formed an organization for purposes of self-government and mutual aid. It relayed complaints to the adminis-

tration, translated government policy announcements, and even started classes for the children. On a less obvious level, the association was an important link in the underground communication channel which joined detainees to San Francisco Chinatown.

In their daily regimen immigrants were confronted with depressing and dehumanizing living conditions. As they awaited decisions on admittance to the United States, they were guarded in locked barracks and allowed little freedom of movement. High fences surrounded the dormitories and the small recreation yards. The men's and women's dormitories were separate large rooms

Chinatown after the San Francisco earthquake and fire, 1906.
(Library of Congress)

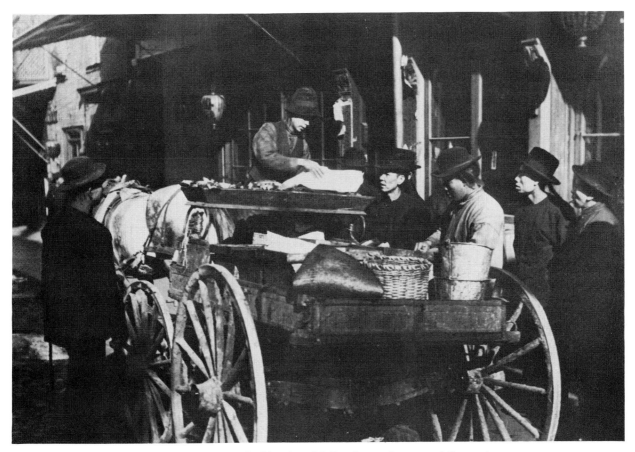

San Francisco bachelor society as photographed by Arnold Genthe at the turn of the century.
(California Historical Society)

filled with double and triple-layered bunk beds. Windows were covered with dark paper. There was no privacy there, or in the bathrooms, where non-partitioned toilets lined the walls. Outside, the chilly bay waters surrounding the Island discouraged any break for freedom. The detainees occasionally found relief for their frustration through a number of revolts and demonstrations. After three decades of use, the barracks were labeled firetraps by the authorities, and finally, after a 1940 fire in the administration building, the Chinese detainees were moved off Angel Island to other quarters in San Francisco. By the early 1950s the detainment of Chinese was discontinued. The task of verifying that immigrants met required qualifications was thereafter conducted by United States consular officials in Hong Kong or other points of departure.

Compared to the experience of other immigrants to the United States at the time, Chinese isolation on Angel Island was a disastrous begin-

ning to American life. The experience of being treated as common criminals upon first arrival left residual scars on the Chinese American psyche. For decades many Chinese endured poor living or working conditions in silence, fearing that if they attracted attention in any way, the fact that they were "paper sons" might be discovered and result in certain deportation.

Chinatown Boundaries

Once released from Angel Island, the Chinese who arrived in San Francisco and other cities across the country had but one choice of neighborhood—Chinatown. This pattern of segregation stemmed from the prejudice of city residents and was encouraged by restrictive housing regulations which excluded the Chinese from other districts. The population of San Francisco Chinatown, the largest

*Fish peddler, San Francisco
Chinatown, early 1900s.*
(California Historical Society)

Chinese community in America, increased steadily during the height of the anti-Chinese movement as Chinese were driven from the countryside and sought protection and work in the city. By 1900, the Broadway-California-Kearny-Stockton Street boundaries of San Francisco Chinatown had been clearly delineated, and the seven-block area within became the "safe zone" for Chinese. Those who ventured across the border streets often met with verbal and physical assault. Previous experiences of anti-Chinese violence led the Chinese to avoid direct confrontation, especially when alone. New

immigrants soon learned to travel in groups for protection and to live within the boundaries of Chinatown. Essentially a bachelor society, the community was a mixture of new immigrants, resident merchants, and workers from the factories, mines, railroads, and farmlands. Chinatown grew in complexity as larger numbers of men arrived and made possible the groupings, loyalties and conflicts with which developing communities must contend.

Most of the men lived in boarding houses, crowded into small rooms with other members of their family or village. To save space, beds were sometimes nailed to the walls, two or three above each other. In some crowded rooms, the men slept in shifts. At the end of each year, expenses were divided among members. These *fongs*, or rooms, were the basic living arrangements in early Chinatowns across the country. Gene Eng describes his experience in New York Chinatown:

The Engs, we are all cousins, so we grouped up. We chipped in and took care of an apartment. If you work out of town, you come back on the weekends, or it's too far away, maybe two or three states, maybe you come two or three times a year, every season. But those who live around the Metropolitan area get together on the weekend, play mahjong. So if you're out of a job, you stay there. That's a good thing, too. Six to ten of us chipped in for this apartment. All the expenses are paid by the whole group but those who are out of work can stay there. No matter where you go, you still chip in for the expenses.[5]

Reassembling a Culture

Because of the scarcity of Chinese women, the Chinese community lacked the traditional stabilizing element of the family. But early residents did their best to maintain other cultural practices and beliefs. Several holidays were faithfully celebrated. Chinese New Year, replete with red paper, fire crackers, and dragon dances, was observed in January or February, depending on the lunar calendar. In the spring, Chinese observed *Qing Ming*, or Memorial Day. In the fall, there was the Moon Festival, a traditional celebration of the harvest in China. The folk religion practiced by most immigrants combined the beliefs of Confucianism, Taoism, and Buddhism. In each Chinatown, the immigrants built altars to honor their deities, who included Kwang Kung, god of literature and war; Bak Ti, god of the north; Hou Yin, the monkey god; Kwan Yin, goddess of mercy. When enough

Festive celebration of Chinese New Year in Los Angeles.
(California Historical Society)

money was raised, traditional temples were constructed for worship, festival celebration, and funeral ceremonies.

Means of communication were initiated. A growing Chinese American press disseminated world and local news. Early newspapers such as the *Golden Hills News* and *California China Mail and Flying Dragon* featured information of interest to businessmen, such as commodity price lists and shipping news. Some publications promoted religious or political beliefs. The Reverend William Speer of the Chinese Presbyterian Church started a bilingual newspaper, *The Oriental*, in 1855. Leaders from both China and the San Francisco community established other newspapers to win support for their particular policies. The *Sacramento Daily News*, the first Chinese daily in America, commenced publication in 1856.

Chinese stores played an important role in the community, whether located in San Francisco Chinatown or other settlements across the country. The stores sold food, herbs, and other products from China. Their backrooms often provided places of relaxation where the men might buy lottery tickets, play mahjong, or smoke opium. They were surrogate banks, used by workers who entrusted storekeepers with their earnings. Lastly, they were centers of communication, as Locktin Eng of Seattle recalls:

A few of the Chinese stores were export and import but some of them did not even have merchandise. They just put up a name because all Chinese came. Not just relatives. They all just like to get together. They talk together. And they teach the younger generation what they're going to do and what they are supposed to do. Sometimes they even get some idea from China. Our village had something to do—they send a letter over here, we get together and talk it over—and send it back. We communicate, see, otherwise you're alone. You know nothing.[6]

Chinatown Evenings

In 1852 a playhouse was shipped from China and assembled in San Francisco, and Chinese theater in America was launched. Subsequently in larger Chinatowns throughout the country, Chinese residents were treated to traveling road shows. A night at the theater was a lively experience, with young vendors selling melon seeds, candles and oranges in the aisles. The theatrical bill of fare was the conventional dramatization of early Chinese history, but plays were also presented in a variety of forms, including histories, romances, comedies, and tales of virtue rewarded.

Gambling was popular in times of economic hardship. When money was scarce, the possibility of a quick fortune was most appealing. While a sojourner might take years to reach his financial goal by saving his wages, a winning streak on the tables could mean success in an evening. Mahjong, fantan and *baakgapbiu*, the precursor of keno, were games which the men had played in China, and now they provided recreation, the excitement of risk, and sociable evenings. Habitual gambling, however was the bane of many a working man. Precious savings could be lost in minutes, prolonging the immigrant's time in America.

Opium parlors and houses of prostitution were the other establishments open to the men of Chinatown in the evenings. The euphoria induced by smoking the opium drug offered escape from daily problems, and the habit was popular among some immigrants. The famous Chinatown opium dens, however, were often commercial tourist attractions. Prostitution flourished in Chinatown, as it does in any settlement where there are so few women. Periodic police raids on brothels, opium dens and gambling parlors limited all three activities. Yet they remained a part of bachelor Chinatown society through the first decades of the twentieth century, although exaggerated by the press.

Kinship Associations

Kinship organizations in early Chinatown were derived from the immigrants' familial and geographic origins in South China. When these immigrants discovered the problems of pioneer life in America, they formed mutual aid associations based on homeland affiliations. At the most basic level, there was the *fong*, composed of close family and village members. But because groups from individual villages were often small, there were also larger groupings formed by surname, called "family" or "clan" associations. Family associations often maintained clubhouses which doubled as social centers and places of residence. The larger associations built altars for worship, conducted council meetings, and transmitted letters from their villages. At Chinese New Year, they provided elaborate banquets for their members. If a member died, the group was responsible for sending his remains back to China. Altogether, the association was a present reminder of familial and village obligations.

As Chinese moved throughout the United States in search of work, particular family groups established themselves in various cities. Ong was the most common surname in Phoenix, Moy and Chin in Chicago, Lee in Washington, D.C., and Yee in Pittsburgh. The Wong, Lee, and Chin families were predominant in San Francisco. Once a clan member had established himself in a locality, he sent word to California or even to China urging his clansmen to join him. Naomi Jung remembers the frequent arrivals of "cousins" from the home district in China:

I still remember when I was a little girl growing up in Albany, there would always be somebody coming from the old country. And as he would come over,

Chinese opera was a popular form of entertainment. The larger Chinatowns had their own theaters; smaller Chinatowns were visited by traveling troops.
(The Museum of the City of New York)

the cousin would be taken downtown and he'd be bought one good suit from a good, conservative store. He'd get a Stetson hat. He'd get Florsheim shoes. He'd be fitted for the next couple of years in good, conservative clothes. He would be given money to start a business. Whether it would be business with them or for himself.

There was always room for one more when he came from the old country. It was always good to see someone come from your village because they brought stories of everybody from the village. And when you come from the same village, with the Chinese this is kinfolk. This is why people would say all the Lees are here. One would come and settle in New York. Before you know it they'd write back and more Lees would come.[7]

District Associations

On a level above the family associations and more powerful in the socio-political scheme of Chinatown were the district associations, or *huiguan*.

Roughly similar to the *Landsmannschaften*, or immigrant aid societies of Germans in America, the *huiguan* were formed when the Chinese community grew large enough to organize according to region. The *huiguan* served some of the same purposes as family associations, but the scope of their activities was much more extensive. They were in contact with new immigrants from the moment of arrival, greeting them at the pier, finding employment for them and providing their initial board and lodging. Their influence, in fact, was felt throughout the entire sojourn of the immigrant, and members needed their clearance on exit permits to the home country. The district association served as arbitrators in the settlement of disputes, avoiding the need to bring cases to the municipal courts. Organized under merchant leadership, the associations became so powerful that an immigrant who refused them his allegiance faced ostracism in the community.

Three major regional groups established district associations in San Francisco Chinatown. The largest number of early immigrant laborers hailed from Sze Yup, or the "Four Districts" of Taishan (Toishan), Xinhui (Sunwui), Enping (Yanping) and Kaiping (Hoiping). The second most numerous were immigrants from Zhongshan (Chungshan). Many of Chinatown's merchants hailed from Sam Yup, or the Three Districts of Nanhai (Namhoi), Panyu (Punyu) and Shunde (Shuntak). A fourth association attended to the interests of the Hakka, a Guangdong minority group. Differences in dialect as well as rivalries brought from China served to reinforce the popularity of the district associations, and emboldened lines of demarcation among the various groups.

Chinese Six Companies

Feuds between clan and district associations were such a problem by the late 1850s that the San Francisco community leadership organized the Chung Wai Wui Koon. Its English name was the Chinese Six Companies, derived from the six original associations, and it served as a board of arbitration with overall jurisdiction within the community. Later, seven districts were represented in the organization: Ning Yung, Sui Hing, Hop Wo, Kong Chow, Yung Wo, Sam Yup, and Yan Wo. In 1880, when the Six Companies became intensely involved in fighting anti-Chinese legislation, the group was officially named the Chinese Consolidated Benevolent Association (CCBA), but it continued to be popularly known as the Six Companies.

In addition to its judiciary power among San Francisco Chinatown's district associations, the Six Companies started a Chinese language school, organized medical and hospitalization services for the sick and indigent, and fought at least twenty-five laws, statutes and regulations which were legal attacks on the Chinese. In the world beyond Chin-

Officials of the Chinese Six Companies, photographed by Louis J. Stellman.
(California State Library, Sacramento)

atown, the Six Companies was recognized as the official representative of the Chinese community.

Merchants' Guilds

Three major economic groups formed the structure of the early Chinatown economy: the merchants, who operated import-export enterprises; the small business owners, who established laundries, groceries, and restaurants; and the workers, who provided labor for Chinese establishments as well as outside industries. Of the three, the merchants had the most influence on the early formation of Chinatown. Merchants controlled the clan and district associations and the Chinese Six Companies as leaders and spokesmen. Their power gave them jurisdiction over most aspects of the lives of Chinatown's working men. Some of the laborers who had accepted merchants' credit for ship passage from China were compelled to work off the debt at high interest rates. Small business owners bought partnerships in merchant stores so they could send for their wives as members of this exempted class.

Perhaps the first Chinese organization in California was a merchant's guild called the Chiu-Yat Gung-so. Although it attempted to settle disputes among merchants, fix price ceilings on goods, and temper over-competitive spirits, the drive for economic control of Chinatown was too strong for the guild to handle. The guild's powerful Sam Yup members were constantly challenged by the Sze Yup merchants, who resented their domination. Sam Yup leader Loke Tung was assassinated in 1880. During the next decade, six Chinese Consul Generals failed to arbitrate the Sam Yup-Sze Yup feud. The hostility led the Sze Yup to form their own guild, which they called the Haak-Seung Wui-kuan. They boycotted Sam Yup enterprises until 1899, when the Chinese government used its leverage to force the lifting of the boycott.

In 1908, the Sam Yup and Sze Yup guilds realized that the advantages of a merger outweighed the disadvantages, and formed the Chinese Chamber of Commerce at the urging of the Chinese Consul General. The Chamber became the meeting ground for divergent business interests in the community, as well as a vehicle for self-promotion in the world outside Chinatown. It spoke out against immigration and trade policies which affected merchants and worked with city officials on such additions to Chinatown as a branch post office and Chinese-style street lamps.

Secret Societies

Partly in response to Chinatown's merchant oligarchy, another kind of organization gained popularity among the immigrants. These were the secret societies or tongs which attracted members according to a set of beliefs rather than clan or district allegiance. As fraternal organizations, the tongs were especially attractive to those without power, money, or the support of Chinatown's major clan groups.

The earliest American tongs took their inspiration from the secret societies of China which were formed to overthrow the Manchu dynasty and to reinstate the rule of the Han Chinese. One of the major societies in South China was the Triad Society, or Heaven and Earth Society. Some of its members fought in the Taiping Rebellion and the Red Turban Uprisings in Guangdong. When its anti-Manchu rebellions proved unsuccessful, some Triad members found outlet for their frustration in illegal activities such as piracy and smuggling. Many Triad members joined the mid-nineteenth century emigration to North America and Southeast Asia, and once settled, founded overseas lodges.

Although the secret societies in Hawaii retained the political goals of the original Triad Society, by the 1870s, a different type of tong had emerged on the United States mainland. These were tongs whose main concerns were more immediate, involving political and economic dominance in American Chinatowns. In subsequent years, rival tongs struggled with each other, and with the *hui-guan* and Six Companies, in several arenas. These included the challenging of monopolistic control of enterprises by single families or associations; establishment of territories in the businesses of opium, gambling, and prostitution; protection of individual members by their sworn brothers; continuation of feuds transplanted from China; and

Merchant stores often served many functions, including that of post office, bank and social center.

(Bishop Museum)

class conflicts between the wealthy and the workers.

When the Sam Yup merchant leadership failed to effect promised changes in the exclusion laws, the Six Companies lost considerable favor with the community. Its role as Chinatown's foremost organization was challenged and it began to lose ground in the intense battle for control of the community in the 1890s. The tongs began to take precedence in Chinatown. Friends in the law enforcement field, paid generously for their inattention, disregarded many of their illegal Chinatown activities. When disputes between the organizations could not be peacefully settled, feuding groups took their battles to the streets. After 1906, the Six Companies, joined by a number of Protestant missionaries and a small police squad, managed to subdue the tong wars, but the skirmishes persisted off and on to the early 1930s.

Because profits from opium, gambling, and prostitution provided the economic base for the tongs, when society members grew older and the overall sex ratio of Chinatown became more balanced, the tongs gradually declined in influence. In some instances they changed the nature of their activities and came to resemble the other associations in Chinatown, providing clubhouses for recreation and fraternization.

Enterprises Beyond Chinatown

The secret societies restricted their activities to Chinatown, and most of Chinatown's legitimate enterpreneurs developed their businesses solely within the community as well. By the end of the nineteenth century, however, some merchants had amassed large savings and initiated more ambitious ventures. Some of this money was invested in China, in projects promoting modernization and progress such as the Sunning Railroad in the Sze Yup region. Nationalist feelings remained strong among Chinese merchants, reinforced by the racism they too had encountered in America. Many believed that a modern China meant a more respected China in the rapidly changing twentieth-century world.

Some merchants joined forces to establish larger enterprises based in the United States. In 1907, one such group formed The Canton Bank in San Francisco, which attracted its principle stockholders from the Chinese community. The China Mail Steamship Company was organized in 1915 to aid in the war effort against Japanese aggression in China. Financial and management problems forced the closing of both enterprises in the 1920s.

A few business ventures succeeded and spread throughout the west. In 1903, Joe Shoong started a small store in Vallejo, California, and two years later relocated to San Francisco. By 1928 he had established a chain of over forty-five department stores called the National Dollar Stores, an enterprise which still exists today. Kenneth Lim, a manager for over thirty years, recalls the early staff effort it took to ensure success:

You know why they call it the National Dollar Store? In the beginning they sold the goods for nothing over a dollar. That's how they started out. . . . Clothing, everything, was under one dollar. You know those five and ten cent stores in the old days, everything was five and ten cents. Coming up, they changed the system a little bit. It was so busy in those old days when I started with the Dollar Store. It's just crowded like anything, because they sold at a pretty low margin. Sometimes, even if it was a little over a dollar, they sold it for a dollar, and when we had that kind of a sale (famous quality sheets), we used to open up

a box, with so many hundred sheets. We collect the money and ring it up, so it was fast. Oh, everything was really fast!

We all worked hard under him (Shoong and his buyers) and very long hours. Early in the morning till after midnight sometimes. Sometimes our families had to help too, especially when we had big sales.

During World War II we expanded into Nevada and up to Oregon and Washington and then over to the Hawaiian Islands. I moved from the Stockton, California store to open up a new store in Spokane, Washington where we even had a grocery department in the basement. When the shipyards were booming, I opened up another new store in Bremerton, Washington where there were many defense workers. I worked in busy stores so I had some bonus. If the stores made money, you got a bonus. . . . But some stores didn't make money, so the manager only got wages.[8]

The Chinese business to prosper most on a large scale in the first decades of the twentieth century was the Wah Chang Corporation, based in New York. It was founded in 1916 by Dr. Kuo Ching Li, credited for discovering the mineral tungsten in China. From 1916 to the outbreak of the Sino-Japanese War in 1937, Wah Chang was the leading company in American-Chinese trade and engineering. It imported minerals and agricultural products from China and exported machinery, chemicals, steel, and other industrial goods to China. In later years, Wah Chang excelled in minerals research, and was commissioned by the United States government to design and operate a tungsten treatment plant in New York, a zirconium-hafnium plant in Albany, Oregon, and a tin smelter in Texas City, Texas. In its international ventures, it developed the world's largest columbium mine and two tungsten mines in Brazil, and engaged in other mining operations in Bolivia and Southeast Asia.

National Dollar Stores and the Wah Chang Corporation were exceptions to the rule. As capital increased in the community, there were a few Chinese who made bold investments in oil wells, mines, canneries and automotive companies. But the vast majority of Chinese businessmen during this period invested in enterprises which needed only nominal seed money to establish. Business-

Mott Street, New York Chinatown's main street, 1900.
(Library of Congress)

men in Chinatown were generally restricted to small-scale enterprises for several reasons. Their managerial experience and capital were limited and competition with expanding American corporations was difficult. Such business experiments as The Canton Bank and the China Mail Steamship Company had failed, and the Depression of the 1930s made matters even more difficult.[9] Finally, racism in the form of institutional restraints handicapped them still further.

In contrast, Chinese merchants in Hawaii encountered the right conditions for steady business expansion, and by 1930 they had become a force to be reckoned with in the local economy. In Ha-

waii, as on the mainland, Chinese businessmen often formed the *hui* to generate capital. In this arrangement, several men, often from the same village or district, placed equal amounts of money into a joint fund. One man was then chosen to use the entire sum for his particular project. The next month, the pool was replenished and the procedure repeated, continuing each month until every member had taken his turn.

Chinatown as Community

The Chinatown "bachelor society" offered situations of mutual aid, a familiar culture, and protection for men who faced hostility outside their own community. The men accepted their isolation because most believed that their American residence was temporary, and that they would eventually retire in China. Chinatown was "home base" for new immigrants as well as men who had lived "long time Californ'" and who returned to the community after seasonal work away from it.

The freeze on unrestricted travel during the Exclusion Era affected individual plans as well as the scope and purpose of the community. Compelled to remain in America to support families at home, the men realized that their bachelor society was no longer temporary. The frustration of being made scapegoats by the labor movement and of being unable to wage a strong fight in return filled the community with tension.

As a result, the leaders of Chinatown became even more important. Rival groups competed for political and economic control of the one area in their overseas lives which they could attempt to direct—Chinatown. And although few people enjoyed the stability of family life, the numerous associations served as surrogate families, and the sense of community, with all its dynamics, grew stronger each year.

5 Women and Family

Until 1970, the ratio of Chinese men to women in the United States was radically disproportionate. This historical imbalance had a number of reasons. In the beginning, Chinese women remained in China by choice, but eventually they were prevented from immigrating by law. During the earliest decades of work in America, few Chinese men brought their wives with them; the migrant nature of their labor in the American West made it impossible for them to establish a home. Moreover, the strong tradition of family and village ties encouraged Chinese wives to remain in the villages with their children and in-laws and to maintain the homes to which their husbands planned to return someday.

During their years in America, the men sent periodic remittances to their families and tried to return for visits every few years. Reunited with their wives, they stayed for perhaps a year, long enough to see the birth of a new baby. Many children did not meet their fathers until they were grown. When eldest sons were old enough to work, they were often sent to America to assist their fathers with the overseas support of their families. Many men never returned to China after their first departure, either out of choice or economic misfortune, and their journey to Gold Mountain passed into family history.

When the Chinese in America left railroad and migratory farm work for jobs in urban settings, and also realized that their sojourns in the United States would be prolonged, many became interested in sending for their wives. But with the 1882 Exclusion Act, the American government initiated a series of laws which restricted travel between China and the United States until 1965. These acts had tremendous effect on Chinese family life.

As a result of the 1888 Scott Act, over 20,000 Chinese laborers, told that they would be barred from re-entry should they leave the United States, looked towards futures alone in America with new despair. From 1882 to 1924, only import-export merchants could bring their wives with them from China, and from 1924 to 1930, no Chinese wives were allowed entry.[1]

Traditional Role of Women in China

Confucian ethics were the mainstay of China's social order for centuries and were still widely accepted at the time of nineteenth-century travel to America. In Confucian China, a well-ordered government was sustained by a rigid social order in which everyone had an established role. The masculine (yin) and feminine (yang) roles, at first evenly divided, in time placed the woman in a position subservient to the man. She was to serve her father when young, serve her husband when married, and serve her son when widowed.

Different treatment of the two sexes began at birth. The Chinese adage, "A boy is born facing in; a girl is born facing out," meant that sons preserved the sacred family lineage, while daughters would be of chief benefit to the family into which they

61

Donaldina Cameron with rescued slave girls.
(California State Library, Sacramento)

married. Marriage was arranged by parents and clan elders, and the bride and groom met for the first time on the day of their wedding. After the ceremony the young woman moved into the house of her husband's family, where she was expected to serve her mother-in-law and have children. With the birth of a son, the young wife secured a lasting place in her husband's family, making it impossible for her to be cast out.

Early Arrivals

The bachelor society of the mining camps and city settlements provided an open market for prostitution. By the mid-1850s the tongs had begun to take advantage of the situation by steadily importing young Chinese women to work as slave girls and prostitutes, making large profits for their treasuries. To their owners, the women were worth $1,000 to $3,000, depending on age and physical appearance. A complex web of Chinese and Americans were involved in their procurement, passage, surreptitious entry into United States and distribution.[2] Frequently, they were stolen and resold from one owner to another. In exchange for their cooperation, deputy sheriffs and constables pocketed as much as $500 in bribe money. In San Francisco, a quarter of the profits made in the importation of prostitutes was earned by non-Chinese. In that city alone, as many as 159 brothels may have existed in Chinatown by 1870.[3]

In 1875, a crackdown on the importation of "lewd or debauched" Chinese women began. An act prohibiting the further importation of coolies and "immoral women" was passed, and a number of Chinatown merchants cooperated with Christian missionaries in an effort to stop the traffic. But the powerful system which involved the American Consular Office in Hong Kong, steamship and immigration personnel and competitive tongs was not easily subdued. During the years of Chinese exclusion from the United States, women became even more valuable, and with increasing tong entrenchment and immigration service corruption, the exploitation of Chinese prostitutes increased. Although the American press made accusations of cultural degradation, Chinese brothels were no more numerous than those of other groups. In mining camps of the 1850s the Chinese women joined prostitutes from Germany, Spain, Chile, France, and the United States.

Many Chinese women were tricked or kidnapped into the journey to Gam San. The story of Wong Ah So is a typical one:

I was born in Canton Province. My father was sometimes a sailor and sometimes he worked on the docks, for we were very poor.

I was 19 when this man came to my mother and said that in America there was a great deal of gold. Even if I just peeled potatoes there, he told my mother I would earn seven or eight dollars a day, and if I was willing to do any work at all I would earn lots of money. He was a laundryman, but he said he earned plenty of money. He was very nice to me, and my mother liked him, so my mother was glad to have me go with him as his wife.

I thought that I was his wife, and was very grateful that he was taking me to such a grand, free country, where everyone was rich and happy.

When we first landed in San Francisco we lived in a hotel in Chinatown, a nice place, but one day, after I had been there for about two weeks, a woman came to see me. She was young, very pretty, and all dressed in silk. She told me that I was not really Huey Yow's wife, but that she had asked him to buy her a slave, that I belonged to her, and must go with her, but she would treat me well, and I could buy back my freedom, if I was willing to please, and be agreeable, and she would let me off in two years, instead of four if I did not make a fuss. She said that so I would be quieter about it. I did not believe her; I thought she was lying to me. So when Huey Yow came I asked him why that woman had come and what she meant by all that lying. But he said that it was true; that he was not my husband, he did not care about me,

and that this was something that happened all the time. Everybody did this, he said, and why be so shocked that I was to be a prostitute instead of a married woman. I asked him, "What is a prostitute? Am I not your wife?" And he said, "Couldn't I just say that you were my wife? That does not make it so. Everybody does this sort of thing. The woman gave me money just to bring you over.[4]

Ah So was forced to work as a prostitute for seven months, and then was seen at a party by a man who knew her father in China. She was afraid to admit who she was when he confronted her, for fear of disgracing her parents. But he persisted, asking "How is it that you have come to this?" He offered his help and Ah So related the whole story. About ten days following the party, she was rescued and given refuge at a San Francisco mission headed by Donaldina Cameron.

Between 1895 and 1938, Cameron, or "Lo Mo" as she was known to Chinatown, led a tireless crusade to liberate Chinese slave girls and prostitutes from houses which held them in bondage. With the important support of many Chinese, she carried out a course of action begun by Margaret Culbertson and the Occidental Board of Foreign Missions, which had been formed in 1874. In the dark of night, Cameron, accompanied by armed police and Chinese women from the mission home, would travel underground tunnels, scale fences, and climb precariously along rooftops to rescue waiting women. Tong highbinders were dispatched to retrieve the women, so they were kept in hiding until Cameron, who returned to court thirty times on one case, could legally free them from their owners.

The mission gave the women the free choice of going back to China or remaining in America, and the ratio of those who stayed and those who left was equal. Those who chose to leave were provided passage back to the homeland. The women opting to remain were taught English, reading and homemaking skills. Many married and started families. Suitors from all over came to the mission and were awarded inspection by Cameron herself. Some women who had grown accustomed to fancier surroundings in brothels or homes of the wealthy regarded conditions at the mission with disinterest and scorn. Others relished the new freedom of choice. One of the first Chinese American women doctors emerged from the mission's program.[5]

Immigration of Wives

At the beginning of the twentieth century, many families in China were still obliged to send able-bodied family members abroad to find work. During this time, the rise of industrialization in China began to change the traditional role of women. Many women joined the work force in the factories and textile mills which were springing up in port cities. Economic necessity prevailed over the tradition which had kept women tied to their village homes. Furthermore, during this period Chinese men in America began sending for their wives. They concluded that the disadvantages of war and poverty in China were worse than the racist abuse in the United States, where, with persistence, a living could be made. And, in contrast to their earlier migratory work, their new jobs in the cities permitted them to establish real homes for the first time.

The wives often made the sea journey across the Pacific alone, and endured quarantine, questioning, and detention on Angel Island for indefinite periods of time. Some left the familiarity of China for life in a strange, new land with the added apprehension of having never met their new husbands. In the traditional manner of arranged marriages, some men returned from America for a wife, and others had a wife chosen for them by relatives while they waited in America. Dottie Mun was one of these women:

When I was seven, my mother died. When my father died, I was nine years old. I stayed in Hong Kong with my cousin. Then this man came back to Hong Kong. He was nineteen. I was supposed to be nineteen too. He married me. He was born in California and our marriage was arranged. So I came here in 1917. I got into Honolulu, then I got to California. I stayed on the Island for about two weeks, in isolation, Angel Island.

Interviewer: Were there other ladies?

Sunday outing, Los Angeles.
(California Historical Society)

Oh yeah, plenty, young girls too. Some of them stayed for a whole year. Can't send them back, can't get out. We eat the same time. We go to sleep the same time. Some of them came because they had husbands here already. Some of them came because their fathers were here. They examined you.

Interviewer: Who arranged your marriage, your cousin?

Yeah, but I don't know if they sold me for money, they might have. At my age, at that time, the people were very stupid, not like today, you know. So I had no choice. They told me I was going with him, that's all.

Interviewer: How did you feel?

I feel scared, that's all. You never met the man, you don't know what's what.[6]

Once they had met all the entry requirements on Angel Island, the women were met by their husbands, who brought them to the cramped Chinatown dwellings which would be their homes. Bachelor quarters were transformed into usable family space by knocking down walls of single rooms to form larger ones. Homes were often small apartments behind or above a store or laundry.

Women and children were an unusual sight in San Francisco Chinatown.
(Library of Congress)

Women as Income Earners

Once settled, immigrant wives of men who owned businesses joined their husbands in running the family enterprise. Women worked as clerks in the stores, as waitresses and cooks in the restaurants, and they washed and ironed in the laundries.

No matter where the Chinese chose to settle across the country, the successful operation of the family business relied on the labor of both wives and children. Tommy Jang's father worked on the railroad and then in the 1920s settled his family in Seligman, Arizona, a rugged western town with a Chinese population of 100:

> After the contract was over he got paid and he left the railroad and wanted to open his own business, the restaurant business. Then when he made enough money, he went back to China and brought my mother over and then also the older brothers . . . and they took the whole family to Arizona, and that's where I was born in 1921.[7]

Jang's father ran the restaurant until his death and then his family carried on. His oldest son was then 16. Eventually, the family moved their enterprise to another Arizona town. They built a large restaurant and dance hall, where cowboys would ride up, tie their horses to the front post, and stride in for food and entertainment in the western fashion.

In groceries, general stores, laundries and restaurants, home life and family livelihood were often inseparable. Husbands and wives ran their business together, training their children to take on added responsibilities as they grew older. Although the families followed the traditional Confucian model with father as the authority figure, children were taught to respect and obey both parents.

The amount of daily work accomplished by Chinese women in the early 1900s is described with great respect by their children. Vera Chong remembers what life was like for her mother, Mary Lee Chong, who supported her husband in his pastoral work in Hawaii:

> Each Sunday she fed the congregation with lunch, and of course there were no supermarkets at which to buy the bread. So on Saturday morning, whenever she was finished with her housework, she would bake

Studio portrait of an early arrival.
(California Historical Society)

> loaves of bread. She milked the cow, churned the butter, and made poha jam.
>
> When my father was busy, my mother would get on a horse to visit the congregation. She helped split wood, trimmed and polished kerosene lamps. We had a well beside our house, and she drew water from there, because there was no water piped in.
>
> My mother did say that the Chinese people were very closely knit over here. To come to church, they walked from a radius of five miles. A very fortunate few came on horseback, which was then the only mode of transportation. They also visited our family during the weekdays and when they did they always came with a basket of food, whatever they had planted. And they always went home with jams and loaves of bread which my mother had baked.[8]

Women whose husbands did not own their own business supplemented the family income by seeking outside employment such as peeling shrimp, sewing in garment factories and canning fruits. Some women, like Wong Shee Chew, became the family's sole provider. Wong's husband was accidentally injured in a tong battle and incapacitated. To support the family, Wong labored in a cannery from 6 a.m. to 8 p.m. six days a week for $9.50 a week. In addition, she cleaned shrimp and sewed garments to add to the earnings. Monetary compensation for their labor, no matter how meager, meant independence from lives weighted with poverty:

You can use your hands to work and to make money. That spelled freedom from want. In China, unless you were willing to climb a hill and chop weed or do some hard labor there was no chance to make money. No escape from poverty. That's what China was. You don't have income, you are going to starve. In America, you have the opportunity to make money, to be independent. So that's important. To survive. The opportunity is much better here.[9]

Support Network

The network of clan associations, labor groups, and tongs which had been organized by the Chinatown bachelors proved unresponsive to the needs of women and families. For help in settling into new homes and facing the problems of this foreign world, women turned to other women. Older, earlier immigrants eased the adjustment process, helping with the practical arrangements of living in Chinatown or in rural areas outside the cities. Churches and missions offered assistance to Chinese women who asked for help or were members of their parishes.

Doing laundry in a Chinese fishing village in Monterey, California.
(Visual Communications)

Margaret Leong Lowe was an immigrant wife who joined her husband in America when she was in her twenties. She was widowed while pregnant with their third child. She then moved from Texas to San Francisco. That child, Erline Lowe Wong, recalls her mother's subsequent struggle:

So when she came here to San Francisco she lived next to a Catholic Church. Now, I don't think we were Catholics then. But she must have had some associations with the Catholic Church. As soon as she came up I guess she got in touch with the Catholic Church. The Father took us under his wing and got

us family aid. Chinese welfare in San Francisco. We call it widow's pension. At that time it was Catholic charity.[10]

Margaret Lowe herself recalls the unrelenting work it took to raise her three children on her own:

I worked about six days a week. Sometimes I bring home work—embroidered flowers to make money. I never go to somebody's house. I haven't got time. Sometimes the next door neighbor comes over to my house to talk a little bit. Sunday? Same work at home. Take three children to Sunday church. I be mother,

In the South and Southwest the grocery store was a major source of Chinese livelihood.
(Courtesy, John and Mamie Kai)

Family dressed in festive clothing for New Year visits.

(Library of Congress)

I be father. I had to make money and take care of children. I sewed evening gowns and wedding dresses. . . . I worked fifty-two years. Seventy-two years old stopped. I worked my whole life."

Keeping Tradition Alive

Passing the Chinese tradition on to the children was one of the mother's major responsibilities. She instilled in the children cultural mores, a sense of

Chinese etiquette and a respect for elders. She cooked special foods and organized celebrations around Chinese holidays. Perhaps the most important traditional celebration was Chinese New Year. Edith Wong recalls the excitement surrounding the special day:

Oh yes—we cleaned the house upside down. My mother saved money and ordered rice. You know it was good luck to have plenty at the start of the New Year. We couldn't buy too much, but a bit of every-

thing. And then there would be oranges and lishee.[12] *We didn't have money for the* lishee—*we used dried nuts for money. My mother would put it all over the house to represent money. But the beauty of it was that we'd wake up in the morning and there was some lishee that was ours to keep. And friends would come and give us* lishee. *And then we had wonderful food. Oh, my mother made the best* zai.[13] *We'd have that . . . for our early meal for New Year's day. We said "Happy New Year and Long Life!" to mother and bowed and gave mother tea. My father wasn't home so when my father came back we went through the same thing.*[14]

As the children took part in school programs to commemorate the holidays, mothers got into the spirit by preparing feasts at home. Chinese women also led their families in adapting to American customs such as Thanksgiving and Christmas. They added their own creative touch however, to traditional American dishes, such as basting a turkey in soy sauce and filling it with a stuffing of sweet rice, vegetables, ham and dried shrimp.

"We owe what we have and what we are to each generation before us," says Esther Tang. Given this respect for the elders, the challenge then became how to integrate the old ways with contemporary ones:

In Chinatown, there was a great big barbecue oven and a trolley where they would hoist a 80- or 100-pound pig and let it down into that particular oven and roast it. You would pay the man or say, if it was a wedding, he would cut it up and help distribute the Chinese wedding cookies and pork. When my brother had his one-month coming out party, we invited our friends and we had a big string of fire-crackers and they hoisted it up via a telephone pole. It burned for at least half an hour. They put a white cap on my brother's head and had gold medallions and even though we weren't people of means, my mother and dad saw it was fitting to do that.

So tradition is a great part of our family and even though I'm third generation, I try to keep some of the better traditions. In the Southwest, we have the Mexican culture, the Indian culture, and of course, we're in America so we're Americans, and then we ourselves have the traditional Chinese culture behind us. What we've done in our family is to take advantage of all

the cultures and it's become a very rich lifestyle. It's nothing for us to come home and decide we want tacos or beans, or that we want an Italian dinner of lasagna or whatever. We might combine our meals with rice and Chinese soup or steak. So we really have the best of all cultures and we enjoy it very much.[15]

One element of Chinese cultural tradition maintained in America was a continued inequality of sexes. The expanded role of the female head of the family improved the situation somewhat, as mothers widened the potentials for their daughters. However, the attitude that boys were more precious than their sisters, ingrained in the Chinese psyche over centuries, persisted. Christian families took a more egalitarian attitude, but generally boys were expected to take more responsibility in the family business and pay more attention to their studies. If both parents were working, it was the girls who stayed home to care for the baby brothers or sisters. Some girls started school for the first time when they were ten or twelve, having stayed home until then to care for younger ones while their mothers and fathers worked.[16]

Children at Work

Regardless of gender, children were given responsibilities at a young age, performing small tasks to alleviate the work load for their parents. As they grew older the chores assigned to them became more difficult. In family laundries, children might first help by folding clean handkerchiefs and towels. A few years later they were taught to operate the presses and perform other more complicated jobs. The English they learned in school soon surpassed that of their parents, and their language became an asset in customer relations.

Mothers who brought home garment piece-work to sew, baskets of shrimp to be shelled and artificial flowers to be constructed often asked their children for assistance. When they reached their teen years, Chinese youngsters would spend summers working full time, finding jobs in town or on nearby farms. Their contributions to the family income were essential. Harry Chew remembers the summers of his youth in California:

Plantation family in Hawaii photographed by On Char.
(Bishop Museum)

(My mother) had to work twice as hard because my father was unable to work from the time he was disabled. We were just born—two youngsters. And she had no education. It was lucky we didn't turn bad. Some of that tragedy rubbed off on us—sensitized us. We knew we had to help. Even when we were 16 or 17 we'd go to the country and pick fruits—two months at $1.25 a day. We worked from six in the morning to evening. We got $1.25, room and board. All the kids helped. We'd make maybe forty dollars the whole summer. We turned all the money over to our parents.[17]

Paul Louie recalls that during his childhood in the Pacific Northwest, the Chinese earned extra income and sometimes filled the family table by tapping the abundance of the land. Children were always brought on the excursions to help:

I lived in a place in Seattle Chinatown called Canton Alley. . . . Many of the families that lived in Canton Alley grew vegetables and they sold those vegetables and my family also sold vegetables. At the same time, we, mother and father and I and some of the children, would go out to some of the nearby areas for water-

Bringing lunch to her father, at work in a goldsmith shop. (California State Library, Sacramento)

These second generation Chinese Americans, raised in the world of laundries, restaurants, groceries, and cramped Chinatown apartments, were cuddled and prized as babies, but then expected to mature quickly and learn filial piety, responsibility and resourcefulness. Although Lily Quock was the youngest of nine children, she soon learned to do her part:

You pick shrimps, you know, you peel the skins for cannings. That's what we did, 6¢ to 7¢ a pound and all my sisters and brothers got together and did that. We had to go to the store and then afterwards, after closing time, we had to bring it to the house. And we opened clams, $1 a box and it was 40–50 pounds a box. That's when I was five years old. They put two boxes so I could stand up where they had the long tables there. It was so wet and damp. I stood up there and I learned how to open those clams.
I learned how to sew when I was about seven years old. My mother went to work in a sewing factory. I learned how to sew a whole smock when I was about eight.[19]

When older brothers and sisters were needed in the daily operations of the family business, the youngest children were sometimes left alone in the apartment during the day. The feelings of neglect or abandonment at this early age no doubt had an effect on the children's development and mental health. But the extended family system which provided child care by grandparents and other family members in China did not exist in this new American society.

cress. In those days in Seattle, with much less population, watercress flourished, and with my Dad's car, we would go out, bring the watercress back, and sell it to the restaurants and stores in Chinatown. . . .

Some of the other things that we did as a family, other families did, such as going out to the beaches of Fauntleroy and Aiki Point for clamdigging. That was not to sell but just to get clams to eat. Also we went out to different beaches for seaweed. There is a kind of seaweed that is edible, which we dry and clean, and some of it was sent back to China to the village. I still remember a number of trips that I made with my Dad and younger sisters to the mountainside or the area near Renton to dig for wild ginger root . . . it's used for medicinal purposes.[18]

Educating the Young

Many Chinese American parents were convinced that education was the key to economic and social improvement for the next generation. Sons were especially encouraged to study hard and avail themselves of the free public school education. It was hoped that education would increase the choice of jobs for young Chinese Americans, freeing them from the long hours of laundry, restaurant and grocery work. Some parents hoped that, skilled with modern scientific and technical

Sunday school class, Chinese Presbyterian Church, San Francisco.
(California State Library, Sacramento)

knowledge, their children could return to China and join in its drive towards modernization.

Another priority for second-generation Chinese was learning the Chinese language and culture. The first Chinese language school was organized in San Francisco in 1884. As the number of Chinese American children increased, language schools were organized in Chinese communities throughout the country. Children were expected to attend Chinese school daily after "English school," and were expected to study hard to maintain their grades in both.

After elementary school, many young Chinese were sent back to China for a period of years to continue their Chinese education. There they joined overseas Chinese youth from Australia, Cuba, and other parts of the Americas to learn the language and culture of "the homeland." Chinese American Jung Oi Won was among the more diligent students who returned to China; he passed

the very competitive provincial examination in 1904, and was named a licentiate. Many other students returned to America to continue the familial support once shouldered by their fathers and grandfathers.

A culture shock awaited these second generation youngsters. During their years in China they were young scholars somewhat spoiled by family, and in some cases, *amahs*, or maids. Upon their return to America, usually in time for high school, the young people once again experienced long workdays in family businesses and a society which treated Chinese as second-class citizens. The fact that families tried to save money for their children's education in China demonstrated how important their Chinese heritage was to them. To return to China someday was a deep desire for many, and a Chinese education for the younger generation was preparation for going home.

In schoolyards across the country many Chinese

Although not much older, eldest children looked after younger siblings while parents worked.
(California State Library, Sacramento)

children faced racist teasing and hostility from their peers. The Chinese mother had the enormous task of reinforcing an ethnic pride in the midst of a society which demeaned the race at every turn. Alice Fong Yu, California's first Chinese American public school teacher, remembers that her mother's message, a common one among Chinese mothers, was "Be proud that you're Chinese":

> [Growing up in the mining town of Washington, California] the children weren't nice to us at all. They yelled these obscenities to us each time we would be approaching the school: 'Ching Chong Chinamen sitting on a rail,' and oh, funny sounds, 'eeyauyauyau-yauyau!'—things like that. Just things to make us mad, but then we always took things calmly because we were told at home, 'Don't pay any attention, they're just barbarians! Just be as nice as possible to them, because you have a superior culture.'

> That's what kept us together because nowadays you hear about this 'identity crisis'. People don't know whether they are Americans. Of course we are Americans by birth. Legally we are told yes, legally we are Americans, but physically, they will never accept us. Our physical features—'Look at your face,' our folks would say, 'But don't worry, just show them how smart you are because you have a superior heritage. And then when you grow up and get a good education, go and help your people in China,' So that's why we always prepared to serve our people in China."[20]

At other times, Chinese children found that the best method of dealing with racism was the direct approach. In school, Chinese children learned more than their three R's. Because the school was a microcosm of society, the children also learned how to cope, and in some cases, fight for their place

Photographer Louis Stellman captured Chinatown children at play.
(California State Library, Sacramento)

in the new society. Jack Don recalls his school days in the Southwest:

The older Chinese believe very much in educating their children. Like my father. He said, "I've worked my fingers to the bones for you boys to get yourself an education. If you cannot be better than they are, try to be their equal anyway, because that way, one of these days, you can be up there too.' He said, 'You don't have to go and fight for it.'

I had a temper. The Mexican people called me Chinese Chino. I used to get mad. Now I think, what did I get mad for? I am Chinese. But when someone would call me "Chink", that was something else. I didn't like that. So, big or small, I didn't care what you were, I'd straighten that up right now.

In fact, I had an incident even here in high school. During study period one of them came up to me and wanted to know how to work a problem. He said, "Hey, Chink, how do you do this?" So I just got up and I let him have it. The study group teacher came over and said "What happened?" I said, "Well, he wanted some help with a problem and I'm showing him the chinky way of doing it." [21]

Chinese Families Apart

Some men carried their families in their memories alone, faithfully sending remittances to wives, children and parents in China. A number of men who believed it impossible ever to bring their wives over married Native American women— Mexican, Hawaiian, and American Indian. Their cultures often seemed to have much in common.

Arizona baker Hi Wo, his Mexican wife and their three children, Soledad, Isabella and Pepe.
(Arizona Historical Society)

American Indians and Chinese, for example, revered the spiritual world, shared an understanding of man's place in the natural world and valued the clan or tribe. A mutual respect developed, and one proof of cultural acceptance was the significant number of marriages and the nurturing of children who often exemplified the best of both worlds.

Other men, like pioneer Arizona grocer Fong Hing Sang, were not able to bring their wives to the United States until immigration laws changed. Fong and his wife lived on separate sides of the Pacific for 34 years of their married life.

When I came to Tucson, I first opened a little Mexican grocery store, serving Mexican food and also American food. There was one street, Meyer St., about three to four blocks long, one street from west to east to the mountains. Those were the only streets that

had business. All around were houses. There were Mexicans, Indians, a lot of Indians. They talked a different language. I left China in 1912. I came here via two months on Angel Island in 1913. Right after the war, some Chinese brought their family. Before, not more than 10 Chinese families. Take care of the family store year after year, make a little money, and then go back to China—then come back.

I went back home and got married in 1917. In the 1940's they changed the law. Chinese could be citizens. After five applications, I got my citizenship papers, to bring her over. Not until 1951. Long time. I went back seven times. I had five children, but no longer. Miscarriage, some get sick. I suffer a lot during this life. She was home and I was here long.[22]

Changing Chinatown

With the decline of the bachelor society, those institutions which primarily served single men, such as the opium dens and brothels, gradually closed down, although gambling retained its popularity. With the disappearance of these enterprises the tongs lost their economic base and eventually their influence declined. By the early 1930s, the tong skirmishes which had sporadically plagued the streets of Chinatowns across the country were ended through peace pacts. Chinatown businesses and families exerted public pressure towards this end.

The social complexion of Chinatown transformed from bachelor to family society as young families increased in number and became a real and permanent part of the Chinese American population. As time passed, pedestrian traffic within the communities reflected the increase of married women and babies, and the decrease of those whose queues, shaven heads, or bound feet were reminiscent of nineteenth-century Chinatown.

Chinatown's new population seemed to make a conscious effort to improve the Chinese image and counteract the scandalous accounts of slave girls, tong hatchetmen and opium eaters. For if America was to be their home and if they were to raise their children here, an atmosphere of stability and respect had to be developed. With the over-

In the Chinatown bachelor society, babies were cherished.
(California State Library, Sacramento)

throw of the Manchu Dynasty and the founding of the Chinese Republic in 1911, renewed pride in the motherland stirred feelings of nationalism in Chinatowns across the country. Perhaps now, a strengthened China in the world circle of nations would gain respect for her people overseas.

6 Last Look Back

Dr. Sun Yat-sen, "Father of the Chinese Republic," left an enduring impression not only on Chinese and world history, but in the grassroots oral history of overseas Chinatowns as well. Chinese oldtimers in America remember him as a man who travelled overseas like them, and who inspired in them hope for a new and strengthened China. When the need for a Chinese revolution became increasingly apparent in the early 1900s, they responded generously with their moral and monetary support.

Sun Yat-sen was born in 1866 in Zhongshan. His home village was thirty miles north of Macao, a major emigration port used by Chinese leaving for overseas work in the latter part of the nineteenth century. Sun received his early schooling in the village. As a boy he listened to the tales of an uncle who was a veteran of the Taiping Rebellion, whose leader Sun came to venerate as a hero. In 1879 when he was 13, Sun was sent to Hawaii to join his older brother Sun Mi, who in turn had been brought to the island by another relative, in the kindred tradition of emigrant Chinese communities. There Sun applied himself to the new world of learning before him. In his three years in a parochial high school, he was exposed to the western democratic principles which later were reflected in the ideals he promoted for China.

Upon return to his home village of Ts'ui Heng, Sun is said to have smashed a Taoist idol; to him it symbolized the superstition and oppression which were respectively the enemies of his new Christian faith and his progressive ideas for China's future. Partly due to this village outburst, Sun was sent to Hong Kong, where he attended college and was trained as a physician in a British mission hospital. While in Hong Kong, Sun discussed the formation of a revolutionary society with anti-Manchu compatriots and left his medical practice for a life of political organizing. In 1894 Sun organized the Hsing Chung Hui, or Revive China Society, in Hawaii, and during the following years he formed over fifteen additional branches in overseas Chinese communities throughout the world. Members of the international secret society dedicated themselves to promoting the modernization and prosperity of China.

In 1895, the society's first revolutionary attempt to take over the provincial government in Guangzhou failed. Several of Sun's comrades were caught and executed, and Sun fled overseas. In subsequent years, Sun, as the exiled leader of the Chinese revolutionary movement, studied political and social theory in Europe and Japan, and intensified organizing efforts in Asia and America. In the United States, his organization raissd funds by selling bonds printed with the design of a flag showing the sun under a clear sky. Each was valued at $10 Chinese and redeemable after the revolution for $10 U.S. Chinese newspapers in San Francisco and Hawaii were used to promote the movement.[1]

Reform Movement

It became increasingly clear that China's traditional dynastic structure was incapable of solving the persistent problems caused by foreign intervention, natural disaster and general disarray of society. From the 1890s through the first decade of the twentieth century, the political stage was shared by both reformers and revolutionaries. Reformist Chinese led by Kang Yu-wei and Liang Chi-chao began in 1898 to work through the Emperor to change China's absolute monarchy to a constitutional one, and to establish programs to modernize the country. The young Emperor began to issue a broad series of reform edicts to diminish official corruption and improve the Chinese economic, educational and governmental network. In opposition to the reform measures, the retired Empress Dowager returned and staged a coup d'état. She then rescinded the Emperor's edicts, executed several reformers and imprisoned the Emperor.

Taken to the logical conclusion, the increasingly popular anti-foreign doctrine implied the expulsion of the Manchus, who were foreigners to the Han Chinese. With continued local uprisings, it became evident that the longevity of the Qing Dynasty would depend on its ability to change with the times. In 1902, the Empress Dowager put forth provisions for reform, and attempted to implement many of the programs proposed in 1898. The most significant area of reform was education.

In the 1920s and 1930s thousands of Chinese students arrived in the United States to earn graduate degrees at American universities.
(California State Library, Sacramento)

A school system was initiated throughout China with a curriculum which combined Chinese and western ideas. In 1905, the classical examination system was abolished. Large numbers of Chinese students went overseas to secure the scientific, technical and economic knowledge needed to modernize the country.

Chinese Students Abroad

The emphasis on strengthening China through modernization led many Chinese students, aware of their role as future leaders, to go overseas to study. While the majority went to Japan, large numbers also enrolled in American universities. From 1901–1920 there were 2,400 students in the United States and from 1921 to 1940, a total of 5,500.

Hundreds of Western-educated students returned to China and were given positions in which their training could affect various areas of policy. One of the most successful in translating theory into practice was Y. C. James Yen, who graduated from Yale in 1918 and returned to work among illiterate Chinese peasants in Tinxien. By the mid-1930s his Mass Education Movement had borne unmistakable fruit—the literacy of millions of farmers and their families. Yen was named one of the era's "ten most outstanding revolutionaries," in the company of Albert Einstein, Orville Wright, John Dewey, and Henry Ford.[2]

Revolutionary Movement

Reform was an insufficient answer to China's mounting problems, however, and Sun Yat-sen and his associates, whose first plan to seize Guangzhou had failed in 1895, continued to organize for revolution. In 1905 Sun formed the revolutionary Tung Meng Hui, or "Sworn Together Society," in the overseas Chinese community in Japan. Other chapters were organized in Singapore, Brussels, San Francisco, Honolulu, Guangzhou and Hubei. Sun traveled from place to place, often under disguise, to rally Chinese around his San Min Chu'i,

Dr. Sun Yat-sen.
(Library of Congress)

or Three Principles of the People: nationalism, which extended the anti-foreign precept to include the Manchus; democracy, which would replace the imperial with a constitutional system; and people's livelihood, which called for a better distribution of material wealth.

After the turn of the century numerous disputes were waged among reformers and revolutionaries in overseas Chinatowns. "Pen fights" erupted between party newspapers and organizations and both sides of the political question gained loyal followers. In Sun Yat-sen's speaking tours of America, he managed to rally opposing groups under one banner of nationalism. Although initially dubious of his ideas, Chinese in the United States and other overseas communities were eventually among Sun's most ardent supporters, giving the revolution major support and encouragement through their generous donations. Some Chinese Americans even commenced military training in preparation for service in the revolutionary army.

Ten revolutionary attempts failed in various sections of China throughout the first decade of the twentieth century but by 1911 the mood of the people was such that revolution could no longer be suppressed. Three thousand New Army soldiers

Chinese Americans celebrate the founding of the Republic in 1911.
(California State Library, Sacramento)

revolted in Wuchang on October 10, and the Manchu government officials fled from the city. The rebellion received spontaneous anti-Manchu support in the city. Although the Tung Meng Hui revolutionaries were not involved in the October 10th uprising, they quickly mobilized supporters in other areas, and by December the South Central and Northwest provinces had also declared themselves independent of Manchu rule.

Republic of China

In January 1912, a provisional government was organized in Nanjin and Dr. Sun Yat-sen was elected President. Chinese communities throughout the United States rose in celebration. In New York City, Sun's Young China Association led a festive rally of 2,000 people. Chinatown residents lined the bend of Mott, Pell and Doyer Streets to watch and applaud a parade of community youth, who hoisted toy guns and the new flag of the Republic of China. In San Francisco, Chicago, Los Angeles and elsewhere, the pride was just as deep. Even in the quiet mountain town of Kula, Maui, where Sun Yat-sen's brother Sun Mi lived, there was no restraint to the elation, as Willie Fong recalls:

They paraded down this main road, and go back there to the society building again. A good two miles. They passed right by our place, you know, some with flute, some with the cymbal, making all kinds of noise, music, and then we would burn firecrackers when they come. Everybody was happy. So we all joined that. Barefooted! Those days we didn't even have a pair of shoes![3]

Meanwhile in Beijing, the Manchu government called General Yuan Shih-kai to fight the revolutionaries. Although Sun Yat-sen had accepted the presidency of the new Republic, he offered to resign if Yuan joined forces with him. In February of that year Yuan convinced the Qing Dynasty to abdicate. Sun then immediately handed Yuan the presidency.

Yuan Shih-kai became enamored of his own military power while the calls for modernization and restoration of China went unheeded. At his death in 1916, China entered the Warlord Period (1916–1928), during which time the country was partitioned by powerful warlords. Their armies pillaged the countryside, robbed the villagers of food and money, and charged exorbitant taxes. China lapsed into a state of chaos, with disruption of trade, widespread sale of opium, deterioration of railroad networks, and the collapse of irrigation and flood control. With the warlords answerable only to their own interests, the country suffered continued poverty and disorder. The Revolution of 1911 had failed to usher in a solid Republic which could function effectively. Nationalism and anti-imperialism had not yet been fully understood. It became apparent that the desire to overthrow the Manchus had been the sole unifying force among the 1911 revolutionaries.

The warlords seized Beijing and established a government which was subsequently recognized by the foreign governments, who realized their own interests would be better served by a weak China. Sun's government, convened in 1917 in Guangzhou when Yuan's betrayal of the revolution became obvious, was ignored by the western powers. Sun worked to refocus the attention of the people on his Three Principles. The Soviet Union was the sole western power which paid attention to Sun's vision and by 1923 the principle of "nationalism" had become that of "anti-imperialism." Before he had time to develop and restate his plans more effectively, Sun died in 1925.

The Kuomintang, a continuation of the revolutionary party formed by Sun, experienced a political split in 1927 and ushered in yet another decade of rivalry for political control of the country. Civil war between the two major contenders, Chiang Kai-shek and the non-communist constituency of the Kuomintang, and Mao Zedong and the Chinese Communist Party, was of tremendous consequence for American Chinese, delineating and characterizing community politics to this day. A temporary truce quieted the rivalry, however, when Japan's militarism posed a threat to all.

Sino-Japanese War

In 1937, Japanese forces invaded North China, marking the onset of the Sino-Japanese war. Chinese in the United States lost no time in organizing a campaign of support for their country under the auspices of the United China War Relief Society, which coordinated activities all over the country. They raised funds for the Chinese military and refugees through benefit events, monthly donations, cultural performances, warm clothing round-ups, and other events. America's Chinese collected over $56 million in war relief funds during the eight years of the duration of the war.[4] Rice Bowl Parties were organized all over the country to raise money for food for the needy during this war, and later, World War II.

On another front, Chinese Americans walked picket lines at major ports in protest against United States corporations which were selling and shipping scrap metal and other materials to the Japanese prior to World War II. Chinese Americans also called for an American boycott of Japanese goods. Many Chinese petitioned Congressmen, government officials and the press with letters such as this:

What can the individual citizens of the democratic nations do to stop the ruthless onslaught of the Japanese aggression? We can do at least one thing: we can show our disapproval of their overt acts by boycotting goods "MADE IN JAPAN" . . . by preventing Japanese goods from landing on our shores, and demanding that the merchants with whom you deal do not carry Japanese goods.

Discourage the selling of gasoline, oil, airplanes, scrap iron, and other war materials to the aggressor. Kindly pass this information along by distributing copies among your friends.

Yours for Justice and Peace,
Chang Chew Kong[5]

Chicago Chinese join the war effort during the Sino-Japanese conflict, 1931.
(Chicago Historical Society)

Alice Fong Yu remembers that in San Francisco young people took a leading role in war relief work:

I was working in Chinatown, and we were in the war relief movement, and we were very busy. You know we had our protests in those days too. We were marching with cotton stockings; boycott Japanese silks, Japanese goods, not to wear silk stockings because they came from Japan. We carried these posters protesting silk stockings, and we had to wear those awful cotton stockings, but we didn't mind.

Then we also organized Rice Bowl fashion shows, which were Chinese fashion shows, with different dynasties, with young people from the community performing the various dances. They were very popular in those days. I was amazed to look back at them— when young people are given a chance, what they can do! The older folks believed in our ability to do all these things . . . writing, producing, training young

people for all these shows, and doing the small towns in chartered buses—San Mateo, Vallejo, Grass Valley.[6]

Americanization

Although most of the young people who worked towards the success of the war relief drive had never been to China, they spoke of China as their mother country. Ironically enough, this was the generation which had every right to call America home and which had been influenced largely by the mainstream culture of the United States. Throughout their lives they had learned American ideals in the public schools and from the media.

As they were embracing the values of middle-class America, however, their first-generation parents grew alarmed at their children's forfeit of

Chinese culture in order to gain acceptance from their peers. Generational conflicts were commonplace within families and were described by Chinese American authors such as Pardee Lowe and Jade Snow Wong. The American virtues of independence, aggressiveness, and progressive thinking were in stark contrast to their parents' conservative Confucian ideology.

The most heated conflicts arose over the subject of dating and marriage. Rather than accept a spouse chosen in the traditional manner by their parents, the young people argued for the right to make their own choice of husband or wife, based on love. Naomi Jung recalls:

I remember when my sister got to be eighteen, a match maker said, "Well, so and so is looking for a wife and has a very good position," such and such. My father, being Chinese, and my sister, being eighteen and living in a small town with no Chinese around—well, he was very concerned that we marry Chinese. So I remember someone was interested in my sister. My sister, being a very reserved person, just went to pot when she found out. She'd always go into tears. And of course, we were so Americanized. My sister would throw up her arms and say to my father, "Don't worry about us." So that went by the board. So when I got to be eighteen, the same thing happened and of course I just said, "Papa, don't worry about me." And

Second generation Chinese Americans had many interests similar to other young Americans. Esther Don Tang and her cousin in front of a new car, 1930s.

(Courtesy, Esther Don Tang)

by that time my father knew and I think all the people in New York Chinatown knew—forget it.[7]

In communities throughout the land, Chinese youth created their own brand of American life. They followed new fashion trends, donning flapper dresses and raccoon coats and speaking the appropriate American slang. They mooned over Valentino and were faithful movie goers and fans of Hollywood stars such as Clark Gable and Carol Lombard. They mirrored the activities of their white classmates with their own dances, sports teams, "sharp" dressing and cars.

Mary Shem and Mamie Chu remember the socializing that occurred among Chinese Americans in their town:

Shem: When I came to Houston, one of the local places of meeting everybody was at the downtown bowling alley. You know everybody also has their soda fountain/drugstore deal but when any visitor from out-of-town came to Houston, they went to the bowling alley and that's where they found the crowd. We were all bowlers. When we were through bowling in the evening, when it was still early, about 6 or 7 o'clock in the afternoon, maybe somebody wanted to have a sock dance at their house that evening. So we'd go out to that person's house and have a sock dance. What's a sock dance? Everybody danced in socks. You don't dance with your shoes on. You went for the phonograph and the records, and you'd have potato chips and sandwiches and the pop and everybody would meet in someone's home. The mother and father would be there to chaperone.

Chu: I remember I used to have parties at my home when my sister was here. I would make a pot of spaghetti and I would make a pot of creamed chicken. I would have some salad. My brother was there then, and we would use the driveway to dance on and we would use the garage for the buffet and we used to have good times.[8]

Chinese American young people understood from an early age that their dating and eventual marriage would take place within the race. Edward and Emily Wong explain that in the South, long distances did not deter the young men and women from meeting each other:

Emily: They didn't have anything like matching you up but you knew. Back when I was growing up, in our minds, we knew pretty much that we would marry Chinese.

Edward: Back then, 'course that was some 30 years ago, well, maybe 22 or so, when we were growing up, like in high school there was a lot of prejudice in this part of the country. We were forced to be social with other Chinese kids because we weren't accepted by the outsiders—so called outsiders, the white race so to speak. We all went to high school with other kids, and you were fine in school, but once 3 o'clock came that was it. Besides that, our parents always preached that you need to marry a Chinese. We used to have dances together.

Emily: People in Mississippi, I know, whenever they had any kind of function, people came from all over the state.

Edward: We used to drive from San Antonio all the way to New Orleans or Houston for a dance on Saturday night and go back home that same night. I remember when I was doing my pre-den (dental studies), I was here in Houston already. I'd go over to San Antonio on Sunday because dances were held on Sunday nights because stores were open on Saturday and Sunday was the only free evening. We would leave here at noon, drive over there and arrive around 5 o'clock, then go to somebody's house, shower, go to the dance, leave there at 1 or 2 o'clock, drive back and then go to school—then make class at 8 o'clock.[9]

Chinese Americans were restricted to certain occupations; they operated small family businesses or worked in the service industries and so experienced a constant strain in the family budget. But children, influenced by the media and white schoolmates, sometimes dreamed of better economic circumstances. Mary Shem recalls:

Window-shopping was one of our favorite pastimes because we couldn't buy anything and we always loved to wish for stuff in the windows. Even though you couldn't afford what your counterparts were wearing, you could always go downtown and look in the windows and drool. That was one of our favorite pastimes—we went down and drooled at those windows.[10]

Dancing the bunny hop at a Texas Dragoneers Club party, 1953.
(Courtesy, Wong Shee Ong)

In Search of the American Dream

For the sons and daughters of Chinese immigrants, American citizenship was a birthright, but skin color was a deterrent to equal participation. In growing numbers they were completing college studies and were ready to use their skills and talents in contributing to American society. In city after city, however, Chinese college graduates who sought employment in their fields could find no work. They were inevitably passed over for white applicants. In utter frustration, graduates in chemistry, physics and engineering found themselves working in restaurants, laundries and stores. Some saved their money and went into private enterprise in the Chinese community, the only other avenue open to them. David Chin owned a New York laundry and remembers limited job options for Chinese:

In those days all the Chinese in New York were in laundry. The American people say any Chinese person was the laundryman. There were some restaurant people but not many, like now. Only after the Second

New York City's Chinatown in the 1930s was still primarily a bachelor society where Chinese lived and worked.

(Museum of the City of New York)

World War did things change around a lot. When Chinese people came before, even if you had an education, there was no other work. One man was a graduate of Columbia University. He couldn't get any job, it was about 1929, '30, somewhere around there. So, he just hung around Chinatown and just did nothing. Where are you going to get a job? They don't pay any attention—they don't bother with you. What do you do? Because he had so much education, he didn't want to work with the laundry or the restaurant. In those days, it was better if you just came over to work hard, not know anything. Just work.[11]

Chinese American women were sometimes hired by large hotels and restaurants as hatcheck girls, elevator operators, cigarette sellers and dancers. Their employers found it helped business to create an exotic milieu in their establishments. So they hired attractive Chinese American women and costumed them in Chinese clothing; to mainstream society, Chinese faces were necessarily accompanied by Chinese costumes.

A number of Chinese who were able to find jobs in offices outside Chinatown encountered problems of their own, walking the uncomfortable margin between both worlds. Emilie Lau recalls working in a San Francisco insurance company as a file clerk in the late 1920s:

Here again is where the prejudice comes in. The whites didn't want me, my own race was jealous, suspicious of how I got the job and as a matter of fact, I was one of the first Chinese girls to get a job there and I got it through the Catholic Church, believe it or not. And gradually after that, I started bringing girls in, one by one. But there, the funny thing about prejudice is the company I worked for did not hire Blacks, Jews and Catholics. But Chinese they did. But even at work it was hard. So through the Depression years, some of the whites would say to me, "You have no right here. By rights you should be in Chinatown, doing laundry."[12]

A few Chinese artists, writers and performers used their culture to advantage, their popularity based on the presentation of an image the wider American public had come to expect. They often did their Confucius-say routine tongue-in-cheek, as was the case of Hugh Liang and the Chung Wah Four barbershop quartet. In 1912 Liang was a student at the University of California at Berkeley when he was asked to join the first Chinese barbershop quartet and tour vaudeville:

We played all around San Francisco and finally, we made the trip to Honolulu—to the Liberty Theater. When we came back, the manager thought we would be a big hit on Broadway so he took us to New

Chung Hwa Four, vaudeville's Chinese American barbershop quartet.
(Courtesy, Hugh Liang)

York. . . . When we got to New York, nobody would believe it. They all said, "We've never heard one Chinaman sing in key, how're you going to get four Chinamen in harmony?" They told us to get out of here. They wouldn't listen to him.

So, finally, one Irish manager said, "I'll take you on. . . . I'll give you a contract for one week at Buffalo. I know it'll be a failure but I'll take a chance. One week and then you'll take your Chinese back to San Francisco."

So, anyway, we went up to Buffalo and you know to our big surprise and to everybody else's surprise, we were a big hit. "Big time," they called it. "You see," he said, "They stopped the show! Nobody could follow them!" We started with a Chinese song, "The Song of the Lily,". . . . We made a joke, saying "When we come to the chorus, we would like everyone to join in." Naturally, no one came in. We didn't even know ourselves if there was a chorus. After the song everyone laughed . . . and then we said, "Gee, maybe you don't like Chinese songs. We'll sing you something American, maybe you'll like better."

The lights dimmed out and . . . I tell you, you could hear a pin drop because it was such a shocking surprise to hear the change from the "crazy Chinese song" to the harmony in the "Chinese Blues.". . . After the song, the house just came down. My goodness, they never dreamed that Chinese could sing like that. From then on, it was a cinch. . . . It was easy sailing for 14 years. We played in America and Canada as the first and only Chinese quartet in the world. So that's it.[13]

There were other Chinese Americans who, through a combination of talent and timing, were able to excel in their career. One such person was James Wong Howe, who was synonymous with the best of Hollywood cinematography from the 1920s until his death in 1976. In 1917, after watching some filming in the Los Angeles Chinatown area, Howe found work sweeping floors for $10 a week at the Famous Players-Lasky Studios. In time he was promoted to assistant cameraman and then cinematographer at the insistence of actress Mary Miles Minter, who was so pleased with his work that she would work with no other cameraman. In the 1920s and 1930s, Howe worked his way to the top of his profession. During his fifty-two year ca-

rer, he collaborated with Hollywood's top directors, from Busbee Berkeley to Martin Ritt and John Sturges, on about 120 feature films. He won Oscars for cinematography in *The Rose Tattoo* (1955) and *Hud* (1964). Sturges called him "the greatest stylist in the business." Without a doubt, his eye for photographic realism helped shape American movies as we know them today.[14]

Returning to China was a common topic of conversation among young second-generation Chinese Americans. They chose courses of study in college which would be of practical use in developing China—engineering, medicine, nutrition, education and the sciences. They talked about "going back," although few had been there before. They knew China through their parents, through Chinese-language schools, through correspondence and remittance to relatives there, through newspaper accounts and through fellow students from China whose commitment to the country was often contagious. Since they felt unaccepted in mainstream America, those who were educated in the universities typically spoke of returning to help in the modernization of China. Many joined China-born students in return trips to the "motherland" or continued their studies at Chinese universities.

Chinese students from the United States and China met on campuses, socialized and discussed China's future. Groups like the Chinese Student Christian Association and the Chinese Christian Youth Conference held annual conferences at Silver Bay on the east coast and Lake Tahoe on the west. A certain comradeship developed between native- and China-born in groups like these. Although the writers of this 1946 letter to *The Nation* magazine were from Hawaii, the United States and China, they shared a dream for a strong Chinese nation:

Dear Sirs:

The civil-war-in-China diet that the American press insists on feeding its readers these days is a source of great unhappiness to us Chinese young people, studying and working in the United States. Not only because civil war will mean years more of unprecedented suffering for our loved ones at home, but because conflicting and unreliable reports may cost us the friendship and understanding of the American people.

Chinese American youth formed their own sports teams and waged keen competition in regional leagues. (California State Library, Sacramento)

We believe too much stress has been laid on the inevitability of internal strife in China and the disunity of the Chinese people. Little mention has been made of the basic and common desire of the Chinese to arrive at a quick and equitable solution of their internal problems and establish a strong and democratic government. . . .

We feel, in reiterating the following national goals, that we are representing the heart-felt desire of all Chinese, regardless of party and faction. 1) China must have unity. . . . 2) China must be democratic. . . . 3) China must maintain her national sovereignty, free from the fear of foreign military aggression or economic imperialism; 4) The new gov-

ernment must observe the principle of people's livelihood.

Janet Chong, May Eng,
Edwin Kwok, Wellington Lee,
Shelley Mark[15]

American-Born Battle for Rights

Second-generation Chinese Americans found that being born in the United States did not necessarily guarantee equal treatment for them. When discrimination was the rule, Chinese Americans often voiced their protest and fought for rectification of the situation. As early as 1895, Walter U. Lum, Joseph K. Lum, and Ng Gunn founded an organization which they called the Native Sons of the Golden State. Their purpose was to defend the rights of Americans of Chinese ancestry. The group made its headquarters in San Francisco and expanded to other cities. By 1915, it was known as the Chinese American Citizens Alliance (CACA). As the foremost Chinese American organization in the civil rights field, it fought against discriminatory exclusion laws and segregation in schools and other public places. CACA's aim was acceptance in American society through active participation—it encouraged Chinese Americans to vote and to speak up for their democratic rights.

Other Chinese Americans fought for their economic rights. Two-thousand members of the Sai Fook Tong, a laundry worker's guild, shut down Chinese laundries in San Francisco for a week in 1929 and won an eleven-hour day. New York's Chinese Hand Laundry Alliance, formed in 1933, grew to more than 3,200 members, and battled discriminatory legislation. During the Great Depression of the 1930s, Chinese joined the massive ranks of America's unemployed.[16] Many marched in demonstrations which pressured the passage of the National Recovery Act. In 1934, the Chinese Workers' Center joined the San Francisco General Strike, shutting down most of Chinatown. This show of solidarity was an important step towards the opening of mainstream union doors to Chinese American workers.

A drive to push Chinese out of the grocery business in Texas was stopped short by an organized and vocal Chinese community in San Antonio in 1937 during the depression years. Rose Don Wu, representing the Chinese grocers, addressed the State Senate with a scathing testimony which made headlines. The bill that she, the Chinese Consul and a Mexican American representative testified against called for restricting Texas property ownership to American citizens or aliens who could become citizens. She reminded the senators that it was the Chinese, her father among them, who had built the railroad which greatly boosted national prosperity.

"Twelve hundred Chinese helped build the railroad and now there are only seven hundred Chinese in Texas and we have to go through all this for those seven hundred," Wu told the Senators. When the bill's sponsor, Senator Franklin Spears, told Wu that as a Chinese American she had the same rights he had, Wu responded, "I know I have the rights, but I do not forget my blood. Everyone can tell I am Chinese by my color. You pass this law and I have to go through much embarrassment if I want to rent a piece of property. Everyone doesn't know I'm a citizen."[17]

During the questioning period, Wu charged that San Antonio chain stores were the architects of the bill to restrict Chinese businesses. In the end the Chinese community won a victory in their fight against the Alien land bill, perhaps forestalling similar measures throughout the country.

Segregation in San Francisco schools was suggested as early as 1858, when State Superintendent of Public Instruction Andrew Moulder called for the exclusion of Africans, Chinese and Indians from the public schools. Two years later, legislation was passed to establish separate schools for non-white children. The legislation neglected the establishment of a school for Chinese children. A fight for such a school escalated in 1885 with a court case suing for the admission of an eight-year-old Chinese girl to Spring Valley Public School. As a result of a ruling in favor of the plaintiff, the State revised its code to permit separate schools for the Chinese. The Chinese Primary School was immediately organized. Today it is known as Commodore Stockton School and still serves as one of the major schools in the San Francisco Chinatown neighborhood.

Several Chinese challenged school segregation in San Francisco in the early 1900s. In 1902, Dr. Wong Him took the Board of Education to court to stop the expulsion of his young daughter from Clement Grammar School, which was closer to the Wong home than the Chinese Public School. The court ruled against Dr. Wong. In 1903, a group of Chinese merchants in San Francisco petitioned the legislature for a dissolution of segregated schools, but was unsuccessful.

Segregation declined in the next decades as public sentiment towards Chinese improved. In the small towns of California, it had become expensive to maintain separate schools for a handful of Chinese. When integration occurred without major incident, more schools experimented. The larger

Although second generation Chinese Americans were born and raised in the United States, employment discrimination restricted many to Chinatown businesses.

(Courtesy, Virginia Wong)

cities followed suit. But anti-Chinese elements continued to oppose integration in various locations until the 1930s.

In Mississippi, Chinese children were, for a period of years, barred from the public schools. Berda Lum Chan recalls what it felt like to be one of those children, and how her father challenged the ruling all the way to the Supreme Court:

I was born in Denoit, Mississippi. So were my sister and brother. I was in the third grade in Rosedale, Mississippi, when they decided that the Chinese could not go to school in Mississippi. And it all came about because there was some Chinese in Cleveland, Mississippi, that opened up a wholesale grocery store and because of professional jealousy, or whatever you call it, they decided that they couldn't compete in business with the Chinese and therefore they did it. According to the law, each nationality had to have their own school.

The next thing we knew, they told us we couldn't go to school. My dad didn't like that so he took it to court. He took it to the United States Supreme Court and paid all the bills. The Supreme Court said that they would turn it back to the states and they had the right to say who they wanted to go to school. . . . (We) moved from Mississippi to Arkansas after we lost the case. So, we went to school in Arkansas and I finished my school there."[18]

Mistreatment in America caused young Chinese Americans to consider a future in China, that faraway land of their ancestors. But the political events of the first half of the twentieth century caused the community to recenter its thoughts on America. Civil War, a World War, and another revolution would bring dramatic changes to China and in turn, Chinatown. And China the Motherland continued to fade gradually, mirage-like, with each passing year.

DEDICATED TO OUR
AMERICAN AND CHINESE
NEIGHBORHOOD BOYS IN SERVICE
DEMOCRACY FOREVER
SNAPPY CLOTHES

7 Turning the Tide

December 7, 1941, is a day which has held a variety of meanings for America. To the United States government and most of its citizens, the attack on Pearl Harbor was a clear call to war against Japan and the Axis powers. To Japanese Americans, it signaled the start of a nightmare which would include their unwarranted mass incarceration. To Chinese Americans, America's entry into World War II provided a set of circumstances which, in retrospect, marked a breakthrough in their acceptance and progress as an ethnic minority.

The mass mobilization of American troops for war created a domestic labor shortage which was intensified by the development of war industries in need of workers. After decades of systematic exclusion from American industry, American Chinese were finally called into its ranks. The United States and China were now allies dedicated to working together against common enemies. Thousands of young Chinese Americans were hired in shipyards, aircraft plants and factories. Many trained architects, engineers, chemists and technicians found work in their fields for the first time, enabling them to leave the Chinatown businesses which had earlier sustained them.

Sociologist Rose Hum Lee reported in 1942 that all over America, the war had qualitatively changed Chinese community life. The exodus of Chinese labor from Chinatown into mainstream industry caused a slowdown in community businesses. Restaurants ran with a fraction of their staff, or closed down completely. Establishments in Phil-

adelphia and Pittsburgh tried to survive by shuttling workers from larger Chinatowns. In Minneapolis, the city's only Chinese gift shop owner liquidated his enterprise and joined a war industry.

"New York's Chinatown cheered itself hoarse when first draft numbers drawn were for Chinese Americans," wrote Lee. "Some below-age boys tried to pass on their 'Chinese age,' which is often a year or two older than the American count. Since their birth certificates told a different tale, they had to be patient and wait."[1] The eleven draft-age Chinese Americans in Butte, Montana all entered some form of service to their country.

The Portland, Oregon, community had a contingent of thirty-three pilots serving with Generalissimo Chiang Kai-shek and sent to China before Pearl Harbor. Others trained for the United States Air Force. San Francisco Chinatown reported raising $18,000 for the Red Cross and more than $30,000 in the Defense Bond drive.

Some 300 laundryworkers in Los Angeles closed their shops and joined the construction crews of the ship *China Victory* in 1944. In California shipyards, Chinese men and women joined other Americans in welding, iron cutting, steel fitting and electrical, mechanical and scientific tasks. Eight thousand young men from the Chinese community enlisted for service in the American military. Restrictions barring their earlier participation were quickly lifted. Chinese could for the first time qualify as apprentice seamen in the United States

Navy and Naval Reserve, whereas earlier they had been relegated to positions as mess men and stewards.

Yet some racism still had to be confronted. William Der Bing, today, head of Protocol and Community Affairs at NASA, tells the story of his application for flight training in the United States Navy:

They were reluctant to give me the application forms. I said, "Either I get them here or I can get them from my Congressman." The minute I mentioned "Congressman," the next thing I knew I had a pile of papers. Even in the Navy, there were some real good men, but the majority didn't want a "Chinaman" in their outfit. They made every remark possible to harass you.

"Personally, I was told that "No Chinaman will ever fly in my outfit." I was told that by a doctor—a Navy doctor. He gave me a physical. He said, "I want you to know that I would do anything I can to fail you in your physical." I looked at him and said, "If you do, it would be the most dishonest thing that an officer in this United States Navy would ever do to another member of the United States Navy." I put it just this way.[2]

Although he was failed by that doctor, Der Bing persisted and was eventually admitted, after seeking a second medical opinion.

Jack Don discovered that the war made entry into new occupations much easier, but treatment from fellow workers showed that attitudes towards the Chinese had not yet changed:

During the War, I went to work at Davis Air Base. I got to be foreman but I couldn't have the title. They paid me the foreman's wages, a senior mechanics rate, and all that, but about every month or so, on payday, they'd say, "We don't want a Chinaman giving them orders." I was working in the Armament Department. I had all the duties of the foreman but the superintendent from the base came down and told me, "Don, we want you to take this job but please take it without the title." That was WW II. Now the Chinese people are having it a little easier.

Before then, I had a grocery store too. There was one time when a lady came from back East, or something, she came into the store there, filled up her basket, brought it out to be checked and then she looked up and said, "Are you Chinese?" I said, "Yes, Ma'am I am." She just left the basket there and took off. She

Hazel Toy was the first member inducted into the air unit of the Women's Army Corps, which was composed of Chinese American women, 1943.
(National Archives)

didn't say a word. Everybody in the store was laughing. They said, "Gee, what happened there, what did you do?" But that's the kind of stuff we had to take.[3]

Opening Chinatown Doors

Despite incidents of racial discrimination, Chinese American soldiers participating in the United States military began to convince American people as a whole that they were loyal citizens. A special Chinese American infantry division, suggested by Madame Chiang Kai-shek, fought in China. While there, many of them realized the extent of their Americanization and discarded thoughts of returning to the motherland after the war. That dream was replaced by one of making Chinese life better in the United States.

The re-opening of American industry to Chinese Americans came at a time of labor shortages, just as it had decades earlier, when Chinese were an important part of the working force in the railroads and California industries. By the 1940s there was a generation of United States citizens, educated in American schools, and already trained

for the blue and white collar jobs which were opening up to them. All their lives their parents had stressed the value of education. Now the scientific and technical knowledge nurtured by those years of study was finally put to appropriate use. Given these new-found opportunities, Chinese generally performed well and earned greater acceptance, paving the way for subsequent generations of Chinese students, workers, young professionals and small business owners. Chinese no longer had to return to Chinatown, nor did they have to think about going back to China to reach personal and professional goals.

Increased prestige in American society provided a psychological lift for the Chinese community. Harold Lui recalls the shift in attitude in New York City's Chinatown:

In the 1940s for the first time Chinese were accepted by Americans as being friends because at that time, Chinese and Americans were fighting against the Japanese and the Germans and the Nazis. Therefore, all of a sudden, we became part of an American dream. We had heroes with Chiang Kai-shek and Madame Chiang Kai-shek and so on. It was just a whole different era and in the community we began to feel

Shu Lee joined the war effort by putting his training in mechanical engineering to use.
(National Archives)

very good about ourselves—within the community, not outside. My own brother went into the service. We were so proud that they were in uniform. It was nice. We felt part of the society at that time. Right after the war, that was the big change.[4]

Repeal of the Exclusion Act

Unprecedented cooperation between the United States and China during World War II served to expose the Chinese exclusion laws as a source of embarrassment to the American government. The Chinese in America were no longer considered a social or economic threat. In order to strengthen the Allied war effort and to counteract Japanese propaganda which accused the United States of being anti-Asian, the need to abolish the Chinese exclusion laws became evident.

Several events led to their final repeal. The Citizen's Community to Repeal Chinese Exclusion was founded in May, 1942. It was composed of over 180 non-Chinese members whose purpose was to educate the public and promote a favorable image of the Chinese. There was initial opposition to the repeal by the American Federation of Labor (AFL), but AFL locals and the Congress of Industrial Organizations (CIO) supported the measure. Patriotic societies such as the Society of Mayflower Descendants, Daughters of the American Revolution, and Native Sons of the Golden West spoke against the repeal.

Support was expressed by religious, business, humanitarian and liberal organizations, and individuals such as author Pearl Buck. An articulate and confident Madame Chiang Kai-shek was a living contradiction of the Chinese stereotype in her speech to the Joint Session of Congress and her national tour in the spring of 1943. Congressman

Chinese American women joined the war effort by folding bandages and packing supplies.
(National Archives)

*Active participation of Chinese Americans in World War II led the United States
government to regard them as loyal Americans. Although discrimination persisted, World
War II was a turning point for Chinese Americans.*

(National Archives)

Warren Magnuson (D-Washington) introduced the repeal bill in the United States House of Representatives in 1942, and following its passage, Senator Charles Andrews of Florida pushed it successfully through the Senate in 1943.

The legislation abolished all existing laws regarding Chinese exclusion in immigration. It granted an annual entry quota of 105 persons of Chinese ancestry, with 75% of that quota for those emigrating from China. More importantly, the bill granted naturalization rights to Chinese in America, allowing them to transfer their citizenship to the United States.

In the decade following the repeal of the exclusion laws, an annual average of only fifty-nine Chinese entered the United States under the quota system. To screen potential immigrants, four preference categories were used, keeping immigrants to a minimal number. The categories were: skilled aliens whose services were needed in the United States; parents of Chinese American citizens over the age of 21; spouses and children of permanent residents; and specified relatives of those in the first three categories.

Fortunately, special acts opened the immigration doors a little wider. Under the 1946 War Bride Act, wives and children of Chinese American citizens were allowed entry under a non-quota category. From 1948–1953, 90% of the immigrants from China were women joining their husbands after years of separation. It was not until 1952 that Chinese American women could send for husbands and children. Then with the Displaced Persons Act, 1948-1954, some 4,000 students and professionals who felt that the 1949 Communist take-over precluded their return to China were allowed to enter or adjust their status to remain in the United States.

From 1953 to 1956, a Refugee Relief Act provided 2,000 visas for Chinese Nationalist refugees outside the normal quota; under the same act, 90,000 German refugees entered the country as well. After over six decades of Chinese exclusion, America began to open her doors. From 1941 to 1960, 44,720 Chinese either immigrated or adjusted their status to that of permanent residents.[5]

After the War

These legal changes did not lead to hordes of new immigrants or inundation of domestic labor markets as some may have feared. But the new laws had great effect on the Chinese in America. They meant that Chinese could apply for American citizenship and qualify for government employment, which has proven a major source of employment for many minorities. This, together with legal changes at the local and state government level, enabled Chinese over the following years to widen employment and income-earning opportunities, buy and own real estate, move into more desirable residential areas, qualify for admission into legal, medical, and scientific schools and professions, and gain public office, on an elected or appointed basis.

According to Harold Lui, New York City's Chinatown community went through visible changes as its female population increased because of the new laws:

Right after the war, with the guys coming from the Army, many of them brought home wives and all of a sudden, all the people who were not born in this country became citizens. And once they became citizens, all their attitudes changed. First of all the attitudes, second of all the numbers. More people began coming here. More families, war brides. There was a combination of American-born and overseas-born.

The Chinatown community began expanding. Communications were better, more people got telephones, carfare was cheaper, the economy was good. People had money, so all of a sudden the Chinese began to spread out to the other schools. And I guess as the Italian community started growing amd making more money themselves, they started moving out and there was a natural kind of moving in.

And as more women started coming over, there was a larger labor market. Factories opened and in 1950, the big thing was making those beads. In 1950-1951 there were more and more jobs for women and whole new lifestyles began to take place.[6]

Chinese American soldiers made use of the GI Bill to go to college or learn a trade. Mary Shem explains:

During WW II, after the kids went into the service, Uncle Sam gave them the opportunity to go back to college; he paid for the college education. So that's how a lot of us were able to get out of the grocery business. My husband was able to go to college, and to learn the air-conditioning/refrigeration business. So when he got to do that his brothers took over the store. Most of the families who have stores, their children do not go back to the stores. Now you have doctors, technicians, engineers, draftsmen, architects. So, you find that this younger generation has broken the gap between the Mama and Papa stores. They go into professions and some of them have set up their own businesses and some are working for other organizations.[7]

From the late 1940s on, some of the states began eliminating anti-Chinese measures such as alien land laws, anti-miscegenation laws, and restrictive housing covenants. In 1952, discriminatory provisions were written off the state constitution in California, where the anti-Chinese movement had been most intense. The state lifted its prohibition of mixed marriage in 1948, but it was not until 1967 that the United States Supreme Court passed an across-the-board ruling against such laws which remained in other states.

With increased acceptance in the period following World War II, the status of Chinese Americans changed from overseas Chinese to that of a bonafide ethnic minority in America. Increased move-

Many Chinese American men enlisted for service in the U.S. military.

(Courtesy, Mary Shem)

ment into the American mainstream included participation in electoral politics. In Arizona, Wing F. Ong was in 1946 the first Chinese elected to a State legislature on the United States mainland. March Fong Eu became a California school board member in 1956, a State Assembly person in 1966, and Secretary of State in 1975. As Hawaii's first Senator in 1959, Hiram Fong was also the first Asian American elected to Congress.

In the 1950s Chinese Americans took an increased interest in the American electoral process, forming Democratic and Republican caucuses in larger Chinatowns and supporting political campaigns. Their involvement was one more sign of a movement outward from the traditional political groupings of Chinatown.

Chinese Americans pulled into the mainstream work force by war industries remained in their new fields, but upward mobility within firms remained difficult. Engineer Him Mark Lai recalls his own experience with college and employment in the mid–1940s:

Even when I was going to college my father was saying, "Why don't you go to the shipyards? You get more money there anyway." And he always pointed out the example, see, he worked for a garment factory and the owner of the garment factory was a graduate, a mining engineer. He ended up operating a garment factory.

By the time I was going to school, the situation had changed slightly. In 1943, it was during the war, some of the Chinese were already working in new fields. Naturally after I graduated I found it was not yet very easy to get a job in those days. You talk about democracy and all that. So a lot of Chinese do go into the Civil Service.

Later I went to the Bechtel Corporation. I worked there in 1953 and I knew all the Chinese because there were not very many of them. Now there are a lot of Chinese, about 10%. I think I became the first Chinese supervisor in my discipline, that's mechanical engineering, and that didn't happen until about 1962–1963. So it's a lot harder for the Chinese than it is for the average white.[8]

In the 1950s, a larger exodus from Chinatown into the suburbs took place. In growing numbers, Chinese bought homes and moved to the Richmond and Sunset districts in San Francisco and the Queens and Brooklyn boroughs in New York City. Residential segregation had begun to wane, but many neighborhoods were still reluctant to accept Chinese Americans. Al Young recalls his parents' house-buying experience in San Francisco's Richmond district:

We block-busted. Yeah, there were no Chinese living in that area and my Dad at the time was a lieutenant colonel—he was the highest-ranking Chinese American officer in the Army and he tried to buy a house. This was after World War II. They wouldn't sell him the house. It was very ironic and he had to get one of his army buddies, whom I believe was partially German, to buy the house and then sell it to my Dad.[9]

America in the 1950s

Following the long years of war, Americans became absorbed in building lives of prosperity and peace. As other world nations recovered from the destruction of war and turned to the United States for assistance, American banks and corporations secured a dominant position in the international economy. Domestically, defense industries had revived a depressed U.S. economy, and regular employment of workers had raised standards of living. A decade earlier, Franklin D. Roosevelt's New Deal had initiated numerous programs in response to the Great Depression, and these continued to improve the quality of life for Americans. They included public works, social security, labor reform, minimum wages, and financial and banking reform.

The ranks of white-collar workers began increasing in the 1940s, and by the 1950s outnumbered blue-collar workers for the first time in United Statem history. With increased earnings, middle-class Americans were able to move from inner cities to homes in the suburbs. Mass-produced middle American communities such as Levittown, Pennsylvania, were developed expediently and inexpensively across the land. The movement to the suburbs also affected the ethnic composition of American cities. In one decade, two million white Americans moved out of the nation's twelve largest cities, as one million eight thousand Blacks and other ethnic Americans moved in.

The fifties also witnessed the growth of conformity. Large corporations stressed teamwork and restricted individualism. Many of them specified the kind of clothes their employees might wear. Schools also perpetuated this standardized lifestyle. Historian Richard Hofstadter writes that in one New York school, the students from grades seven through ten were required to take a course in Home and Family Living, which featured discussions on "developing the school spirit," "clicking with the crowd," and "how to be liked."[10]

Television replaced radio as the central form of entertainment in the American household. Programs such as *Father Knows Best* and *Ozzie and Harriet* idealized American family life. In the cult of true domesticity, the aproned wife remained at home to care for the children, awaiting her husband's return from the office to solve the day's problems. And "keeping up with the Joneses" was an attitude which pressed all neighbors in suburban America towards the proverbial horn of plenty.

Architect Charles Chan and his family, 1952.
(Courtesy, Charles and Berda Lum Chan)

Chinese American Middle Class

The fifties was a relatively quiet decade for Chinese Americans. The majority of those living outside of Chinatown were pleased with their newly-acquired status. The American dream seemed so close that they ignored lingering signs of discrimination. Not surprisingly, the generation that left Chinatown, with acceptance in middle America foremost on their minds, incorporated little traditional Chinese culture into their family lives. Their children often understood but could not speak Chinese. The usefulness of the Chinese language in America was a matter of some debate, as Charles Chan reflects:

Our children don't even speak Chinese. During the war, we were in Detroit and we ran around with a bunch of college students. There was a school of nursing there and the woman told us that we shouldn't teach our children Chinese until they go to school because if you do and they go to school, they'll find out that they're different and they'll have an inferiority complex.

They started a Chinese school one time and we sent our kids there. They each had a different teacher and they couldn't even agree on pronunciation. They came home and had a big fight and I said, "That's enough, you don't go to Chinese school!" No sense in going to school, coming back and fighting about how to say "one", "two". I think the main thing is that if I use Chinese as a means of making a living, I would be reading or writing Chinese. But it's no more useful to me than Japanese is.[11]

The acculturation process in the suburbs meant the loss of a lifestyle familiar to Chinatown families. For a segment of the Chinese American population, the process continues to this day, as Elsie Huang reflects:

I have not accepted all the Chinese customs because I was born here, educated here, and I pick and choose the things I think are fine. I still respect many of the Chinese customs. But more and more people of my daughter's generation are marrying Caucasians. They go to school with them, and the things that the Caucasians do are maybe more suited to them.

The aspiration of many Chinese Americans in the fifties was to move to the suburbs and blend into the American cultural melting pot.

(Courtesy, Esther Don Tang)

We speak English at home. Our kids can't speak Chinese, not unless you train them when they are very little. In a sense, I can't blame my kids or others brought up like ours, that they are married to Caucasians because it's so much alike. For instance, we work five days a week. We eat dinner right around 6:30. Whereas, my sister has a grocery store. She goes to work, maybe about 9 a.m., they don't go home until 9 o'clock at night and they are opened 6½ days a week.[12]

Politically-active Chinese Americans who observed the continuing restrictions society placed on their people began voicing the need for Chinese American organizations similar to the National Association for Advancement of Colored People

(NAACP) and the National Urban League. They warned that the doors of industry and the professions had been opened to the Chinese only because of a wartime scarcity of the labor market. When the economic boom was over, they warned, minority groups would feel it first.[13]

Chinatown Fifties

In the 1950s Chinatowns across the United States dwindled in population. Those residents who remained had specific reasons for doing so. Merchants preferred the close proximity to their place of business. Elderly bachelors found Chinatown residence their only choice because of their limited English and finances, and because they shared surrogate families in the community through district associations. Of the newly-arriving immigrants, only those with families in Chinatowns went there. The trend was to outward movement. By 1960, only 4,000 of 32,000 Chinese in New York City lived in Chinatown.[14]

McCarthyism and Chinatown

The massive American military establishment developed for World War II was not dismantled after the war, but was maintained as a ready force in an atmosphere of growing tension with the Soviet Union over the issue of world influence. American economic and political dominance overseas was further altered by the completion of the Chinese Revolution in 1949. When Mao Zedong and the Chinese Communist Party established the People's Republic of China (PRC) that year, the United States refused to recognize the government and instead continued diplomatic relations with Chiang Kai-shek's Republic of China government, exiled in Taiwan. Kuomintang (KMT) forces took advantage of the United States-PRC hostility to strengthen their influence in American Chinatowns. Their politics were reflected in community newspapers, language schools and the more conservative Chinatown organizations. The KMT position was reinforced by the anti-Communist fervor of the Korean War and the McCarthy period.

Anti-Communist Leagues scoured the community for leftist elements and any feelings of attachment to the People's Republic of China were quelled in the rising paranoia.

In 1955, Everett F. Drumwright, United States Consul in Hong Kong, claimed that many Chinese were illegal aliens and that some of them were possible communist agents. FBI director J. Edgar Hoover voiced similar suspicions. Distressed by this renewal of the yellow-horde image, Chinese Consolidated Benevolent Association delegates from all over the nation formed the National Chinese Welfare Council in 1957 to lobby against mass persecution and deportation of the Chinese. As a result, the Confession program was established. It called for those who had entered America with fraudulent immigration papers to step forward and confess. In return, the government promised to consider the readjustment of their status. Thousands of cases were processed in San Francisco and elsewhere. Soon it became clear to the community's PRC sympathizers that much of the program was aimed in their direction. *San Francisco Journal* publisher Maurice Chuck discusses his personal experience with the Confession program:

My grandfather used the name of Chuck to come to this country, so naturally my father was under the same name and became a citizen of this country. So it's also true for me to use the same last name, to become a citizen.

But what happened was, they used the 'confession' evidence against those they felt were not friendly or loyal to the government and this is exactly what happened to me. They arrested me and tried me and used my father's confession as evidence against me. They didn't use it against my father. But. . . if you call it a crime, it was my father or my grandfather, not me. So it's very obvious that the reason that they put on this so-called 'confession' program was to aim it at some particular individuals.

They tried to deport me to Taiwan but my activities here in this country were so totally against the Chiang Kai-shek government, it's like sending me to a firing squad. So I got all these professors from U. C. Berkeley and other places to prove that because of my political activities, it's absolutely impossible for the government to deport me to Taiwan. So I just keep fighting and fighting the government ever since.[15]

As Chinatown's progressive activists were hauled through the Confession program and threatened with deportation and loss of citizenship, their organizations one by one succumbed to the repression and disbanded. San Francisco's Chinese American Democratic Youth League and Chinese Worker's Mutual Aid Association were two casualties of the McCarthy Era.

Stranded Students

Another group of Chinese joined the ranks of Chinese in America after World War II. About 5,000 foreign-born Chinese in America who had immigrated for purposes of higher education, specialized training and research, business represen-

tation or work experience found themselves stranded in the United States after the 1949 Communist takeover in China. The majority of this number were graduate students attending such institutions as Harvard, M.I.T., Columbia and the Universities of California, Illinois, Pennsylvania, Michigan and Washington.

Donald Tsai, who arrived in 1941 to study at Pomona College and later at M.I.T., explains the wealth of intellectual talent among the students from China during that period:

Many students came from China on scholarships from the Chinese government, although I myself did not come as a scholarship student. Those were very difficult scholarships to obtain, through competitive examinations, and so on. And the reason why you see so many Chinese people in the United States who are

Chinese students at M.I.T., 1944.
(Courtesy, Donald and Sylvia Tsai)

eminent professionals, teachers, and so forth is that many of these were, indeed, the scholarship students. . . . When they arrived, the war occurred and they were either cut off or decided not to return, and they have indeed made out very well.[16]

While they found different ways to support themselves, the students' common intention, says Tsai, was to study and gain practical experience, and then return home:

Some of us had to work, as did numerous other people. I did various kinds of jobs, library, binding room, tutor. We were paid thirty-five cents an hour. So after a whole month of work, maybe fifty hours a month, we would get a check for about twenty to twenty-five dollars. China Institute helped a little bit by giving us tuition scholarships of various kinds. But we worked, and worked pretty hard.

I went to M.I.T. for graduate school. M.I.T. was my father's school also. He studied mining engineering there in 1910 or thereabouts. I don't know whether they considered that a factor or not. They admitted me, giving me some kind of scholarship, but my funds were really running out. So I went to work in a machine tool factory in Springfield, Vermont for two months. This was part of the apprenticeship program for me because really all of the students were planning to go back to China. There was no thought of staying.[17]

The largest number of stranded students and professionals were Mandarin-speaking individuals from Northern China. Beyond eating at Chinatown restaurants and purchasing Chinese ingredients from its stores, many Northern Chinese students and professionals felt little identification with the earlier Cantonese immigrants and their families. They spoke different dialects of Chinese, formed their own social organizations, and experienced different problems. Their first difficulty was to accept the alteration of life and career goals. While their western education would have guaranteed them a professional job and status in China, this was forfeited for an undefined position in American society. Status deprivation and occupational immobility were the two main areas of discontent among this group of students and professionals. In America, displaced persons not only lacked citizenship rights, but were severely disadvantaged in the job market due to the discriminatory nature of their host country.

In the following years, a brain drain of intellectual talent continued from Taiwan, Hong Kong, and Southeast Asia. Many students who came to American colleges for graduate study found work in their academic fields and remained in the United States. Beng Ho, a pharmacologist who came to America as a student in the 1950s, explains his decision to remain here:

My family is all in Singapore and actually I enjoy life there because it's my hometown. My brother came with me to the United States. We both finished school and we got married, one after the other. He went back, and now he is an Associate Professor at the University of Singapore Medical School. He is an entymologist, and being an entymologist in Singapore, you can establish yourself. But as a chemist, a pharmacologist who wants to do research, this country has by far the best opportunities for me.

If I went to Singapore, my duties most likely would involve teaching, so I wouldn't have a chance to do the research I am doing now. The reason is that research funds are quite limited in Singapore and other Asian countries in comparison to the U.S. That's the primary reason why I stayed here, because of the opportunity and the funds that are available for doing research.[18]

On every university campus with sizeable numbers of foreign-born students, social organizations were formed. In addition to dances and outings, the students celebrated Chinese New Year and other holidays, sometimes producing cultural performances for the rest of the student body. Social contacts were retained after graduation as well. Herbert King explains that this was the case with Houston's Chinese Professional Club (CPC):

The CPC was originally called the Chinese University Club. Then as the people got older, and the University students were not joining the club anymore and all the members were professional people, that's when the name was changed, maybe eight to ten years ago. I was the President of the CPC back in 1975. I would say now, three to four hundred families are members, most of them are professionals. Mainly this is a social function club, then back around four to five years ago, we were talking about instead of being socially-oriented, we should do something for the community, so the thing that we did is award a scholarship. The money is from an annual dance. Then two years ago, we established a permanent scholarship fund with donations from the members as well as the money we get from the annual ball. Right now, we have about ten to fifteen thousand dollars in the permanent fund; drawing interest on that will be the scholarship.[19]

During the post-war years, American-born Chinese began to enjoy the fruits of their labor and loyalty. Chinese Americans entered new occupations, new neighborhoods, new social and political arenas. The internal nature of the community also changed dramatically. There was now a heterogenous population of Chinese in America: original immigrants from Southern China, who were now elderly bachelors in Chinatown; American-born Chinese who lived in the suburbs; foreign-born students and professionals. Although world views and life experiences differed among the groups, all benefitted from America's changing attitudes towards Chinese Americans. A place was secured and America was home.

8 Problems of a Model Minority

By the 1960s, a new image of the Chinese American community had found its way into the mainstream media. The Chinese were America's model minority. In 1966, *U.S. News and World Report* published a landmark article, entitled "Success Story of One Minority Group in the United States," in which it upheld Chinese Americans as an exemplary minority which had integrated well into the melting pot of American society. "At a time when Americans are awash in worry over the plight of racial minorities," said the article, "one such minority, the nation's 300,000 Chinese-Americans, is winning wealth and respect by dint of its own hard work."[1]

The article claimed that Chinese Americans were proof that minorities could find success in America and questioned the need for the growing civil rights movement. "At a time when it is being proposed that hundreds of billions be spent to uplift Negroes and other minorities, the nation's 300,000 Chinese Americans are moving ahead on their own—with no help from anyone else. . . . Not all Chinese Americans are rich. Many, especially recent arrivals from Hong Kong are poor and cannot speak English. But the larger majority are moving ahead by applying the traditional virtues of hard work, thrift and morality."[2]

Chinatown's traditional leadership took great pleasure in this article, agreeing that the Chinese had always met the needs of their own community and would continue to do so. Middle-class Chinese who had secured homes in the suburbs and jobs outside Chinatown were gratified by the laudatory tone of the article. After years of discrimination, these Chinese appreciated their new status. Hard work and educational attainment seemed to be opening opportunities in the once impenetrable mainstream world.

Reports of Chinese American success were, unfortunately, greatly exaggerated. Indeed, there was evidence of substantial economic improvement in the sixties decade. According to the 1970 census, the average income of Chinese families was higher than that of families in the population at large. A fuller inspection of other census statistics, however, reveals that family income, especially for Chinese Americans, was a faulty indicator of economic progress. In the 1940s, 1950s and 1960s, the individual income earned by Chinese males ranked consistently below the national average income, even though Chinese men had made steady progress up the occupational ladder. For purposes of family survival, however, more Chinese wives and family members had found it necessary to work, pooling their wages for the benefit of the whole family. In Chinese families, generally larger than the American average, the total income was higher but it was divided among more members, and actually amounted to a lower per capita income. Because of such incomplete readings of statistical indicators, and because it was believed that the Chinese always took care of their own anyway, Chinatown problems were ignored by the government and funding for community services was difficult to obtain. In addition, the "model minority" stereotype dissociated the Chinese from other eth-

nic groups, in the minds of the general public, those groups, and the Chinese themselves. In reality, however, Chinese Americans and other minorities had much in common. Like other groups, Chinese Americans faced housing, employment and health problems as well as difficulties stemming from bicultural lifestyles.

Influx of New Immigrants

In the sixties decade the Chinese American population experienced social and economic changes which forced recognition of its problems. An un-

precedented increase in Chinese immigration to the United States occurred after the passage of the Immigration and Nationality Act Amendment of 1965 in which the discriminatory national origin quotas[3] were abolished. The Eastern Hemisphere was allowed an annual maximum of 20,000 immigrants from each country, with a total limit of 170,000 per year. The Western Hemisphere was permitted a yearly limit of 120,000 but without specified country limits. As a colony of Great Britain, Hong Kong was allowed a quota of 600 emigrants annually to the United States.

For the Eastern Hemisphere, the amendment established eight preference categories to unite families under a non-quota system and to admit persons with special skills. As a result, two groups of Chinese immigrants began to arrive. The first group were relatives of Chinese in America, including older women who were allowed to join their husbands for the first time in some thirty years; many of these immigrants settled with their families in Chinatown. The second group of immigrants was composed of professionals whose high level of education and good spoken English gained them good jobs and homes in the suburbs.

The Chinese American population increased from 237,292 in 1960 to 435,062 in 1970. By 1980 the number of foreign-born Chinese in the United States had exceeded that of the American-born, constituting 54% of the total Chinese population in America. Thousands of Chinese immigrants settled in San Francisco and New York Chinatowns, injecting new vitality into streets stilled by the movement to the suburbs in the 1950s. Joining the earlier groups of Guangdong immigrants and post-1949 students and professionals were new immigrants from Hong Kong, Taiwan, and Southeast Asia. Unlike the previous groups of immigrants, many entered the United States with their families. But like their predecessors their dream of a good life in America was soon replaced by the sobering reality of their first home, a community beset with growing difficulties.

Chinatowns throughout the nation were revitalized and traditional festivities were celebrated with new energy.
(Harry Jew)

Chinatown Housing Conditions

The problem of overcrowding in Chinatown, which became visibly serious in the late 1960s, steadily worsened each year as thousands of new immigrants sought housing in the community. With the rising cost of housing throughout the country, lower income families continued to look towards Chinatowns for places in which they could afford to live. Immigrants who did not speak English needed to live in Chinatown in order to survive. By 1970 San Francisco Chinatown had developed a population density eleven times that of the rest of the city. It had the second highest density rate in the nation. The only location more crowded was New York Chinatown. There a population of 4,000 in 1960 experienced a phenomenal increase to 24,000 by 1970.[4]

Within New York and San Francisco Chinatowns, waiting lists for apartments were hopelessly long. It was not unusual for a family of six to live in a two-room apartment with no heat or hot water and a bathroom and kitchen which had to be shared with other tenants. Sometimes families separated when living areas were simply too small and sent their older children to live with relatives.

Because of the demand for space, Chinatown landlords charged key money totalling hundreds or even thousands of dollars to guarantee reservation of an apartment. Because of this heavy investment, most families could not afford to move out, and newer immigrants found few vacancy signs posted. With little leverage for complaint, tenants were forced to accept the delapidated conditions which persisted in Chinatown.

In 1972, a study conducted by the Department of Housing and Urban Development concluded that San Francisco Chinatown, composed mainly of buildings constructed shortly after the 1906 earthquake, possessed the worst housing in the western United States. The construction of the Ping Yuen projects alleviated the problem, but with only 234 apartments completed between 1950 and 1952 and another 194 ready in 1961, the Ping Yuen complex was quickly filled to capacity. As a result, the San Francisco Chinatown housing problem was mitigated but not resolved. It was not until 1979 that further housing construction, the 185-unit Mei-Lun Project, commenced.

In the late 1970s the nine-block area in the center of New York Chinatown was composed of 500 restaurants and retail shops and 2,318 dwelling units which housed 9,900 people. Eighty-five percent of the community's buildings were tenements constructed prior to 1901, and they were in constant need of repair due to the poor building stan-

A resident in his Ping Yuen Housing Project apartment.
(Ginger Chih)

dards in force when they were built. Only two percent of the family units were serviced by elevators.[5] In the mid-1960s a few Chinatown leaders began to discuss the question of housing, and launched the Confucius Plaza project, which was completed in 1978. Sponsored by the Chinese Chamber of Commerce and the Association for Chinatown Housing, and subsidized by funds from the city government, it consisted of housing units for 3,000 residents, an elementary school, and commercial space.

Employment Issues

For Chinese in America, a major issue was not unemployment, but underemployment. Many immigrants who held skilled and professional jobs in Hong Kong, Taiwan, or other places of origin, found themselves handicapped by limited proficiency in English, or by the fact that their professional licenses or diplomas were not valid in the United States. Chinese Americans continued to experience job discrimination in fields such as the construction industry, in which unions barred minority workers from gainful employment. With no other recourse, they supported themselves and their families by working at menial, and uniformly low-paying jobs; they often held two or three jobs at once. Sylvia Lee's father, a Hong Kong accountant, could only find employment as a grocery stock man and a janitor, and the women of his family went to work for the first time:

He used to work in a grocery store and he had to pick up heavy stuff. Long working hours, ten hours a day, six days a week. Also, the income was real low. My mom started to work too, as a seamstress and also myself and two sisters worked—also sewing. We went to school in the morning and sewed in the factory in the afternoon. We never sewed before. Just go into a factory and then they start to explain to us. It's real easy to learn when you want to learn something.[6]

Like the Lees, most Chinatown families survived financially through the joint efforts of all members who were able to work. Wives were often joint "rice winners," working in garment shops,

Limited employment opportunities were aggravated by the closing of businesses. This garment shop succumbed to the competition. (Ginger Chih)

canneries or at other factory jobs. In 1970 the percentage of Chinese working wives was higher than that of white and Black American women. The overall ratio of wives who worked in the United States in 1970 was 39%, as compared to 48% of the Chinese American wives,[7] whose work was often crucial for family survival.

Through the 1970s, the major employer among Chinatown women, especially of those who had recently immigrated, continued to be the garment industry. In 1978, 400 of New York City's more than 1,000 garment factories are were located in Chinatown. They employed about 12,000 Chinese, or 10% of the workforce in the fashion industry. Over 90% of New York's Chinese garment workers were unionized, and collected such benefits as unemployment and health insurance.[8] But union in-

In urban centers throughout the United States, the number of Chinese laundryworkers has decreased, due to the advent of dry cleaning as well as more options available to the younger generations. (Ginger Chih)

volvement stopped here. Because family income was so dependent on the women's garment shop jobs, most women were unwilling to testify against sweatshop conditions and substandard pay offered in the piecework system. With unions paying attention only to specific complaints, rather than to overall contractual agreements, working conditions were seldom improved. Furthermore, because of the large number of factories, manufacturers were able to use the fierce competition to their advantage and to keep the bidding for contracts very low; consequently the wages paid to the workers remained extremely depressed.

In the larger Chinatowns, restaurant work continued to be a major source of employment for Chinese men. There were no benefits such as sick leave, vacations or retirement pension plans. Those who could not find work in Chinatown sought work in surrounding areas. Suburban restaurants sent vans to shuttle cooks and waiters to and from work. At times Chinese men lived closer to their place of work than to their families and were unable to go home more than once a week.

Pat Wong was a teenager when his eleven-member family immigrated from Hong Kong. The family supported itself by separating and working in Chinese restaurants in New Jersey, Connecticut and New York. In a few years, they had collectively saved enough for their own family restaurant. Wong says he would like to work outside of the business but feels he must participate in the family effort:

My older brother and my third brother work in the kitchen as cooks and they know how to make the dim sum and the baked goods. My father manages outside here, taking orders, serving the people. My kid brothers all go to school. After school, they come and wash dishes, answer the telephone, do a little delivery. My sister is ten years old. She's too young, so we don't want her to stay in the restaurant. My mother does all kinds of things, helping my brothers wash dishes, preparing some meals.

I work at least twelve hours a day—sometimes even more like fourteen. Restaurant is a very tough business. For me and my brother, we don't like it. We don't mind working hard. But we're interested in something else that we want to try, and there's not much chance for us to prove ourselves. I could find a job, not so easy, but I still could find a job. But I have to consider my family—my father, my mother and my older brothers.[9]

Tom Tam immigrated to New York from Hong Kong in the mid 1960s with his family. He recalls that employment outside the usual Chinatown businesses was considered enviable advancement:

I worked in those big laundry places where they do bed sheets and tablecloths with big machines, a rag wash. The laundry was in Brooklyn somewhere. When I came home I would just collapse and fall asleep and then the next morning, get up real early and then go back to work. I worked there for a few months and then I left and worked in a restaurant for a few months and then I went to work at Macy's as a stock room boy. And that was quite some news to some people when I got a job there. They thought, I guess, that it was a step away from Chinatown. Everybody thought it was fantastic that I got a job at Macy's.[10]

It is not uncommon to see children in garment shops waiting for their mothers to finish work. The inadequacy of day care and after-school facilities make this an inevitable choice.
(Ginger Chih)

Restaurant work is a major source of employment for new Chinese immigrants, since language is not a necessary skill.

(San Francisco Journal)

Health Conditions

Overcrowded living arrangements in Chinatown caused major health problems. In San Francisco, a 1965 Public Health Survey revealed that Chinese led the city in cases of tuberculosis, with a death rate three times that of whites and Blacks. Lack of prompt medical attention was probably the reason for the high number of fatalities from heart disease and cancer. A 1967 survey conducted by the San Francisco Chinatown-North Beach Economic Opportunity Council found that 34% of the Chinese polled had never had a complete physical examination and a higher percentage had never had dental or eye examinations.[11]

Health problems in Chinatown were compounded by the lack of bilingual medical staff in

area hospitals. As a result, many Chinese sought help at hospitals only when their illnesses were severe. Some fatalities occurred when the patients or their families were unable to explain the extent of the medical problem or even call for an ambulance.

Mental health and hypertension problems were also common to those living in Chinatown through the 1970s. According to Tom Tam, first director of New York's Chinatown Health Clinic, the difficulty of adjusting to the American culture and environment can cause tremendous stress, especially among older Chinese. But because of the stigma attached to mental health disorders, and the image of Chinese as traditionally self-sufficient, the problems have yet to be fully acknowledged by the community or even by many experts in the field:

An elderly bachelor in his single hotel room in San Francisco.
(Ginger Chih)

The suicide rate of Chinese is very high and in the past, the suicide rate for the Chinese has been about four times as high as the national average. In the 1970s the situation changed a bit. Generally, the suicide rate for the males has gone down more than for the females. For the females, the overall is still twice as high as the general population within New York City, and it's especially true for older people. The high rate reflects on the mental health problems of Chinatown, because for every case of someone who commits suicide, there are many cases of depression and other things that are not reported.

Suicide prevention programs have been started in many, many places, but none of them have been started in the Chinese community, which is really ridiculous because the Chinese have the highest suicide rate. Many people use Chinatown as an example of rationality, good families, things like that, that this is one community that knows how to take care of itself. They say that a suicide prevention program does not have to be included and this statement has been made by many people who are suicide experts.[12]

Many Chinatown residents have shown a preference for the Chinese system of herbal medicine rather than the Western system of health care. The adherence to one or the other, or to a combination of both, depends on the individual's age, nativity, medical experience, education, and identification with the traditional Chinese culture. A 1970 survey of 200 residents of Boston Chinatown revealed a wide diversity in the seeking of health care among community members. With growing Chinese American communities, there has been a demonstrated need for research studies and health care policies which are not only culturally sensitive, but take cultural diversity into account as well.[13]

Youth Gangs

With their parents forced to work long shifts throughout the days and evenings, many Chinatown young people were left on their own and spent their time out of the crowded apartments and on the streets. Chinatown was by all practical definitions a ghetto and the frustration of confinement among its youth was acute. David Chin observes that with continued financial strain, such problems are aggravated:

Some people come from China, and can't speak English. They can only go into the kitchen and learn how to be cooks. I say why don't they go down to take English classes? There are a lot of things that they should learn. In Chinatown now, some kids are bad. Why? All those years, the Chinese children should be good children, respecting the elders, respecting the laws, but now they're going the opposite way. Why? Because when they come over here, [their

parents are] so busy working they don't have time to take care of them. You can't just work, work, have all the money and be all right. Still now, we need a lot of help in Chinatown.[14]

Many Chinese immigrant teenagers faced problems adjusting to American life. Unlike their younger brothers and sisters, it was difficult for them to learn English, especially if they spent all their time with Chinese-speaking friends. Many lost interest in school and dropped out, but others struggled through. Mabel Jung, a former San Francisco teacher, recalls the difficulty her students had in learning English and the cultural tension that sometimes arose:

Many of the students were in their early teens when they arrived from Hong Kong. They had very little or no knowledge of the English language. They faced a real struggle living in Chinatown and getting adjusted to the American way of life. Nevertheless, they had the ambition at an early age to stick to it and tried their best to make something of themselves.

To encourage my ninth graders, chiefly from the Chinatown area, I made a ruling on the black board: SPEAK ENGLISH ONLY. When I asked an absentee why he was not in school the day before, unable to express himself in English, he replied in Chinese, "Yee Ming Kuk," I answered, "Immigration Station." Wrote it on the black board, "Immigration Station." Whereupon a student in the back said, "You are Chinese, but you don't speak it." "I do speak Chinese," I answered, "but I am an English teacher."[15]

Outside the classroom, however, these immigrant youths discovered that many of their native-born counterparts could not speak Chinese. There were also other cultural differences, which were magnified as Chinatown became more crowded. In the tension that developed, various slang terms were coined: American-born Chinese were called "ABC," or *jook sing*, signifying the hollow part of the bamboo, or a Chinese person devoid of culture. In turn, the American-born called the foreign-born Chinese "FOB", for fresh off the boat. They were also referred to as *jook-kock*, the inflexible joint of the bamboo.

In time, both ABC and FOB youth formed their own clubs and gangs for a sense of social belonging

Youths participating in a three-legged race at a summer fair in New York Chinatown.
(Ginger Chih)

and protection in the Chinatown neighborhood. With more youth arriving during the 1960s, the battle for space was heightened. Some of those who had dropped out of school drifted towards tong-related jobs such as being look-see boys for busy gambling parlors. Gang members became increasingly daring, employing more sophisticated weaponry and fighting over higher stakes. Gang murders and retaliatory killings occurred with increased frequency towards the end of the decade of the sixties.

George Woo, San Francisco State University instructor and former spokesman for the Wah Ching, a large San Francisco gang, explains some of the reasons and results of Chinatown gang formation:

You go back in the newspapers—and begin to see some reported Chinese gangs and Chinese juvenile delinquency coming up in the late fifties. It was at that time that there were some people like me, around fourteen to fifteen, coming over . . . cannot relate to school, they cut out of school. Then they get in fights with each other. And as a rule, at least at that time, the people who came from China were a little smaller. [To the American-born], a fair fight is one-to-one but if you're 110 pounds and I'm 200 pounds. . . . One day the immigrant kids all got together and shared experiences and decided to fight them Chinese-style. What is Chinese style? All for one and one for all. So if someone challenged you to a fair fight, you said, "Yeah, I'm going to meet you at 6 o'clock out in Portsmouth Square; and all ten of us go and jump him. That's the beginning of the Chinese gang, Wah Ching. They came here, they can't relate to school, they can't really find a job and their parents usually are not doing that well—so they steal. And they find it's very lucrative.

This is one of the real tragedies about the subsequent gang killings. Many of the people who killed each other were all comrades. They all remember their birthdays—how they used to steal to feed each other and all that. That group subsequently became gang leaders. Many of them died out there—caught up with groups that end up killing each other.[16]

On the evening of February 2, 1968, Woo represented the Wah Ching at a Human Rights Commission open hearing on the subject of Chinatown youth. Before an audience of Chinatown groups and the mass media, a vehement Woo outlined the problems of Chinatown's youth, condemned the inaction of the Chinatown establishment and warned of a potential riot situation should nothing be done for the youth. He likened the plight of Chinatown's youth to that of other poor people, with the additional handicap of language.

This departure from Chinatown's traditional manner of solving problems within the community itself astounded the gathering. John Yehall Chin of the Six Companies and the Human Rights Commission's Chinatown Advisory Board called for an uncompromising stand:

They have not shown that they are sorry or that they will change their ways. They have threatened the community. If you give in to this group, you are only going to have another hundred immigrants come in and have a whole series of threats and demands.[17]

Wah Ching's request for federal assistance was turned down. The group eventually broke up into factions, some returning to the streets and some finding employment with the tongs. A few attempted to work individually towards a better future.

In New York City, Chinese gangs were supported by certain Chinatown tongs. In exchange for guarding the gambling houses, the youth were given money and a place of their own. But as the gangs grew more powerful, rivalry increased, and they then extorted money from Chinatown restaurants and stores. Gang fights publicized by the media frightened away the tourists, and with the subsequent loss of business and potential extortion money, the gangs expanded their activities to restaurants in the suburbs.

David Eng, former director of Project Hing Dai, a social service agency for youth gangs which is now defunct due to lack of funding, says that if alternatives such as education or employment were attainable, gang members would opt for them:

Being a gang leader or gang member in Chinatown is not really a good life, because you're always worried about somebody coming behind you and pulling a piece and blowing you away. You live in a constant state of fear. The money is good, the fun is there, but so is the fear. But, there's nowhere for them to go. And that's the reason they're doing what they're doing today. If there was a way for them to get out . . . they would do it.[18]

The 1960s brought a deepening dichotomy between the myth of the model minority and the reality of the Chinatown ghetto. Tourists window-shopping on Grant Avenue in San Francisco or Mott Street in New York were usually oblivious to the health, housing and employment problems in the streets just beyond.

Because its purpose had so long been the upgrading of the Chinese image in the American eye, the Chinatown establishment did little to expose these community problems. In a press release dated October 2, 1967, San Francisco's Chinese Consolidated Benevolent Association discussed the topic of transition:

Today the new immigrants have swollen Chinatown's population to the largest in its history, much more than its peak of 1880. This one single factor—a matter of individual efforts to migrate to the United States— a matter certainly outside of any official controls of any Chinese organizations, has unbalanced the pendulum.[19]

While the CCBA admitted the existence of problems in Chinatown, it was quick to emphasize the more positive aspects of the Chinese community. The report contended that the same problems occurred in other sectors of society, implying that press accounts about Chinatown were exaggerated. It assured readers that the CCBA, "the voice of the entire Chinese community," had matters under control.

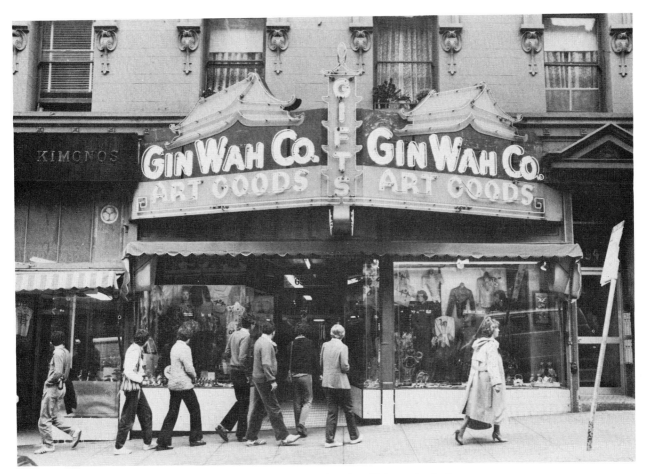

For the tourists who delight in shopping for souvenirs and eating Chinese food, San Francisco Chinatown means Grant Avenue.

(Ginger Chih)

9 Toward Social Change

The promise of socio-economic equality for Chinese Americans following World War II faded amidst community and national changes in the decade of the 1960s. New immigrants encountered Chinatown ghettos beset with housing shortages, hazardous health conditions and unemployment. In the suburbs, middle-class Chinese Americans owned homes and held white-collar jobs, but they too discovered some incongruities between the American Dream and their lives as Chinese. The popular belief that Chinese Americans were a model minority who were self-sufficient and highly successful in society had adverse effects on both Chinatown and suburban sectors of the community. It diverted needed funding and attention from the former and placed undue pressure on the latter to maintain high levels of achievement and model behavior. In the mid-1960s, a number of factors combined to make way for a clear articulation of Chinese American problems and the mustering of new forces for social change within the community.

The Civil Rights Movement

One of the primary influences on Chinese American activism in the 1960s was the civil rights movement. As the vanguard of contemporary domestic reform, the movement developed an idealism which inspired other American social struggles later launched by students, women, Third World activists, anti-war proponents and the poor.

In 1954, the United States Supreme Court had ruled against school segregation and in subsequent decisions declared illegal any forms of segregation in public transportation, recreational facilities, parks and buildings. When their treatment by society remained largely unchanged, Black Americans began to organize more intensely for the civil rights being denied them. Without responsible enforcement by the government, everyday infractions continued.

Although Dr. Martin Luther King, Jr., and other leaders and organizations attracted thousands to the civil rights movement with their philosophy of non-violent protest, patience wore thin as communities experienced increased police harassment in the 1960s. By 1965, growing organizations such as the Black Muslims and the Black Panthers had emerged as vocal forces in the movement. Although the Civil Rights Acts of 1964 and 1965 legislated against racial discrimination, the translation from paper to practice was negligible. Growing discontent over worsening ghetto conditions erupted in violent rioting in Watts in 1965 and in Newark in 1967.

Young Chinese Americans were among those influenced and made politically conscious by the civil rights movement and other areas of protest which the movement inspired. Doreen Der, a staff member at San Francisco's Cameron House, recalls her own decision of social commitment:

1964 to 1965 was the year of the Free Speech Movement at Berkeley and I got involved in that, really as a matter of conscience. I don't think I was political as a freshman, sophomore, junior, not even as a senior. But in our senior year, part of the issue of the Free Speech Movement was that different organizations were not being allowed to just give information out on Spraul Plaza, and that seemed very strange to me. Very undemocratic. All the values we were raised with in terms of the American government I think were challenged at that point. And it was a matter of deciding: was that an issue, or wasn't it, or were you there just for school?

At that point, I felt it was an important issue to take a stand on. A lot of people, if they had just read about it in the paper, thought it was just a bunch of students having a good time. The national student uprising, students vocalizing on issues, was just coming into the fore at that time. I had people challenging me, saying, "Why did you become involved in that? I thought you knew better."

But out of that came the commitment to work in VISTA for one year and basically I began to express that I was willing to do more than just boycott classes or strike, that there was a commitment to work with people. I came back from VISTA not knowing what I would do, and was asked to work here at Cameron House, and began to realize that they did a whole different type of work, not just with youth, but with adults who needed help, whether it was concrete services or getting English classes so that they could get jobs, or Americanization classes so they could become citizens. From that, I decided to go into social work.[1]

Social Service Agencies

In 1964, President Lyndon Johnson's Great Society Program led to the creation of social service agencies within urban ghettos. In New York City, the Chinatown Planning Council (CPC), a multi-service agency, was founded. During the summer of 1965, it received funding for a Head Start project and a youth program. It attracted Chinese American professionals, social workers and students who returned to Chinatown to teach English or otherwise apply their skills to help the community. Harold Lui discusses CPC's pioneering effort and the early volunteers who embraced its concept:

In 1965, when CPC first began setting up services, there were no other agencies which were essentially run by Chinese. There really were no social services. CPC began to get more and more requests for help and what it did was begin to set off, in the other institutions, especially churches, the recognition that there was a need for more outreach services and there were some government monies available.

Our volunteers consisted of second-generation Chinese who came through the Second World War and Korean War and identified with Chinatown in its small, local days, knowing everybody. And they were vitally concerned about the kids growing up in Chinatown. They envisioned having a major role to play and getting it back to the way it used to be. They helped the CPC in getting started. They were doctors, nurses, teachers.

We had a large group of volunteers and the more successful we got, the more people were attracted to us. All the agencies that got started from the 1960s started with volunteers. People felt there was a gap and they wanted to see services of a certain nature be developed.[2]

The creation of effective social services within Chinatown, for all the initial enthusiasm, was a difficult task. It required an understanding of the

Ethnic pride was one concept of the Asian American movement.

Social service agencies like the Chinatown Planning Council in New York started classes
in English and citizenship.

(Ginger Chih)

community's history, an organizational network, and changed attitudes towards government-sponsored projects. In Chinatown agencies in New York and San Francisco, the learning process was often reciprocal: client and staff workers learned from each other. Liz Young recalls that her studies in social work were only a partial preparation for work with gang members in New York Chinatown:

We wanted to really help these kids but it was more hit and miss. All my social work techniques, my ability to empathize could only go so far with the kids because I didn't understand the street culture where a lot of these kids were from. I didn't understand, in a deep way, the Chinese way of looking at things culturally because I was very Americanized and I didn't have the language skills to help me bridge some of that communication gap.

I was asked to teach a course on the Asian American experience at Hunter College and I had to do reading

for the course. I started reading about Chinese American and Asian American history and a lot of things fell into place that maybe if I had understood and known before I started the program, it would have given me some perspective to work out of.[3]

In San Francisco Chinatown, federally-funded agencies such as the Economic Opportunity Council were set up to assist immigrants and the poor in their adjustment to and survival in the United States. The organizations offered English tutoring, health referrals, job banks and subsidized food programs.

Chinatown social service agencies introduced new attitudes about Chinese Americans. Their very establishment and stated purposes brought Chinatown's multiple problems to light. As Chinatown became one host to the network of government-funded agencies in urban ghettos throughout the country, Chinese communities were drawn further

By the late 1960s the postwar generation had come of age to express their opinions.
(Ginger Chih)

out of their isolation. Agencies handled a number of services originally performed by district associations, and they had growing numbers of elderly residents and immigrants participating in their programs. In community politics, the social service workers introduced alternatives, and therefore challenges, to the influence of the traditional leadership of Chinatown.

Young America

In addition to the momentum of the civil rights movement and the establishment of social service agencies, the new activism was stimulated by America's large youth population. Throughout the nation, the post-war baby boom drew visible effect

as that generation came of age to vote, attend college, be drafted, and become vocal on the day's issues. By their sheer numbers and idealism they constituted a "counter-culture," rejecting an American society which seemed to them to worship materialism run rampant at the expense of humanity. Folk and rock musicians chronicled the times in America's popular music. All accepted customs of American life were defied, including those of dress, hairstyle, relationships and behavior.

From the late 1960s to the early 1970s, political activists directed general feeling of rebellion toward protest concerning specific issues. While many Chinese American youth on college campuses remained absorbed in their studies and ignored the demonstrations, others felt compelled to listen and participate, and eventually applied what they had learned to their lives as Asian Americans.

Vietnam War

The anti-war movement attracted tens of thousands of protestors over the controversial subject of American intervention in Vietnam. Asian American activists took special issue with this war, identifying with the Asians being napalmed and slaughtered across the ocean by the United States military. The Vietnam War, they said, also had ramifications for Asians here in America, as had World War II and the Korean War. The American public's perception of Asian Americans was unduly affected by wars in which Asians were the enemy.

Asian American G.I.s told tales of pre-Vietnam bootcamp maneuvers in which they were singled out to play the "gook." Some of them spoke of the intense degredation and trauma they experienced. Vietnam veteran Norman Nakamura wrote in 1970:

> For some GI.s in Vietnam there are no Vietnamese people. To them the land is not populated by people but by "Gooks," considered inferior, unhuman animals by racist-educated G.I.s. Relieved in his mind of human responsibility by this grotesque stereotype, numerous barbarities have been committed against these Asian peoples, since "they're only Gooks."[4]

Upon their return to America, some Vietnam veterans failed to change their concepts of Asians. They saw Asian faces in war-time flashback. Young Asian American women were propositioned in street Vietnamese by returned G.I.s who were reminded of Vietnamese girlfriends and prostitutes.

American children incorporated some of the war-time attitudes into their young worlds as well, reviving the label "gook" in schoolyard fights. Whether it was "chink," "jap," "slant-eyes" or "gook," Asian American children still found themselves with one more layer of societal labeling to shed before having the chance to discover who they really were.

Asian Americans organized vocal contingents at anti-war demonstrations across the country. The insight that the Vietnam war was racist as well as imperialist was constantly articulated by Asian community speakers. Chants such as "Ho-Ho-Ho Chi Minh, Vietnam is sure to win" reflected their feeling of solidarity with another Asian people.

Films about China, Vietnam, and Asian America were featured in film festivals at campuses and community centers.

(Poster Courtesy of Yuri Kochiyama)

Asian American spokespersons also argued that the same racist mentality which shaped the United States government's policies in Vietnam were evident in its policies for minority communities at home.

Asian American Studies

By the end of the sixties decade, college campuses across the country found themselves host to the issues of the day, especially with regard to curricular relevance. Political consciousness and ethnic pride motivated Third World students to demonstrate in favor of Ethnic Studies courses.

Chinese American students joined the pioneer Third World Strikes at San Francisco State University in 1968 and at the University of California at Berkeley in 1969. Ethnic Studies programs were established as a result of the sometimes violent

A wall mural by John Woo in Seattle's International District shows the role of Chinese in the development of the Pacific Northwest.

(Ginger Chih)

agitation on both campuses. Students at other universities throughout the country followed suit. In New York, students demonstrated for Asian American studies at Columbia and the City Colleges. When attempts to work through the normal administrative channels failed, activists organized demonstrations to publicize their demands. Even small, private institutions like the all-women Mills College in Oakland allocated funds for Ethnic Studies after the mass pressure of rallies and sit-ins.

Within various Ethnic Studies programs, Asian American courses were organized. Classes were created for the study of identity, history, literature, language, and community issues. After decades of rejecting their Asian heritage in order to be accepted by mainstream society, second- and third-generation Chinese Americans realized that they had a history of which they could be proud and a culture which was their own. They began to con-

sider what might have been lost in the Americanization process.

Liz Young remembers father-daughter discussions about being Chinese in America and her own road to self-acceptance:

I remember telling him that I was an American first and that being Chinese wasn't so hot. He said that one day I'm going to want to know everything there is to know about being Chinese and I thought he was just crazy and that was one of his old-fashioned ideas. But it was true, eventually that need was there in me—a craving to know more about myself after so many years of self-denial about being Chinese and Asian. There was a need to fill the vacuum, of what was missing in me, about who I was and what my culture was, what my past was, and more importantly, because I needed it like a missing piece of a puzzle, I wanted to deal as an effective person, as a whole person. I had to understand it to accept myself. I couldn't accept myself without accepting that I was Chinese.[5]

Young Asian Americans who had grown up in the suburbs in the 1950s and 1960s began to rediscover their roots in Chinatown. A number of Asian American Studies courses gave students credit for participation in programs of social service to the Asian community. With study, they discovered parallels in Chinese, Japanese and Pilipino immigration experiences, labor struggles, and assimilation. And in the study of their communities they became aware of conditions which had existed without radical change for decades.

Chinatown Youth

The coming-of-age of postwar Chinese American babies and the influx of immigrant teenagers combined to increase the youth population of Chinese America dramatically. The community's provision for them, however, remained scant. In San Francisco, Cameron House, St. Mary's Church, the YMCA, and the YWCA served as social and recreation centers for young people from both Chinatown and the suburbs. But by the late 1960s such organizations were unable to handle the scope of Chinatown's youth problems. Gang warfare had escalated, and several murders and revenge murders took place.

Because of the reputation of delinquency which had been attached to them, street youth, regardless of whether or not they participated in gang activities, faced greater difficulties in their day-to-day lives. Realizing that no assistance was forthcoming, a group of American-born street youth started a self-help organization, Leways, Inc., in 1967. Alex Hing, a founding member, recalls why Leways was organized:

I think that just about everybody who grew up in Chinatown had some kind of social conscience. I mean it was impossible not to have a social conscience, because everyone knew that they individually were not to blame for the hole that we were in, that there was something wrong with society. There was no future

outside of Chinatown—there was no future inside Chinatown. People got in trouble and there was no place to turn to, so it was obviously some kind of social phenomena that was going wrong. So between the mid-sixties and the late sixties, people started to search for solutions. One of the first programs that developed out of that was a group called Leways, which stood for Legitimate Ways. A group of youth, basically, bought this pool hall and saw the pool hall as a social meeting ground and a place where people could discuss their problems. The pool hall would generate a source of income which could be used for a number of things—particularly legal defense, because a lot of people had legal problems. . . . A press conference was called to point out the problem that existed and people started to awaken. Leways became a basis for a lot of progressive youth to come out, pointing out the plight of Chinatown.[6]

Leways was supported by several prominent community members, and organizations such as the Chinese YMCA and Youth for Service. The police, however, remained unconvinced by the legitimate-ways concept, and persisted in regular harassment of the Leways headquarters, with reported cases of brutality inflicted upon youth who were said to have resisted arrest. In addition, lack of support from establishment organizations such as the Chinese Chamber of Commerce closed opportunities for gainful employment. Repression of Leways continued in the form of high rent and accusations that they were instigating violence on the streets. Two years after its inception, Leways put its original ideas of job training, employment, and recreation and educational programs to rest.

The Leways experience embittered the youth of the community, and served to sharpen the political understanding of some of the group's members. They began to acquire a political understanding of their world in response to opposition from Chinatown's Kuomintang loyalists who labeled Leways communist and to increased awareness of new China and the teachings of Char iman Mao Zedong. Surveying the ghetto conditions surrounding them, they concluded that a basic social change was necessary in Chinatown and in 1968 formed the Red Guard Party, a revolutionary organization.[7] Alex Hing, the group's Minister of Information, describes the formation of the organization:

The Black Panther Party (BPP) inspired a lot of youth at that time because of what they stood for, revolution. They stood for overturning the present system. So a number of people from Leways started to make contact with the BPP and the BPP came into Chinatown.

During that time, the Panthers were into organizing youth gangs. So what happened is that the Panthers came into Leways and started to teach revolution via the thoughts of Chairman Mao. They distributed a Red Book and started to give political education classes to the people who hung out around there and their ideas caught on.

So a group of more advanced people down there started to see that the Leways organization in and of itself and cooperative capitalism was not enough. What needed to be done was to develop a revolutionary organization to deal with some of the questions that people in Chinatown faced and what happened was that these people got together and formed the Red Guard Party which basically adopted the BPP program and started to make revolution in the community—or tried to make revolution in the community.[8]

The Red Guard initiated a breakfast program for children, a free food program and a community film series. It collected 5,000 signatures on a petition protesting the closing of Chinatown's only tuberculosis clinic. Some of its members took courses in anti-draft law and worked with Asian Legal Services, an office which helped over 1,000 young men to get Vietnam War draft deferments.

In their dramatic and sometimes violent confrontations with Chinatown's Kuomintang supporters, the Red Guard spoke in favor of the People's Republic of China, breaking a silence which had been maintained since the McCarthy era on the leftist end of Chinatown's political spectrum. Because of residual fears brought about by the repression of a decade earlier, the Red Guard's Maoist rhetoric fell on apprehensive ears and met limited response. In 1972, San Francisco's Red Guard merged with the New York Chinatown-based I Wor Kuen to form a national group with a more studied Marxist-Leninist interpretation of Chinatown conditions.

Community Organizing

It had become clear to Chinese American activists that the federal government's war on poverty and social service agencies could provide only temporary relief from deep-seated and complex Chinatown problems. Within the country's major Chinatowns, progressive organizations proliferated through the turn of the decade. They called for broad changes in Chinatown's political and economic structures. They put various interpretations of leftist theory into practice by initiating serve-the-people programs to meet community needs and to develop a base among Chinatown's poor, aged, new immigrants and workers.

From the late 1960s, the 800 block of Kearny Street in San Francisco housed several Asian American organizations formed by Chinatown activists and students from area campuses. The Kearny Street Workshop provided space for a collective of community artists. The Chinese Progressive Association and I Wor Kuen organized worker-student discussions, a nursery school, film showings, and internal study of Marxist-Leninist-Maoist theory. Asian Legal Services handled draft and other legal cases, and Everybody's Bookstore stocked progressive literature and items from China. The Asian Community Center (ACC) and Wei Min She (For the People Organization), founded in 1971, organized a food project for 300 Chinatown families, cultural and political programs, language classes, summer workshops for youth, political study groups and the *Wei Min Bao*, a bilingual community newspaper. The May 4th Singers, who composed and performed music of political relevance, marked its beginnings in the basement of ACC in 1973. The Chinatown Cooperative Garment Factory was formed by Berkeley students and a group of Chinatown seamstresses as an alternative to factories which exploited the workers.

Above the row of Kearny Street storefronts was the International Hotel, which became a rallying point for resistance to urban development at the expense of the poor. Black ghettos had been forced to face the urban renewal sweep of their communities a few years earlier, and now San Francisco's Chinatown, Manilatown and Japantown, all prime property areas, confronted the same threat. In these districts, developers sought to raze old buildings and replace them with commercial complexes and parking lots which would increase property revenues. The buildings in question were often low-rent hotels which provided housing for the poor and elderly of the community. Residents and community activists called the urban renewal process "urban removal."

Even when the plans included housing, tenants could not afford the new, high rents. As residents were evicted, they were forced to separate and find housing in other areas of the city. Redevelopment destroyed not only buildings, but often, the community itself. Residents of the International Hotel, insisting on their right to low-cost housing, fought eviction for nearly a decade through court battles and demonstrations. They were finally evicted in 1977, but not without a final fight in which a force of club-wielding police, many of them mounted on horseback, had to break through throngs of supporters to evict the residents bodily.[9]

Tenant organizing occurred in two dozen other San Francisco Chinatown buildings during the 1970s. Residents aired grievances over unsafe conditions, protested evictions, and fought rent in-

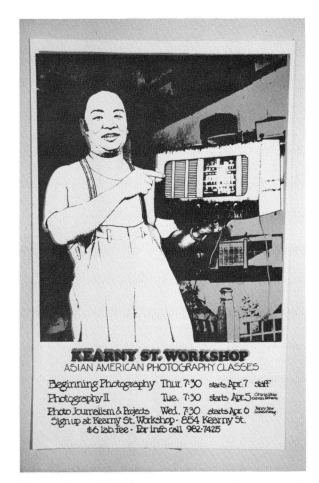

Kearny Street Workshop was a center for community artists. (Russ Lowe)

creases. The most successful of these was the Ping Yuen Rent Strike, which lasted for four months in 1978. George Lee, president of the Ping Yuen Tenants Association, explains his involvement, and the course taken by the strike:

On August 23, 1978, a girl got killed; she fell from a balcony here. So the people organized, and said we need security guards. The Housing Authority said they had no money—they couldn't afford it. We said, "That housing project has a security guard, this one has, another one has, we want a security guard." So they said, "Well, ask for it" So we went on rent strike. That was October 1978, we called a rent strike. We went on rent strike for four months. Finally they got afraid, they said we'll give you this, we'll give you that. Then we called off the rent strike. That's how we got the gates, and all the security guards. Before, nobody cared. But I cared. I came out. I saw the situation getting worse and worse every day. We had to do something.

Other community groups supported us. We got a lot of good supporters. And then the supervisor supported us. And the students supported us. So that's how we were successful in this rent strike. You need outside help if you want to organize. Even if they don't fight for you—they support you—makes a lot of difference and it encourages people.[10]

In New York City, a variety of organizations were formed to make public Asian American

views. These included the Asian Americans for Action, which participated in anti-war and other mainstream movements; I Wor Kuen and Asian Americans for Equal Employment (AAFEE), which concentrated on organizing workers in the Asian community; the Basement Workshop and *Bridge Magazine*, which began to define Asian American culture through the arts; the Asian Study Group, which examined Marxist-Leninism as an approach to the problems of society, as were numerous other movement organizations; and the Asian American Legal Defense and Education Fund, a law collective which provided legal services and education.

Chinese students and professionals became in-

Hundreds of supporters attempted to stop the 1977 eviction of the tenants of the International Hotel.

(San Francisco Journal)

volved with the Lower East Side Neighborhood Health Council Center, funded by the federal government to insure community participation in health care. The activists discovered that although many Chinatown residents used the nearby Gouverneur Hospital, only twenty-five of the total of 800 people on the staff were Chinese. As a consequence there were communication problems often resulting in misdiagnosis and incorrect treatment. To dramatize the need for more responsive health care, activists organized the Chinatown Health Fair in 1971, turning the streets of Chinatown into a free clinic for ten days. Over a hundred community volunteers, college students and medical professionals distributed health information and administered blood pressure and tuberculosis tests and eye examinations to about 2,500 Chinatown residents. The Chinatown Health Clinic was later established as a result of the community's overwhelming response to the Health Fair.[11]

Other activists protested the failure of the New York construction industry to hire members of minority groups, using the Confucius Plaza Project as a prime example. The Confucius Plaza housing construction site in Chinatown was the focus of three months of agitation in 1974. The major point of dispute was employment for Asian American construction workers by the project contractors. The protest was organized by members of the community group AAFEE and the unemployed Asian workers, who were joined by Black and Puerto Rican supporters. At one point, demonstrators brought construction to a standstill. Community supporters who walked the picket lines included the Golden Age Club for the elderly and garment factory workers who demonstrated during their breaks. Fifty-seven arrests were made in the first two weeks of confrontation.

Even a sector of the Chinatown establishment became involved. The President of the Chinese Consolidated Benevolent Association, M. B. Lee, accompanied AAFEE representatives to mediation sessions. Differences in strategy and tactics led to some diffusion of the protest, but the brief united effort did bear fruit. The issue, a political hot potato among the CCBA, government officials, and contractors, was resolved in July 1974, and arrangements were made to provide jobs for Asian Americans.[12] Even in victory, however, community activists were clearly aware that because of inad-

Basement Workshop in New York produced a traveling multimedia exhibition on the history of the Chinese in America. (Ginger Chih)

equate legal guidelines for minority hiring on construction sites, this was only one fight among many to come.

The Chinese community further demonstrated its commitment to social justice by staging in the following year the most massive Chinese American protest ever held in the United States. On May 19, 1975, 20,000 Chinese took to the streets of New York to protest rising police brutality. The mobilization took place over the case of Peter Yew, a Hong Kong architect and Chinatown waiter who had witnessed an auto accident on April 26 and protested police mistreatment of a member of the crowd which had gathered. Yew had been immediately singled out as an example, beaten, and arrested for obstruction of justice. The march from Mott Street in Chinatown to City Hall climaxed a week of intense demonstrations. Most of the Chinatown factories, shops, and restaurants closed for the morning so that workers could participate.

Urban renewal process in Honolulu Chinatown.
(Ginger Chih)

Many doors posted the sign "Closed to Protest Police Brutality."[13]

Asian Americans in Hawaii, because of their long history in the Islands and because they formed such a large part of the population, did not face the same issues of minority rights. Instead, their activism concentrated on economic issues such as corporate development, tourism and unionization. The Chinese joined native Hawaiians, Japanese, Pilipinos, Koreans, haoles and others in various land and community struggles. The first of these protests in contemporary history was the Kokua Kalama struggle in 1970, during which Kalama Valley farmers, residents and their supporters unsuccessfully fought eviction. The land was subsequently developed by the Kaiser-Aetna Corporation for a golf course and for middle- to upper-income housing.

In following years, local people fought eviction from their homes in Ota Camp, Waiahole-Waikane Valley, Sand Island, Chinatown and other areas. Third Arm, a Chinatown organization composed of students, young workers, and returnees from American mainland campuses, set up a health clinic, weekend block activities, and a newspaper published in Illocano, Chinese and English. When Honolulu's plans for urban renewal were revealed, residents formed an organization called People Against Chinatown Eviction (P.A.C.E.) and protested the high rents that would be charged in the new housing; for them, it was tantamount to eviction, and eviction, they said, heralded the destruction of the Chinatown community.

Within major Chinatowns, progressive organizations continued in the 1970s to call attention to exploitation and supported the community's struggles against high rents, eviction, and inadequate social services. Activists also played supportive roles in labor disputes involving Asian workers, such as San Francisco's Jung Sai garment workers' strike in 1975 and the drives to unionize New York City's Chinese restaurants in the late 1970s. Community residents and activists attempted to alleviate Chinatown problems by maintaining health clinics, food cooperatives, daycare programs, multi-service community centers and legal collectives such as the Asian Law Caucus in San Francisco and the Asian American Legal Defense and Education Fund in New York.

In the mid- and late seventies, various Chinese American leftist groups merged with larger revolutionary organizations whose membership included whites, Chicanos, Puerto Ricans, Blacks, and other Asian Americans. Members shifted some of their focus from specific community problems to learn of and become involved in other issues facing the American working class as a whole. Some of these national organizations included the Revolutionary Communist Party, the League for Revolutionary Struggle, and the Communist Workers Party.

While these progressive organizations proceeded with work on another level, other Asian American movement groups dissolved because of

Asian, Latino, Black and Native American activists provided Third World perspectives
for numerous political causes throughout the 1970s.

(Yuri Kochiyama)

political factionalism or loss of purpose. The Vietnam protest groups were an example of the latter. A common criticism of the Asian American movement from 1968 to 1975 was that activists had relied too heavily on rhetoric and not enough on a genuine understanding of Chinatown and other Asian American communities. Yet the role of Asian American activists during those years should not be underestimated. The energies they expended at demonstrations, picket lines, work sites, and seemingly endless meetings bore fruit in the establishment of Ethnic Studies curriculum on campus and direct action programs which served community needs. Their articulation of Asian American concerns vociferously challenged the myth of the model minority. Although the organizations did not have the resources to transform the dominant structure of Chinatown, their radical points of view presented persistent challenges to establishment leaders and the status quo.

For young Chinese Americans from the suburbs, the late sixties and early seventies was a time to seek out a lost identity in the ghetto their parents had left behind in the 1940s and 1950s. For Chinatown's street youth, it was also time to be heard. In the face of growing problems following the influx of new Chinese immigrants after 1965, movement activists called for political solutions to serious community conditions which seemed insoluble in traditional ways.

10 Stereotypes vs. Self-Expression

Throughout their history in this country, Chinese Americans have been caught in a web of social stereotyping. Although the images assigned to them have improved since the days of the China Trade and Opium War, the present-day task of defining a Chinese American identity can be very arduous. Are the Chinese America's model minority? Do all Chinese work in restaurants and laundries? Are Chinese American women exotic and demure? Many Americans, because of biased portrayals of Chinese in the media or limited personal experience with Chinese Americans, still consider the Chinese a cultural oddity and know little about their lives and role in American society.

American perceptions of Chinese people have been formed principally in two ways. One was through the force of domestic economics. During the California labor struggles of the 1870s, for instance, Chinese workers were made the scapegoats. Cartoons which depicted the Chinese as locusts destroying the riches of the land conveniently directed attention away from the corporate barons who were responsible for the exploitation of all workers. A second factor affecting American perceptions of the Chinese is the fact that Chinese stereotypes have evolved according to the changing political relationships between the two countries. When they were on friendly terms, the Chinese stereotype was a positive one; when relations were strained or ambiguous, the stereotype was negative. These early, negative portrayals of the Chinese were successfully circulated among the American people through newspapers, periodicals and even textbooks. With the advent of film and television in the twentieth century, these images were reinforced even more effectively. As popular entertainment, the visual media undoubtedly wield an informal but important influence on American attitudes towards Chinese Americans.

From Yellow Peril to Fortune Cookie Wisdom

Chinese were first portrayed in the silent film era as novel and culturally-submerged curiosities. The films were also vehicles for the anti-Chinese prejudice of the period, caricaturing Chinese as villainous, immoral, odd and laughable. Produced by such companies as the American Mutoscope and Biograph Company, these included *The Chinese Rubbernecks* (1903), *Heathen Chinese and the Sunday School Teacher* (1904), *The Yellow Peril* (1908) and *Dr. Foo* (1914).

The silent-film classic *Broken Blossoms*, produced in 1919 by D. W. Griffith, paved the way for Chinese characterization to come. Originally titled *The Chink and the Child*, the film starred Richard Barthelmess as "The Yellow Man" and Lillian Gish as an abused white child to whom he opens his home and whom he grows to love. Barthelmess, one of the first white actors to don a yellow face for film, played his character as stoop-shouldered and fragile, his eyes dulled with the effects of smoking opium. The child's drunken father is furious to find his daughter with the Chink, and the scene's subtitle reads: "Above all, Battling hates those not born in the same great country as himself." The plot is resolved in a manner which became typical of future cinematic Asian-white love relationships: the Chink kills himself, for society condemns his affection for the child, and the threat to white womanhood is eradicated.

The long-running Fu Manchu series brought the Chinese image on film to its heights of villainy. Created by the English novelist Sax Rohmer, the character of Fu Manchu was adapted to the screen and brought to American audiences by Paramount Studios in 1929. In *The Mysterious Dr. Fu Manchu*, the Doctor stealthily stalks British officer Petrie in London, seeking revenge for the killing of his wife and child in China.

The subsequent series of thrillers, starring Warner Oland and later Boris Karloff in the title role, reinforced the fear of the "Yellow Peril" at a time when immigration laws excluding the Chinese were strongly, and according to the series, justifiably, in effect. The sinister scientist brought terror to the silver screen for four decades, ending with *Brides of Fu Manchu* in 1967. Then after a thirteen-year lull, the character was revived in 1980 in a movie starring Peter Sellers.

The Chinese villain reappears constantly: in the

Richard Barthelmess as the Chink and Lillian Gish as the Child in Broken Blossoms.
(Museum of Modern Art)

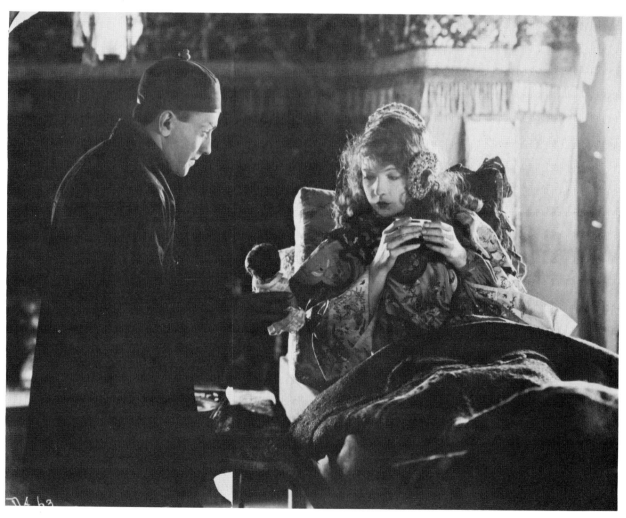

The diabolical Dr. Fu Manchu.
(Museum of Modern Art)

Oland, Sidney Toler and Roland Winters in over fifty movies, possessed a keen intelligence and an unfailing ability to outwit the white police. This film image of the Chinese, although more positive than earlier ones, upon closer examination also turns out to be a product of white racism. Charlie Chan speaks fortune-cookie wisdom, twisting the analects of Confucius for a laugh, cloaking himself in inscrutability. With no real knowledge of Chinese behavior, the white actors who played Chan relied on a placid demeanor, a stooped stance, a pigeon-toed walk, and a fake accent.

In 1980, the announcement of the production of the newest addition to the Charlie Chan legacy, *Charlie Chan and the Curse of the Dragon Queen*, brought immediate protest from the San Francisco Chinatown community, where it was scheduled to be filmed. The producers, however, ignored the "Can Charlie Chan" demonstrations, held in both San Francisco and Hollywood, and proceeded with their perpetuation of the stereotype.

Gung Fu Mania

Martial arts films made in Hong Kong and Taiwan became popular entertainment in the larger Chinese communities in the United States, especially after the influx of new immigrants in the sixties. To Chinese audiences, the films were a welcome respite from Hollywood's ludicrous portrayals. Although production houses recycled one essential plot and village set through many of the films, Chinese Americans delighted in portrayals closer to real Chinese men and women with a range of human emotions and qualities. Superhuman feats touched with movie magic showed the art of gung fu at its most developed stage. To Chinese American viewers, here were surrogate fighters for justice whose pride and skill gave them inspiration in a hostile world.

Martial artist Bruce Lee was born in San Francisco and raised in Hong Kong. He broke international box office records with his gung fu films, first produced in Hong Kong, but later in collaboration with Hollywood in the early 1970s. Lee's charisma and quicksilver authenticity offered stark contrast to the *Kung Fu* series of the American tele-

Shadow of Chinatown, a serial starring Bela Lugosi in the mid 1930s; in the *Flash Gordon* serial of the same period, featuring arch-rival Ming the Merciless; in *The Manchurian Candidate*, in 1962; and in the *Hawaii 5-0* and *Mission Impossible* television series.[1]

In the light of Fu Manchu's tremendous popularity, Hollywood producers were at first unsure of the marketability of an "Oriental good guy." They introduced the character Charlie Chan, created by novelist Earl Derr Biggers in the 1920s, very cautiously. Charlie Chan first appeared in *The House Without a Key* (1926) and was played by Japanese actor George Kuwa, but the role was a very small one. Not until Warner Oland of Fu Manchu experience portrayed Chan did the character become popular. Perhaps not insignificantly at this time, anti-Chinese feeling had relaxed due to the enactment of more stringent exclusion laws, and the American audience was more able to accept a benevolent Asian screen character.

The Charlie Chan character, played in turn by

vision industry, in which white actor David Carradine played a poker-faced Shaolin monk wandering, dazed, through the wild West.

With Hollywood's realization that gung fu was big business, a rash of films was released and distributed to the theaters. New Hong Kong productions were booked with unprecedented frequency. The films were extremely popular with another American minority, the Black community, perhaps because its viewers enjoyed the action and identified with the fight for justice.

For Asian American men, the image of the Chinese as gung fu expert was a step forward from the diabolical mad scientist, the war-mongering Japanese officer, the walking dictionary of Confucian aphorisms or the subservient houseboy. But the gung fu cult brought with it a new stereotype—that of the martial arts expert. In school yards and inner city streets, the false image proved to be just as troublesome.

Our Exotic Selves

Asian women in the media invariably appear as one of a few stock characters: the Dragon Lady, the docile geisha, the sexy Suzy Wong. The movie industry's first experiment with bankable exotica, and a successful one in box-office terms, was the promotion of Anna May Wong, born in Los Angeles Chinatown. From the silent movie era of the 1920s until 1960, the talented Wong appeared in 100 films and enjoyed international popularity. Her first role was in *The Thief of Baghdad* (1924), a movie which made unprecedented use of exotic costuming and sets and which launched Wong's career. In subsequent years she became the Chinese Flapper, the villainess, the vamp, the other woman, the sometime protagonist. She even played the progeny of Dr. Fu Manchu in *Daughter of the Dragon* (1931).

As the first popular Asian American film personality, Wong's acceptance was based on roles which called for an Oriental mystique, coupled with the Western dress, speech, and mannerisms understood by the viewing public. The ultra-Westernized life Wong led as a result of stardom alienated her from her roots in the Chinese community, but apparently not from some feelings

Bruce Lee in Enter the Dragon.
(Museum of Modern Art)

for China as motherland. In 1936, she was one of the many second-generation Chinese Americans who returned to China "to observe" as she said, "the Oriental culture for one year." There she was confronted with the issues of identity and responsibility to her people. "Because I had been the villainess so often in pictures, it was thought I had not been true to my people," she told the *Hollywood Citizen News* in 1958. "It took four hours one afternoon to convince the Chinese government this was not so. I couldn't give up my career because I feel it is really drawing China nearer and making it better understood and liked."[2] During World War II Anna May Wong left show business to work for the USO and United China Relief. Although she made a film comeback in the late 1940s, her career never regained its former momentum.

The exotic-erotic stock image of Asian women, however, was alive and well in Hollywood. In the early 1960s, a demand for Polynesian and Asian actresses drew many young hopefuls to California. Eurasian actress Pilar Seurat said of the boom: "The industry has more confidence in Oriental and Eur-

Nancy Kwan and William Holden in The World of Suzie Wong, *which boosted the erotic-exotic stereotype of Asian women.* (Museum of Modern Art)

asian actresses and will use them in bigger parts. Recently I played a Polynesian girl who was anything but the sarong style native. I wore a two-piece bathing suit."[3] Progress is indeed relative. Most Asian and Pacific American actresses who longed for more substantial roles than bar hostesses, club dancers and Chinatown scenery were disappointed.

In movies such as *The World of Suzy Wong, Love is a Many Splendored Thing, Sayonara,* and *Diamond Head,* the love between a white man and an Asian woman was allowed to blossom on the screen. Conversely, but reflective of social mores which regarded Asian men as a threat to white women, Asian men, from Sessue Hayakawa in *The Cheat* (1915) to the present, have not broken the interracial love taboo.

One Step Forward, Two Steps Back

By the 1960s, popular stereotypes of Chinatown were translated into Hollywood-style song and dance. *Flower Drum Song* (1961) gave us such memorable tunes as "A Hundred Million Miracles" and "Grant Avenue," but resembled a convention of Chinese American stereotypes, past and present. In Hollywood productions, sensitive portrayals of Chinese were few and far between. Occasionally, a Chinese character was allowed to triumph over an adversary or express a deeper range of feelings than the earlier Charlie Chan and Fu Manchu characters. For example, in *Walk Like a Dragon* (1960), James Shigeta portrayed a Chinese gunslinger who

The cast of Flower Drum Song *dance to "Grant Avenue, San Francisco, California, U.S.A."*
(Museum of Modern Art)

was a quicker draw than his white rival. In *The Sand Pebbles* (1966), Mako gave a heart-felt performance as the Chinese engine-room apprentice, Pohan, for which he received an Academy Award nomination.

But more often than not, Chinese characters were flat or stereotypic: the houseboy, the agent of evil, the exotic barmaid, the demure daughter of Old China. Despite protests and indignant letters, the stock characters continued to appear in film and television scripts, through the 1970s and into the 1980s. In the long-running television series, *Hawaii 5-0*, Jack Lord's Hawaiian and Chinese sidekicks were rarely scripted substantially beyond "Okay, Boss." Comic impersonations of Asians were uniformly performed with thick glasses, pidgin accents, and buck teeth. Saturday morning cartoons spread such perceptions of the Chinese to the younger generation through animated char-

acters like Hong Kong Flewis, who first appeared in the 1970–'71 season (*Will the Real Jerry Lewis Please Sit Down?*), sporting slanted eyes, protruding teeth and mock-Confucian adages.[4]

Veteran Hollywood actress Beulah Quo, who has been active in the struggle for decent Asian characterizations, observes that the industry is out of touch with reality, rarely perceiving Asians and Asian Americans as normal human beings:

The media is 50 years behind when it comes to Asians. They still think of us as adding color to a show, rather than being an actor or actress who has a character role that is important to the story. You know, you don't see an Asian woman who's a doctor, you don't even see an Asian woman in one of those medical shows who's a nurse. And today, in life, for instance, you go into a hospital, half of the staff, the nursing staff, are Asian women.

Substantial roles for Asian actors and actresses are rare, says the California-born Quo:

The character role that I've enjoyed and found the most challenging was the Empress Dowager of China, of the Qing Dynasty. I think every actress looks for a role like that. The one gripe I have is the roles that are given to Asian women are very seldom full character roles and you really can't bite your teeth into them. There's very little meat to them and too often . . . they think of very surface and stereotype portrayals. Back in the 60's some independent producer was going to do a show portraying Chinese girls in cages as prostitutes. And the whole acting community protested and I was in the forefront of the protest. None of us would accept any work in that, but more than that, we organized ourselves and protested to the production company about this film and insisted they make changes. They did go ahead and do it. But we made a lot of noise about it.[5]

Chinese American Culture

In the sixties, American minorities experienced a resurgence of ethnic pride which led them to work towards greater control of their own lives, not only in a political and economic sense, but in terms of culture as well. The seventies brought a real renaissance to Asian America. Creative artists reached out to each other, found parallel experiences, learned from differences in perspectives. They examined the history of images of Chinese Americans in books and the media and found unacceptable portraits of themselves which had been fostered by economic and political conditions, racist attitudes, and to some extent, image acceptance by Chinese Americans as well.

Upon closer examination, these cultural workers found that there was indeed a Chinese American culture that had remained intact and was developing in new ways, despite decades of suppression.

Chinese American actors and film crew on location in the 1920s.
(Courtesy, Kenneth and Ida Lim)

They saw how the historical experience of Chinese America had shaped outlook, behavior and expression. With each new day, they found other voices — in literature, art, dance, music, film — and with them, celebrated.

Chinese Protest Literature

While most pioneer Chinese gold miners and railroad workers were peasants who had received little or no education in China, some literate men had made the ocean voyages to Gam San. Accounts of the Chinese experience in America were also written by authors in China.

Themes of bitterness over mistreatment and frustration over the inability of the Chinese government to aid its emigrant citizens filled the literature of the period. Chinese writers took up the cause in such pieces as "An Essay on the Expulsion of the Guests," written by San Francisco Consul Huang Tsun Hsien in the 1880s. The 1905 anti-American boycott prompted Chinese writers to protest the exclusion laws through novels like *Ashes After Catastrophe, Tears of the Overseas Chinese* and *The Golden World,* as well as in poetry, essays and songs.[6]

In music, simple songs and elaborate operas alike expressed the suffering and humiliation of the immigrants. A set of Cantonese songs entitled "The Prisoner in the Wooden Shed Suffered the Utmost in Hardships," written in 1911 or 1912, touched the heart of the matter in the following stanza:

> *My family is poor and suffers from shortages of fire-wood and rice.*
> *So I borrowed money to come to the Golden Mountains.*
> *But it is difficult to escape from the interrogation of the immigration officer.*
> *And I was sent to the Island like a prisoner.*
> *Arriving here, I sighed deeply in a dark room.*
> *When a country is weak, others often treat it with contempt.*
> *She is like a domesticated animal passively awaiting destruction.*[7]

Chinese newspapers and magazines carried stories and editorials which exposed the hardship of the Angel Island detention experience. This heritage of fiction, poetry, music, and journalism reveals that from the beginning, many Chinese were outraged by the institutionalized racism of the Exclusion Era. Although they were diplomatically helpless and legally at the mercy of the United States courts, many of them protested in other ways. They were very successful in alerting others to the ordeal to be faced at Angel Island.

Chinese American Literature

In the early twentieth century, several Chinese government officials and scholars published books in English which were meant to explain the Chinese people to Americans, apparently in the hope that with knowledge would come improved treatment. Books of this nature included Yung Wing's *My Life in China and America* (1909) and J. S. Tow's *The Real Chinese in America* (1923).

Perhaps the first writer to express the true voices of early Chinese American pioneers in the English language was English-born Eurasian Sui Sin Fah. In her Exclusion Era writing, she was not as concerned with presenting a humble, law-abiding por-trait of the Chinese as she was with replacing the John Chinaman caricature with realistic Chinese characters on the Pacific Coast. Her short stories were published by the California magazine *Land of Sunshine* in 1896, and in a volume of her own, *Mrs. Spring Fragrance*, in 1912.[8]

The popularization of the fictional character Charlie Chan in the mid-1920s suggested that Chinese Americans walked daily between two cultures, speaking flowery English rich with ancient Eastern adages. Chinese Americans were thought to have dual personalities, a Chinese half and an American half, and the ability to respond to situations with the appropriate mode. *Chinatown Inside Out* (1938) by Leong Gor Yun, *Father and Glorious Descendant* (1943) by Pardee Lowe, *Fifth Chinese Daughter* (1945) by Jade Snow Wong, and *The House That Tai Ming Built* (1963) by Virginia Lee continued to explain Chinese Americans from this perspective. In the years in which little else had been

Mei-mei Berssenbrugge, poet.
(Ginger Chih)

written for the American public about Chinese Americans, these first books by Chinese American authors, autobiographical and semi-autobiographical in nature, were eased into the book market and reinforced the image of Chinese as non-threatening ethnic novelties. There is also evidence that the American patriotism expressed in Lowe's and Wong's autobiographies was used by the United States government in its anti-Japanese propaganda during World War II.[9]

Louis Chu's *Eat A Bowl of Tea* (1961) signalled a radical departure from the Chinatown-as-novelty novels, capturing the Chinatown streets with unprecedented honesty. Chu wrote of New York Chinatown's bachelor society, of loneliness, depression, impotence and inner-society dynamics. His translation of Cantonese colloquialisms was a stark contrast to the flowery, stilted prose of many earlier works.

New York novelist and poet Diana Chang teaches at Barnard College, and is one of the most widely-published Chinese American writers. Although much of her writing has focused on subjects other than the Chinese American experience, her first, eloquent novel, *The Frontiers of Love* (1956) speaks to the East-West conflict from the perspective of a Eurasian living in China; she examines the choices of cultural and political identity which face the bicultural citizen of the world. Chang has also written four other novels, *A Woman of Thirty, A Passion for Life, The Only Game in Town,* and *Eye to Eye.* Her poetry has been published widely and she is an editor of *The American Pen.*

Shawn Wong's *Homebase* (1979) was, despite its late date in Chinese American history, the first novel by an American-born Chinese male ever published. In language easily balanced between poetic fluidity and discernment, Wong tells the story of Rainsford Chan, a fourth-generation Chinese American, and his quest to discover and retouch his family's historical presence in America. The California-born Wong, who lives in Seattle, remembers discovering in his college years that not only were there other Asian American writers around, but quite possibly a whole tradition. He first came in contact with writers Jeffery Chan and Frank Chin:

> I met Jeff Chan and that was real unusual for me because I was writing and here was another Chinese American guy who was writing short stories. He said, "Gee, you live only about a block away from Frank Chin in Berkeley. He's a Chinese guy and he writes too." So, I called him up on the phone. I said, "My name is Shawn Wong. I'm Chinese and I write." I didn't know what to say. It was like trying to get a blind date.

> Jeff, Frank and I, we decided well, if there's three of us, there's got to be more. We can't be the first ones, it's impossible. So we started looking and we were in a book store one day and we saw a book called **Down at the Santa Fe Depot** and we looked in there and there was a picture of Lawson Inada. So we wrote to the editor and got his phone number and called him up. Same kind of conversation—"We read your poems, we think they're great, we're writers too." He said, "You guys write, you're Asians? I'll be right down." So he drove down from Ashland and met us and we went to this party . . . we just sat and talked all night.

> And then we kind of went around and talked to other people and that's how we started AIIIEEEEE![10] We'd find one writer and then that writer would give us names of other people that they had known twenty years ago—maybe they'd still be writing. We'd send students from San Francisco State out to used bookstores and to the University of California library to look up every Chinese name, Japanese name they could think of. Send them to these junky bookstores— they wouldn't read the titles, they'd just stand back about ten feet and look for bamboo lettering.[11]

Most popular with the mainstream critics and public recently has been Maxine Hong Kingston, whose novel *The Woman Warrior: A Girlhood Among Ghosts* won a 1976 National Book Critics' Circle award and whose second book, *China Men* (1980) became a best seller as well. Although her books were classified as non-fiction, Kingston took poetic license in telling the stories of the women and men of her California Chinese family from her unique perspective. Both works weave reality with dreams and Chinese lore, a technque which has elicited praise from mainstream critics who call the writing "dizzying" and "elemental,"[12] and criticism from a number of Chinese American writers who fear the formation of new stereotypes.

In children's literature, Lawrence Yep has treated children and grown-ups alike to poignant and humorous slices of Chinese American life in his novels *Sweetwater* (1976), *Child of the Owl* (1977) and the award-winning *Dragonwings* (1975). With writing that is fine-tuned to Chinese American language, he portrays realistic community relationships, whether among railroad workers in the snowy Sierras or between a grandmother and granddaughter in a one-room Chinatown apartment.

The ranks of Chinese American poets continue to grow. Among contemporary members are Nellie Wong, Alan Chong Lau, George Leong, Mei-mei Berssenbrugge, Fay Chiang, Wing Tek Lum, Laureen Mar and Kitty Tsui. While a few Chinese American poets have published volumes of their works, the vast majority are published only in anthologies, or in periodicals such as the *Yardbird Reader, Bridge,* and the *Bamboo Ridge.*

Asian American poets and writers' collectives were formed in the 1970s to sharpen technique and lend mutual support. The first Asian American Writers Conference was convened in Oakland in 1975, and the nation's writers met in subsequent years in Seattle and Honolulu. At the end of the decade, two women writers' workshops, the Pacific Asian American Women Writers West in Los Angeles and the Unbound Feet Collective in San Francisco, offered public readings of original poetry and drama.

A play by Frank Chin.
(Poster Courtesy of Russ Lowe)

Drama

Perhaps the most outspoken proponent of the theory that Chinese Americans have a unique cultural sensibility to express is California-born writer Frank Chin. Chin has taught, organized conferences, and co-edited numerous collections of Asian American literature. He has been instrumental in bringing the work of older Asian American writers, whose writing over the years proves the existence of a literary tradition, to public attention. Although he has published many essays and short stories, he is primarily known as a playwright.

The Chickencoop Chinaman was produced in New York in 1972 and Chin became the first Asian American to have a play performed in mainstream theater. His play *Year of the Dragon* was written to commemorate the American Bicentennial, and reached a nation-wide audience on the PBS television network in 1975. "The Chinese came from

a tradition of never being passive," Chin told a Honolulu newspaper reporter in 1979. "They came across the Pacific, settled here, learned two languages. That was not passive! I am not passive! I even sleep restlessly. If I go out and get hit by a car, it's my fault! . . . People in my plays are victims of history, struggling, raging against history. They know something's wrong, but they don't know what."[13]

While still a student at Stanford University, David Henry Hwang received word that his play *FOB* had been chosen for performance at the 1979 O'Neill National Playwrights Conference at Waterford, Connecticut. *FOB* then enjoyed an extended run at New York's Public Theater in 1980, and staging by Asian American theater groups in Los Angeles and San Francisco. It won an OBIE award for the best new play of the 1980–'81 season. The play explores the cultural clash between the ABC, or American-born Chinese, and the foreign-born FOB who is "fresh-off-the-boat," and examines the spirit which wrenches apart, and eventually binds. Actor John Lone was named one of the promising talents of the new season by *The New York Times* and awarded on OBIE for his performance as the play's protagonist. In 1981, Hwang featured Lone and actor Tzi Ma in *The Dance and the Railroad*, a play performed in New York which explores the lives of two Chinese railroad workers during the historic 1867 strike. Hwang was named Playwright-in-Residence for the 1981–'82 New York Shakespeare Festival. His other works include *Family Devotions, Mad Love in Gardena, Love That Waits,* and *The House of Sleeping Beauties.*

With the scarcity of substantial non-stereotypic, Asian roles in theater, film and television, the Asian and Pacific American acting community developed alternatives and organized itself on both coasts through the 1970s. Various repertory groups were formed and provided opportunities and exposure for Asian American actors and playwrights. These included the East West Players in Los Angeles, the Asian American Theater Workshop in San Francisco and the Pan-Asian Repertory Theater in New York.

Art

Although painting as an art form has been part of traditional Chinese culture from the earliest dynasties, a few Chinese American artists are taking some uncharted routes.

Dora Fugh Lee displayed early artistic talent as a child in her native Beijing and began studying painting with traditional masters at the age of eleven. While living in Tokyo in the 1950s, she became a protegee of China's foremost scholar-painter, Prince Pu Ju. Since settling in Bethesda, Maryland, with her family in the 1960s, Lee has exhibited her work in numerous one-woman and group shows and has received over thirty awards for watercolors and sculpture. While she keeps traditional art alive through her teaching, she has also evolved a unique style of her own in response to her life in the western world:

In the late 1960s I started to paint Washington D.C. in my traditional brushwork. The paintings came out somewhat not right. I tried and tried to find a way to depict the cityscape scenes that I love. Material-wise, I still use Chinese colors, brushes, and paper, which are different from western materials. Although my subjects are western, the composition and coloring is very much Chinese. Most of the time, I omit the sky, I don't fill it in with color. The Chinese way is to omit certain sections of the painting and leave it to the viewer's imagination.[14]

Doug Young studied art in Iowa and New York and returned to his native Hawaii in 1973, where he began to employ the intricate watercolor techniques of photorealism to interpret the local environment. His subjects included tourists and hula dancers juxtaposed against large pineapple cans, somen-ramen noodles on store shelves, fish on ice at Chinatown markets.

The underlying basis for my work is my love for the Islands, producing contemporary images of the Hawaii we see today. I'm dealing with local subjects but there are Chinatowns everywhere. Although it (a painting) does specifically deal with images from Honolulu's Chinatown, it could be a scene of a Chinatown in New York or San Francisco. . . . They're straight shots of very mundane imagery. What I'm trying to do is push the scene beyond the mundane sense, identify it but try to make it more interesting, break up the space.[15]

"I'm fascinated by American culture," says artist John Woo, "because it has the potential to include cultures from around the world. It's a salad bowl, not a melting pot. But there has to be a point where people give up their cultural chauvinism and accept other cultures." Woo takes on a variety of assignments as a freelance artist in New York City. He says that Asian themes that emerge in his work are usually "not a conscious effort, but just there."[16] This is not to say that Woo has not, in specific instances, expressed his sense of Chinese America, and the positive contributions of her working people. His works include a mural in the International District of his native Seattle showing Chinese contributions to the Pacific Northwest and a dramatic time-line mural for the New York Basement Workshop's photo exhibit, "Images of a Neglected Past: The Work and Culture of the Chinese in America."

Dora Fugh Lee's traditional landscape painting and a modern depiction of Washington D.C.
(Courtesy Dora Fugh Lee)

Music

To the Chinese American community, musical expression in the past has taken the form of classical ensembles and Chinese opera, the marching xylophone bands of Chinatown parades, and the dance bands of the 1940s and rock bands of the 1960s which mirrored mainstream trends. In recent years, a number of musicians have composed and performed music more specifically about Chinese and Asian Americans.

Composer-musician-poet "Charlie" Chin of New York worked the folk music circuit in Greenwich Village and toured nationally with a rock band in the sixties, but in the early 1970s began to focus his music on the expression of the Asian American experience:

It was around 1971. I remember very clearly. There was a Chinese brother who came into a bar I was working at and he asked me if I knew of any Asian musicians. I was working behind the bar at that time, and I thought "Well, gee, you know, I play a little." So he says, "We're looking for some guys to play at an Asian conference at Pace College." I said, "Well, okay, I'll come down." I had no idea what was going on. And I was startled to find out that there was an Asian American movement.

I decided to start devoting more time to try to get involved in it. There were a lot of young Asians, and some older Asians who were trying to sink back into their communities, into a sense of being Asian American. At this particular time, Asian Americans in this

Poet Fay Chiang and "Charlie" Chin perform at Basement Workshop, New York.
(Ginger Chih)

Scene from the rock opera Chop Suey, *by Benny Yee, Los Angeles, 1979.*
(Diane Mark)

country had been keeping an extremely low profile, even to the point of disappearing. Simultaneously, the Black movement had been going on. And also the war in Vietnam, which made it especially crucial for Asian Americans to at least stand up and make a statement about how they felt. It was not unusual to come home at dinner time, turn on the TV and see people who looked like your uncle or your aunt being shot through the head or burnt out of huts. Emotionally, it was very moving, and I know for myself personally, I had to say something, I had to do something.

You try to contribute something that you can do to the overall movement. And since I was playing music, I was very lucky to meet two other people, Nobuko Miyamoto and Chris Iijima, and I hooked up with them, and we played around the country in the different communities, for about three years. Our responsibility, we felt, was to try to offer an alternative

to some of the things that Asian Americans were exposed to. It wasn't just us doing it, there were many different people working in different areas, and this work is continuing. There had to be an Asian American music, an Asian American literature, and an Asian American art that would speak about us, and where we stand.[17]

Benny Yee grew up playing the piano in the back of his father's laundry in Los Angeles. He helped to organize the Asian American band Hiroshima in the 1960s and later formed Warriors of the Rainbow with vocalist Nobuko Miyamoto and other west-coast musicians. Yee's rock opera, *Chop Suey*, which is about growing up Chinese in Los Angeles, was first staged in the summer of 1979 as part of the East West Players' revue *Made in America*.

The PEARLS *film* Ourselves *featured Asian American women expressing their own experiences through dance, poetry, music, and dialogue.*
(Diane Mark)

Dance

A number of Asian American dance groups have choreographed and performed original works relating to the Chinese American experience. Yen Lu Wong in 1977 presented her *Golden Mountain* in La Jolla, California. As the first major work of dance theater focused on the Chinese American historical experience, it combined sound and visual imagery against a setting of sea and sky. Choreographers and dancers developed their art in other regions as well, in groups such as the Asian American Dance Collective in San Francisco, and the Morita Dance Company and Asian American Dance Theater in New York City. New York choreographer

Chiang Ching worked with both Chinese and American techniques. In 1978, Winston Tong was awarded an OBIE for his choreography in *Bound Feet.*

Film, Television, and Radio

As Hollywood persisted in its recycling of Oriental stereotypes, Asian Americans interested in more realistic portrayals felt compelled to provide alternatives. On the community level, independent filmmakers put limited resources to effective use of produce a wide variety of works. During the seventies, Asian American film festivals screened documentary, short and full-length features, animated and avant-garde pieces. Visual Communications in Los Angeles produced numerous films which circulated within the Asian American communities. Writer Connie Young Yu was the subject of *Jung Sai: Chinese Americans*, a personal/universal pursuit of history. *From Spikes to Spindles* was produced by Chris Choy in New York; it examined the working-class world of Chinese Americans.

Asian Cine-Vision (ACV), based in New York Chinatown, worked toward the combination of professional excellence and community commitment. It organized television training workshops, launched a weekly cable program in Cantonese and Mandarin dialects, sponsored the annual Asian American Film Festival, and developed an Asian American media archive. In 1981 ACV and the National Endowment for the Humanities sponsored the Asian American Media and Humanities Conference to develop communication among filmmakers, scholars, and community resource persons.

In San Francisco, educational programs such as *Yut, Yee, Sahm, Asians Now!, Gum San Haak*, and the Emmy-award-winning *Sut Yung Ying Yee* were aired by local television stations. Producer Loni Ding's *Bean Sprouts* featured a cast of Chinatown community children. Boston's *Rebop* show for children included Chinese American episodes. *Pacific Bridges* and *Pearls*, two Asian American film series produced by the Educational Film Center in Virginia, were aired by the Public Broadcasting System.

Dupont Guy, a pioneer radio series produced by Asian American media activists in San Francisco, featured "Portholes to the Past," dramatic vignettes of Chinese American history, as well as discussion of community issues. The program's east coast counterpart, *Gold Mountain D.C.*, was produced for Pacifica radio by a collective of Asian Americans in Washington, D.C. The monthly program served as a forum for community news and commentary and also featured the work of Asian American musicians, poets and other creative artists.

In the seventies, Chinese Americans explored many areas of self-expression, often in response to media portrayals which colored perceptions of Chinese and other Asians in America. Chinese American writers, artists, performers and filmmakers worked both individually and collectively on their crafts. Once rid of the layers of conditioning by society, inner voices which spoke in new terms, their own terms, were heard in communities across the land. The next task would be to assure those voices be heard by the rest of America.

11 Contemporary Profile

Since 1950, the Chinese American population has doubled in every decade. The number of Chinese increased from 117,629 that year to 237,292 in 1960, to 435,062 in 1970. The 1980 U.S. Census tabulated 806,027 Chinese in the country, and for the first time in seven decades the Chinese replaced Japanese Americans as the largest sub-group in the Asian American populace.

The growth in population was due in major part to the lifting of discriminatory immigration policies in 1965 and to the admission of many ethnic Chinese refugees from Southeast Asia after 1975. Accompanying the dramatic increase in people were changes in demography and socio-economic concerns. New Chinese and other Asian American organizations were formed to voice growing concerns, lobby on Capitol Hill, and advocate the rights of Asian Americans to funding and inclusion in minority programs.

One of the primary obstacles to improvement of conditions for Chinese Americans was the persistent myth of the model minority. In proclaiming the first Asian and Pacific American Heritage Week in 1979, President Jimmy Carter praised Asian Americans for their past triumph over discrimination and concluded: "We have succeeded in removing the barriers to full participation in American life. . . . Their successful integration into American society and their positive and active participation in our national life demonstrates the soundness of America's policy of continued openness to peoples from Asia and the Pacific."[1]

In celebration of Heritage Week 1981, President Ronald Reagan repeated the opinion which seems to cross party lines: "Overcoming great hardships, they have lived the American dream and continue as exemplars of hope and inspiration not only to their fellow Americans but also to the new groups of Asian and Pacific peoples who even now are joining the American family."[2]

In addition to acceptance in the Oval Office, the success story of Chinese Americans continues to be popular in the institutions of government, education and the mass media. The idea is offensive in its failure to recognize the problems of the Chinese American population and the consequent failure of institutions to direct funding and programming where it is needed.

Occupational Dichotomy

Chinese Americans are increasingly well represented in the labor force, but there is a bipolarity in their employment pattern. Although many men are employed in professional and technical fields, many more perform service work in restaurants and laundries for very low wages. One quarter of the Chinese American women who work are employed in professional and managerial positions, comparable to other populations of working women, but the largest category consists of low-status white-collar jobs such as typists, secretaries and sales clerks. In addition, one quarter of the Chinese female work force provides semi-skilled labor for garment and other factories.

Chinese Americans are still excluded from participation in a number of fields. In various trades or crafts they are simply denied apprenticeship, which is a prerequisite to union membership. Consistent with a history of discrimination in the United States, Chinese workers remain employed in industries which pay low hourly wages. Lingering inequities exist in the professions as well.

Although statistics show that a sizeable number of Chinese American men are in managerial work, a closer look reveals that most of these managers have their own businesses, such as restaurants or small companies. Few Chinese men are employed as managers in American corporations.

But perhaps the most dramatic evidence that the body of Chinese Americans has not yet achieved the American Dream is the incidence of poverty among the population, especially in San Francisco and New York Chinatowns. In 1970, 13% of the Chinese American people lived in poverty. Some 41% of all Chinese men earned less than $4,000 a year, while the national average was 31%. This comparatively large percentage represents the many elderly and immigrant men who work at low-paying jobs.

In Hawaii, where the Chinese have had greater opportunities for managerial or professional advancement, the median family income is $14,936, per annum, and is at the high end of the spectrum for all Chinese Americans. In New York City, the median income for Chinese families is $7,809, or about half the Hawaiian figure. According to the Department of Education and Welfare, in 1974, 86% of the Chinese families in New York earned less than $6,000. The per capita income in New York Chinatown was $2,264 compared to an average of $3,720 for New York City as a whole.

Despite this poverty, Chinese families have consistently received less help from the government than any other groups. There are a number of reasons: the lack of bilingual information regarding welfare and social security, the social stigma attached to public assistance and the desire to maintain a clear record should the need arise to sponsor relatives who want to immigrate.

Although many Chinese Americans have joined the ranks of professionals, others, especially the newer immigrants and older bachelors, are employed in service work.

Overcrowding in New York Chinatown affects both the physical and mental health of residents. (Ginger Chih)

Mental Health

Chinese Americans are subject to the same kinds of stress that confront all Americans, with the addition of the social, political, and economic inequities they experience as a national minority. But more so than other minorities, Chinese Americans are said to take care of their own, and their mental health problems are largely unaddressed by institutional programming and government funding.

The issue of Chinese American mental health has been approached from two opposing points of view. Those who regard statistics on the Chinese American's limited use of mental health facilities, low divorce rate, and educational and occupational achievements as indicators of emotional stability,

conclude that Chinese Americans enjoy exemplary mental health. There are social workers and health professionals, however, who claim that the empirical evidence stops short of the truth. For every person who seeks help, they say, there are many others who remain unrecorded in official statistics because of their fear of the social stigma of mental illness, or because of language or cultural difficulties, or the unresponsiveness of programs supposedly designed to help them.

New York school psychologist Le Min Chin discusses the general reticence towards handling problems of mental illness outside the family:

There are many reasons why Chinese American mental health data, generally, show spuriously low inci-

dence of emotional disturbance. Mental health problems aren't acknowledged unless you have something like a full-blown psychosis that cannot be handled at home or hidden from neighbors. Other problems, such as personal conflicts or adjustment difficulties—for example, marital problems—for which some middle-class Americans often seek help, are not usually taken outside the Chinese home. These are often resolved within the family. Problems can also be denied or suppressed. Somehow the individual or the family learn to live with the problem in a way that would not mar the family image. Each individual represents the family and can bring shame to it.

Many Chinese families adhere to tradition unquestioningly. If the members do not deviate from convention, there is less likelihood that friction will occur. Each person knows his role and his duties. In a way, introspection and individuality, which are associated with the acceptance or at least acknowledgement of outside influences and psychotherapy, are not encouraged.[3]

Psychology professor Stanley Sue of the University of Washington believes that alternative strategies for the study of Chinese American mental health are necessary:

I propose that Chinese-American mental health be examined in terms of a stressors and resources model. . . . For many Chinese Americans, it is true that prejudice and discrimination affect self-esteem and well-being; it is true that poverty and limited social-economic mobility creates feelings of frustration, anger, and helplessness; it is true that many Chinese-Americans have not fully resolved their identities as bicultural Americans.

We must begin to identify Chinese-American resources. What are the personal strengths, family and community systems, informal support networks, herbalists, etc., that help to alleviate emotional problems? What are the attitudes of nutritional health practices that contribute to feelings of well-being?

What this means with respect to mental health is that psychological well-being is enhanced when individuals have low levels of stress and high levels of resources. On the other hand, Chinese-Americans who encounter a great deal of stress and possess few resources are likely to experience significant emotional

disturbance. The task that is before us is to identify stressors and resources for Chinese-Americans and then to devise strategies that can be used to decrease stressors and increase resources.[4]

Evelyn Lee, Director of the Mental Health and Social Service Division of Boston's South Cove Mental Health Center, voices the frustration of working with inadequate funding and government attention to Chinese American needs:

I had a lady who was separated from her husband for nearly seventeen years. By the time that she arrived at the United States, her husband died on the same day. She cried to me yesterday, asking "What right does the government have, separating my husband and myself for seventeen years"? It's indeed very difficult for me to reply to such a question. . . . I also have a lot of young clients who have no idea whether they are Chinese or American. Many lonely elderly are dying daily in Chinatown, with neither adequate health care nor attention from anyone else.[5]

In 1980 Chalsa Loo and Connie Young Yu of San Francisco's Chinatown Housing and Health Research Project (CHHRP) reported the findings of a comprehensive survey of 108 San Francisco Chinatown residents who were a representative sample of the community. They said that while one-half of the nation's population speaks enthusiastically about life, less than one-tenth of Chinatown's residents share those sentiments. Chinatown residents place a lower limit on their hopes for better futures, expecting less than other Americans. About one-half of the respondents were dissatisfied with their educational attainment, and one-third were disheartened by the accomplishments of their lives. The study further concluded that Chinatown residents felt that overcrowding and noise pollution were hazardous to their health. Like other Americans, they said they would much prefer a quiet, clean and peaceful neighborhood.[6]

For Chinese immigrants and the elderly, the advantages to living in Chinatown include the sense of community, the proximity to grocery shopping and friends, and the use of the Chinese language for those who speak no English. The disadvantages of Chinatown ghetto life cause depression, frustration and suicide among its residents. The deteriorating physical conditions of the nation's large Chinatowns have critically affected the quality of life and mental outlook of their residents. Contrary to popular opinion, mental health has been and continues to be an urgent problem for Chinese Americans.

The Elderly

When Victorina Peralta, Director of Adult Services, City for Philadelphia's Social Services Department, approached the municipal Corporation on Aging in regards to funding for services for elderly Asian Americans in 1975, she was asked, "Where are those Asian American elderly? We have not seen them. We don't even know they're around."[7] Although Peralta proceeded to conduct a study on the needs of the Asian American elderly in Philadelphia, upon completion of the study in 1978, the Corporation on Aging told her they had no funds for new programs.

According to the 1970 census, there were 26,856 Chinese sixty-five years and older in the United States, comprising 6.2% of the Chinese American population. The actual number of Chinese American elderly is probably higher than the census shows, however, because this sector of the popu-

One segment of the Chinatown population is composed of pioneers who arrived in America in the first decades of the twentieth century to support their families in China.

lation is very distrustful of government questioning. Their apprehensive attitude has developed in the historical context of Angel Island interrogations, fears of deportation, experiences of racial prejudice and lack of information available in the Chinese language. Elderly Chinese Americans are not spending their sunset years enjoying the fruits of their labor. The median income for elderly Chinese men in 1970 was $1,943; for women, it was $1,188.

Among the visible results of Asian American activism were community-based organizations created to serve the needs and problems of the elderly. San Francisco's Chinatown's Self-Help for the Elderly was a prototype program for the procurement of health and other social services for elderly people who had until then been neglected by both the government and the Chinatown establishment. During the 1970s, a number of new programs for research and services in various cities received public funding. Among them were the Pacific/Asian Elderly Research Project in Los Angeles, the On Lok Senior Health Services and the Chinatown Neighborhood Improvement Resource Center in San Francisco and the Chinese Information and Service Center in Seattle.

Although regular recreational activities are planned for the elderly, the major work of those community centers has been the direct daily services of information and referral, translation, counselling and guidance in application for welfare or other assistance. Francis Hong, Project Director of the Chinatown Senior Citizen Service Center in Los Angeles, notes that Chinese projects differ from other programs for the elderly:

> *Some of the projects in other parts of the country or city deal with something which I term luxuries. We talk about loneliness, the notion of death, companionship, but we cannot afford that type of luxury in Chinatown when, at the same time, we spend all of our time on the survival assistance programs to get them going on a daily basis, make sure they have enough to eat, make sure that someone takes them to hospitals, make sure that their problems are dealt with. That's what I would term the differences.*[8]

In Chinese tradition the elderly held a revered position in the family and in society. Although this system has disintegrated somewhat in the context

Social service agencies such as the Golden Age Club provide a center for seniors to socialize with each other and have a balanced, hot lunch.

(Ginger Chih)

of American society, many elderly still cling to that ideal. Poling Eng, Director of the New York Chinatown Planning Council's Project Open Door, notes that this tradition has prevented many elderly Chinese from seeking the assistance they desperately need:

> *Seven years ago, nobody knew where to get benefits from the government. I would say to them "I know, you have lots of problems, could I try to help you to apply for benefits?" They were afraid. They are afraid to lose their children's face because someone might ask, "Who supports you?" If you say, "My children," then you are very proud of your family, for your children are very respectful of you. And if someone says, "Who supports you?" and you say that you get benefits, something from the government, they say, "Oh, your children are so terrible, they don't respect you, they are not concerned about you," and they will lose their face.*[9]

Eng reports that with increased concern for the elderly and the implementation of programs that are sensitive to their needs, a change of attitude has occurred:

> *At the beginning, seven years ago when our center opened, August 14, 1972, nobody was interested in the English class or educational classes. They would say, "Poling, I am too old." "I feel very tired," "It is hard for me to catch anything." I would tell them in a group, or individually, "Never too old." Nobody knows when they will pass away; young people die too. When you're still living you better take some time for study and enjoy your life. If you have language problems, this is a handicap like not having eyes, a mouth, ears, if you don't have feet, you can't walk.*
>
> *And we have many students right now. It is hard to learn English. Even before, with A B C's, they were afraid to speak up. The instructor would have to say, "Please, speak louder." They would be embarrassed, say that their voice was so horrible, their pronunciation was terrible. I would say, "If you don't speak up, who knows how to correct you, nobody." They say, "Oh, yes." Sometimes, we have a vacation or holidays, they always say, "Poling, we don't want to get holiday and vacation. We want it opened for the whole year. Not just during the weekday, everyday." So this means we have improved our program already. They want to enjoy everyday. They have changed their mind.*[10]

Indochinese Refugees

Another problem of pressing importance to the Chinese American community is the welfare of the newest arrivals, the ethnic Chinese refugees from Southeast Asia. The collapse of the South Vietnamese regime in April, 1975, ended an era of American presence in Indochina. It also precipitated a massive exodus of ethnic Chinese from the region. As members of the disenfranchised merchant class or persons who had been affiliated with the United States, they were forced to flee for their survival, an action seemingly encouraged by the Vietnamese government and the Pathet Lao.

The first 220,000 refugees were airlifted out of their homeland in 1975, and most went directly to the United States or France. The exodus diminished as quickly as it had begun. But the political upheaval, racial persecution and starvation continued, and after October, 1978, tens of thousands of people attempted to escape every month from Vietnam, Cambodia, and Laos. Only about half of the refugees survived the sea voyage in the overcrowded boats and sea-worn freighters which brought them to makeshift camps in Malaysia, Indonesia, Thailand and Hong Kong. They remained there for months, or even years, until sponsors for them were found in other countries.

By August, 1980, the United States had admitted 395,000 Indochinese refugees. Although the State Department was responsible for the initial reception of the Indochinese, the participation of three major federal agencies and numerous independent organizations in the resettlement program resulted in overlapping efforts and general bureaucratic confusion.

The absence of a well-coordinated national resettlement program has aggravated a number of problems which Indochinese refugees have faced since their arrival. The radical changes in their environments and the sudden departures—most refugees who left Vietnam in 1975 had from two hours to two days to leave the country—caused them tremendous disorientation, stress and other mental health problems.[11]

Employment concerns abound. For the professionals, restrictive licensing regulations and their status as refugees prevent their entry into the fields for which they have been trained. While these refugees must resort to blue-collar work to support

Thousands protested the U.S. government's handling of the Indochinese refugee crisis at a United Nation's rally organized by OCA in 1979.

their families, the uneducated refugees, often illiterate, face difficulties of their own. A failure in communication between Vietnamese and local fishermen on the Texas coast erupted in racial violence and the expulsion of about 150 Vietnamese shrimpers from one town.

A two-year limit on services for the Indochinese, minimal funding for programs and the lack of bilingual social workers testify to the unrealistic approach of the government in helping the refugees to adjust to American society. The refugees initially settled wherever their sponsors lived, but later migrated towards milder climates or established Asian and Pacific American communities in such states as California, Washington, Florida, New York and Texas.

In Chinatowns, the refugees can join a community and lose their sense of isolation. By observing other Indochinese, they realize that they are not alone in their struggles in the new world. Turning to Chinatown agencies for assistance, these new arrivals have overwhelmed such organizations as Seattle's Chinese Information and Service Center, New York's Immigrant Social Service and San Francisco's Chinese Newcomers Service Center, whose caseloads were already very heavy.

Education

With the continuing arrival of Asian families, the need for bilingual and bicultural education becomes more pressing. In 1974, the Lau v. Nichols case prompted a landmark Supreme Court decision. Lau v. Nichols was a class-action suit filed in 1970 by thirteen Chinese American students in San Francisco on behalf of 3,000 Chinese-speaking youth in the city's school district. It claimed their right to an education responsive to their English-language handicap. While the Brown v. Board of Education decision two decades earlier had repudiated Black-white segregation in the schools, Lau v. Nichols upheld rights of other children of color, the non-English-speaking Chinese, Korean, Pilipino and Mexican American students.

To meet the mandate of the Lau v. Nichols ruling, Congress passed in 1974 the Bilingual Education Act, which earmarked upwards of $700 million over a five-year period for bilingual-bicultural programs. The new law outlined bilingual-bicultural education as the only effective means to equal educational opportunity for youngsters who spoke little or no English.

Unfortunately, implementation of this ruling in the following years met resistance in various school districts and funding cuts by such legislation as California's Proposition 13. President Ronald Reagan's first educational policy decision was a drastic curtailment of support for bilingual education. The value of a bilingual-bicultural approach to learning has been proven in Los Angeles Chinatown's Castellar Elementary School where it has met wih great success. In 1979 the student population of the school was 75–80% non-English

With the increase of immigrant children, the need for bilingual education has increased.
(International Examiner)

speaking; 300 of the 1,100 students were from Southeast Asia. Principal William Chun Hoon explains the value of bilingual education in his school:

We have a bilingual program in Chinese and Spanish. We encourage kids and parents to speak any language that they feel they can communicate in. We encourage kids to be verbal and we encourage them to speak their native language while they're learning English. Of course, we teach English, this is an English-speaking school, but we utilize their primary language to assist the child in making the transition to learn concepts, understand directions, and communicate with parents.

We've hired additional ESL (English as a Second Language) teachers who reinforce what the teachers do in the classroom. Because when the kids come in, I mean, you have one shock already coming in to a new country and then the second shock is that they go into the classroom and they can't understand what's going on. And I think the beauty of the program is that the teachers can immediately start to communicate with the kids. And just start teaching them right away, from Day 1.[12]

The educational issues which had been defined by Asian American student radicals beginning in the late 1960s were also arousing concern in the latter half of the 1970s. By the mid-1970s, Asian American studies programs on college campuses throughout the nation faced the reduction of budget and course offerings. But student activism is alive. The west-coast Asian/Pacific Student Union, a body of over forty-five student organizations, held its third annual conference in 1980, and discussed funding cutbacks, the oppression of Asian women and the effect of the draft on Asian and Pacific Americans. Various community projects give students the opportunity to develop their professional skills as well as their commitment to their people. In New York's Project AHEAD, for example, students in the health profession collect data and document health issues and gain a community perspective which is likely to effect future professional decisions.

Fighting Extinction

Like other Americans, Chinese Americans have been a mobile people. Regional concentrations have developed in areas of economic opportunity, or where there was need for a community, or as a result of the search for better living conditions. In the 1950s, people moved from Chinatowns to the suburbs. The 1960s brought huge population growth to selected Chinatowns, while one pattern of the 1970s was that of forced eviction through the process of urban renewal.

Because the Chinese were among the oldest residents of many major American cities, they settled in areas bordering the centers of towns. As the towns grew, however, the communities came to occupy prime real-estate areas in many cities. Inattention and lack of funding for renovation over the years have forced Chinatowns into the sub-standard conditions shared by neighboring tenderloin districts.

Across the country, planners and businessmen are refurbishing areas of the cities. The razing of old Chinatown buildings has been motivated by the ready market for higher-priced housing units corresponding to the real estate value of central city locations. It signals the replacement of one economic class with another.

A number of American cities have demonstrated their lack of concern for Chinatown residents. In the 1960s Detroit Chinatown was destroyed to make way for a freeway. Pittsburgh Chinatown was razed by bulldozers for the same purpose. Boston built an expressway which cut through its Chinatown, displacing half of its population. In 1960, when Philadelphia Chinatown heard that it might suffer the same fate, for a cross-Chinatown expressway was planned in order to rejuvenate city businesses, the community organized a Save Chinatown campaign. First launched by the Chinese Consolidated Benevolent Association whose own building was threatened, the struggle was later carried on by a student group called the Yellow Seeds. The community demonstrated and met with government officials. Although it managed to delay wholesale dispersal, some demolition and loss of housing occurred, portending more trouble in the future.

Los Angeles, Sacramento and Honolulu have transitional Chinatowns—partly original, partly developed for purposes of tourism and increased revenue. Community residents, elderly bachelors and immigrant families seem to be living on borrowed time. But having learned from Chinatown evictions throughout the country, residents in cities such as Honolulu have demanded provisions for low-cost housing in the city's plans.

One of the most effectively organized Asian American communities in the country is Seattle's International District (ID). Under the leadership of organizations such as Inter*Im, the community has been able to fight off the adjacent construction of a mass-transit terminal which, combined with the already-built King Dome stadium and freeway, would have meant pollution, traffic congestion, and a threat to the ID's future existence. The ID has made steady progress towards the long-range goal of 1,000 units of decent and affordable housing for its people.

Los Angeles Chinatown is a mixture of commercial and traditional structures.
(Ginger Chih)

Most residents of Chinatowns across the country would be the first to agree that unsafe and dilapidated buildings need to be replaced. But questions concerning the types of development which should be allowed and who should make those decisions have provoked heated debate among the various interest groups. The survival of Chinatowns in the nation's larger cities is important for several reasons. The communities are currently populated by the elderly, immigrant families who arrived after 1965 and refugees from Southeast Asia. Some, like the elderly bachelors, have lived there a long time. Chinatown is their home. For new immigrants and refugees, Chinatown serves as a first stop, a place in which to become adjusted to America. It may also be the only place in which they can find employment while learning English. Until they have attained a proficiency in the new language, residence in or proximity to Chinatown is necessary for survival.

Asian and Pacific American Advocacy

An increasingly vocal number of Chinese Americans with liberal and progressive ideas began in the 1970s to promote a Chinese American presence within the electoral and governmental systems. They see their task as one of organizing constituencies in order to gain political power within the existing institutions. In San Francisco, the Chinese American Democratic Club, the Chinese for Affirmative Action (CAA) and Asian, Inc. have launched a three-way offensive in electoral politics, civil rights and small business advocacy. In 1977, the CAA successfully backed the candidacy of one of its own members, lawyer Gordon Lau, who became the first Chinese American elected to the city's Board of Supervisors. The tenacity of such political success was thrown into question, however, when Lau was defeated in a bid for re-election a term later.

On a national level, the Asian and Pacific American Affairs Unit was established in the Democratic National Committee in 1977. Its participation in the Carter campaign led to a few governmental appointments for Chinese Americans, although none were on a policy-making level.

In Washington D.C., a few federal agencies have begun to consider problems of Chinese American and other Asian and Pacific American peoples. The first to do so was the Department of Health, Education and Welfare, which in 1973 established an advisory office now called the Division of Asian American Affairs. The Asian and Pacific American Concerns Staff of the U.S. Office of Education is working towards identification of and policy strategy for educational problems. Two other agencies, the Office of Civil Rights and the Equal Employment Opportunity Commission, have completed preliminary studies and hearings on discrimination against Asian Americans.

The Organization of Chinese Americans, Inc. (OCA), formed in 1973, addresses the rights of Chinese American citizens and permanent residents in the United States. As a national advocacy

In 1959, Hawaii's Hiram Fong was the first Asian American to be elected to the United States Senate.
(OCA)

organization, it maintains a coordinating office in Washington, D.C., where it has joined the Japanese American Citizen's League in educational lobbying efforts on Capitol Hill in the interest of Asian Americans. Joint efforts with other concerned Asian and Pacific American organizations has resulted in the passage of the 1975 Rice Production Act, which lowered rice prices, the declaration of Asian-Pacific American Heritage Week, and the inclusion of Asian Americans in the Small Business Administration's minority development programs. With over 20 chapters throughout the nation, OCA's concerns for the 1980s include Asian refugee resettlement, liberalization of immigration laws, bilingual and bicultural education, vocational training and equal opportunity employment.

The Asian and Pacific American Federal Employees Council and caucuses within government agencies call attention to specific concerns regarding matters of national policy which will affect Asian Americans. Professional organizations such as the American Public Health Association, the American Psychiatric Association, the American Psychological Association and the American Librarian Association also have Asian American caucuses within their national ranks.

The nation's only State Commission on Asian American Affairs has its headquarters in Olympia, Washington. The twenty-four-member body advises the governor of the State and proposes legislation. The scope of the work is wide, and the response to it emphasizes the need for the formation of similar commissions in other states. Former Executive Director Diane Wong describes the efforts in Washington:

> *The Commission was given basic charge of enhancing the lives of Asian Americans and in order to do that we were given tasks of fact-finding, getting recommendations to the governor, to State agencies, Department heads, other officials. And we were also given the responsibility of making sure that Asians had more involvement and more participation in government, business, etc.*
>
> *We've been involved in Federal legislative issues, busing, Indochinese refugee assistance, proposed immigration assistance. We also do community education. We respond to a lot of requests for information. During two and a half months, we responded to over forty-five requests that came in, and this is on top of all the things we initiated on our own.[13]*

While many Chinese Americans welcomed the normalization of US-China relations,
others felt the United States was betraying its pacts with Taiwan.
(Ginger Chih)

Politically-active Asian American women have voiced the particular concerns of stereotyping, and the lack of educational and occupational equity. Such groups as the Organization of Pan Asian Women and the Organization of Chinese American Women in Washington, D.C., and Asian Women United in New York provide formats for sharing common experiences and organizing for change. A national conference on the topic of Asian and Pacific American Women's Educational Equity was held in August, 1980, in Washington, D.C. It stressed the importance of the formation of a network of women and organizations throughout the country.

Normalization and Chinese Americans

On January 1, 1979, the United States and the People's Republic of China established diplomatic relations. As an important condition, the United States agreed to abrogate the 1954 United States-Taiwan Mutual Defense Treaty by the end of 1979, and to sever relations with the Kuomintang government, which it had previously considered the official government of China. In America's major Chinatowns, supporters of both the People's Republic of China and Taiwan took to the streets to celebrate or protest. The former spoke joyously of being at last able to visit their relatives in China and to feel a renewed pride in being Chinese. The latter accused the United States of betraying Nationalist China and the free world. The concept that loyal Americans were Kuomintang supporters and that the American and Nationalist Chinese flags should necessarily hang together in Chinatown was no longer fully operative. In this sense, normalization of U.S.-China relations had a liberating quality about it, opening up options for Chinese American travel, self-concept and political thought.

Maurice Chuck notes the change of attitude in Chinatown:

I'm not saying it's going to be 100% support of New China. But the situation is changing. People are no longer afraid and that's a big change. You open the Chinese Times *or the* San Francisco Journal, *every single travel service is doing business with China. They are making money, a lot of money. OK? So, it's a trend. They have to face the facts. They want to do business with the Kuomintang, fine, but they have to recognize the fact that they also run businesses and it's going to be a huge market—business with China. And also, the gift shops—a lot of Chinese gift items are selling in most of the gift shops and the grocery stores. You name it, practically every business has something to do with China nowadays.*[14]

Expanding Horizons

Since World War II, Chinese Americans have overcome legal and social barriers in industry, business, government service, the professions, and many other areas of American life. Although substantial discrimination still exists, each step forward has inspired others and has helped open the door to full participation a little wider.

The achievements of some of the Chinese America's most accomplished men and women have received widespread mainstream recognition. Chen Ning Yang and Tsung Dao Lee won the Nobel Prize for Physics in 1957, and Samuel Ting was winner of the coveted prize in 1976. Experimental physicist Chien-Shiun Wu conducted the tests which proved the Yang-Lee theory and led to their Nobel Prize. Wu was the first woman to receive the Cyrus B. Comstock Award of the National Academy of Sciences, given every five years for the most important discovery in electricity, magnetism, or radiation. The Albert Lasker Medical Research Award was presented to Choh-Hao Li, the world's top authority on the pituitary gland, in 1962. Medical researcher Min-Cheuh Chang was co-discoverer of the birth control pill. The California Museum of Science and Industry named Shing-Tung Yau California Scientist of 1979 for his solution of the Calabi conjecture, a geometric problem which had puzzled the world's leading mathematicians since the mid-1950's. Yau's attention is now turned to the phenomenon of "black holes" in space.

I. M. (Ieoh Ming) Pei is a name at the forefront of modern American architecture. Pei was awarded the Gold Medal of the American Institute of Architecture, the highest honor in the profession in 1979. His commissions have included the East Wing of the National Gallery of Art, the Convention Center of New York City and a resort hotel in Beijing. In private industry, An Wang guided the growth of his one-man computer and word processing company, Wang Laboratories, into a highly successful international conglomerate.

Although Chinese had previously been involved in production work in the mass media, the seventies decade brought several Chinese American news personalities under the lights, including Suzanne Joe, Christopher Chow and Connie Chung, the first Chinese American to anchor regional network news. San Francisco television producer Felicia Lowe took her cameras to China to shoot a documentary, *China: Land of My Father.* Journalists Charles Chung and Melinda Liu received choice assignments in Beijing after diplomatic normalization.

Composers Dai-Keong Lee and Chou Wen-Chung have made unique contributions to popular and classical American music. Cellist Yo-Yo Ma, whom Isaac Stern has called "one of the greatest instrumental talents alive," tours internationally, performing with major American and European orchestras. Imaginative set designer Ming Cho Lee teaches at the Yale Drama School and is the principal designer of the New York Shakespeare Festival and the Julliard School Opera Theater. Singapore-born Choo San Goh is one of the contemporary dance world's most sought-after choreographers. Heralded for his fresh and exciting style, he has choreographed for the Houston Ballet, the Pennsylvania Ballet, Joffrey II Dancers, and presently works with the Washington Ballet.

In the judiciary, several Chinese Americans were appointed to the bench. They included William Richardson, Chief Justice of the Hawaii State Supreme Court; Thomas Tang, Federal Appellate Judge, Arizona; Warren Chan, Superior Court Judge, Seattle. The nation's first mayors of Chinese ancestry were John Wing, elected mayor of Jonestown, Mississippi, in 1965, and William Soo Hoo, who became mayor of Oxnard, California, in 1966.

Al Young was the 1978 National Hot Rod Association Division 6 Champion and the Division 7 Champion in the following year. He won a series of races throughout the country in a Plymouth Barracuda named *Lion Dance.* Seattle tennis pro Amy Yee earned a large number of titles including number one rankings in the Pacific Northwest in women's singles in 1951 and 1954, in the United States Lawn Tennis Association's (USTA) national senior women's (50's) singles in 1973, and in the USTA women's doubles (50's) in 1974. Her summer

The *East Wing* of the National Gallery of Art, designed by architect I. M. Pei.
(Courtesy, I. M. Pei)

Champion racer Al Young and Lion Dance.

(Nick Gundersen)

tennis clinics in Seattle introduced hundreds of children to the sport. During the past three decades, Yee and her four children, including her youngest son Gary, a tennis pro in Los Angeles, won over 1,000 tennis titles. The extended family has done equally well; her nieces Marcie and Peanut Louie of San Francisco are professional players on the women's circuit.

The list of Chinese American "stars" could go on and on, for there are many. The scientist, the seamstress, the restaurant worker, the playwright, the medical researcher—all make a contribution to the growing concept of Chinese America. But then this has always been the case. And as early as the 1860s, when they built the railroad, the Chinese were not only expanding their own horizons, but America's as well.

CBS anchorperson Connie Chung.

(Courtesy, Connie Chung)

12 Epilogue

The story of Chinese America is one of survival and integrity, with many chapters yet to be written. Chinese pioneers in 1850 called this land the Mountain of Gold, but few realized the promise of quick riches. For most Chinese, America came to mean hard work, long separations from loved ones, and sinophobic racism born even before Chinese emigration to the United States. Although some immigrants came with the intention of starting new lives in America, others kept the homeland in their hearts, and looked forward to retiring there. As a result of incessant village poverty, social unrest, and foreign invasion and civil war in China, however, by the 1930s and 1940s America had come to be regarded as home.

Chinese American politics, culture and the community itself have been continually revitalized by debate and change. Chinese community leadership, long held by traditional Chinatown organizations such as the Chinese Consolidated Benevolent Association and Chinese Chamber of Commerce, were challenged by newer interest groups beginning in the 1960s. The traditional groups continue to serve a function within the community. They represent the conservative element of Chinese society and sustain cultural tradition through support of Chinese New Year celebrations, association clubhouses and altars, and language schools. A few established leaders have sponsored such community projects as New York's Confucius Plaza housing development and have shown interest in finding solutions to other Chinatown problems. Several factors, however, have diminished the influence of the traditional organizations in recent decades. First is the question of purpose. After 1911, feelings of solidarity with the Chinese Republic overshadowed loyalties to specific villages or districts. Chinatown associations which were organized for these regional connections also found it difficult to gain the interest of American-born Chinese whose concern was acculturation in this country. Secondly, fewer property holdings and the loss of its former influence over new immigrants has limited the economic base of the Chinatown establishment. Most important, however, has been the failure the traditional power structure to grapple with drastic changes in community conditions on its own.

After the mid-sixties Asian American radicals, inspired by a climate of social change in America, challenged the Chinatown establishment with unprecedented fervor. The conflict had two elements: on one level was the issue of community welfare, and on the other was the political clash between supporters of Taiwan and the People's Republic of China. During this period, many programs and drop-in centers were established for health care, child care, subsidized food distribution, legal help, and activities for youth and the elderly. Young Chinese Americans also began to point to the existence of a unique Chinese American culture, and to encourage its expression.

The demographic face of Chinese America has undergone several major changes since the first mass immigration in the 1850s. As miners, railroad laborers and farm and factory workers, most

Chinese remained in the west coast and Rocky Mountain areas through the 1880s. Anti-Chinese agitation and the fact that the railroad was completed and the mining industry was declining prompted some movement eastward to the Midwest and Atlantic coast from the 1880s to the early 1900s. Some Chinese workers who built the railroad through the South and Southwest settled in those regions as shrimp fishermen, plantation workers and small business owners.

After the turn of the century, many small Chinatowns such as Grass Valley, Nevada, which were tied to boom towns, declined as economic bases gave way. In the first four decades of the 1900s, Chinese moved to urban centers where jobs were more plentiful; they went to San Francisco, Chicago, and New York City. As more women arrived and family life became possible, conditions improved a little in communities once inhabited solely by single men.

By the 1940s, there was a sizeable population of American-born, college-educated Chinese Americans. Many served in the Armed Forces and participated in the civilian war effort during World War II, and after subsequent legislative changes in their favor, Chinese Americans began to move to the suburbs in the 1950s.

In the 1960s thousands of new immigrants and refugees began to arrive from Hong Kong, Taiwan and Southeast Asia and settled in the nation's Chinatowns or in cities where high concentrations of fellow Chinese had established communities. By the 1970s, redevelopment plans, sometimes funded with capital from Asia, portended the aggravation of such Chinatown problems as the lack of housing space. A number of those plans, such as the razing of the low-income residential International Hotel, the transformation of Locke Chinatown into a tourist attraction and the commercial development of a Hong Kong-U.S.A. concept in Oakland met intense resistance from activists of all ages.

Although many of the man-made structures from Chinese America's past have been torn down since the 1850s, a few natural reminders still flourish. In Hawaii, Chinese immigrants brought peach, sa-li and pomelo seeds from China and tended the trees for fruit in the new land. On the United States mainland, Chinese Californians planted the Tree of Heaven, or *Ailanthus altissima*, which blossoms green and grows free where Chinese pioneers once worked the land. And the legacy is this original, beautiful spirit, passed through the generations to those who struggle for Chinese America today.

Appendices

Chinese American Population of Selected States by Rank

Rank	State 1980	% of U.S. Total	State 1970	% of U.S. Total	State 1960	% of U.S. Total
1.	California	40.0	California	39.1	California	40.3
2.	New York	18.4	New York	18.8	Hawaii	16.1
3.	Hawaii	7.0	Hawaii	12.0	New York	15.8
4.	Illinois	3.5	Illinois	3.2	Illinois	3.0
5.	Texas	3.2	Massachusetts	3.2	Massachusetts	2.8
6.	Massachusetts	3.1	New Jersey	2.1	Washington	2.3
7.	New Jersey	2.9	Washington	2.1	Texas	1.8
8.	Washington	2.2	Texas	1.8	New Jersey	1.6
9.	Maryland	1.8	Pennsylvania	1.7	Pennsylvania	1.6
10.	Florida	1.7	Maryland	1.5	Michigan	1.4
11.	Pennsylvania	1.6	Michigan	1.5	Oregon	1.3
12.	Michigan	1.4	Ohio	1.2	Arizona	1.2

Source: U.S. Bureau of Census, *Race of the Population by States:* 1980 (PC80-SI-3) and U.S. Bureau of Census *Subject Reports* (PC(2) 1C-1960, PC (2) 1G1970).

Compiled by K. L. Wang

Chinese Population in U.S. by Sex — 1860-1970

Date	Total	Male	Female	Males per 100 Females
1860	34,933	33,149	1,784	1,858.1
1870	63,199	58,633	4,566	1,284.1
1880	105,465	100,686	4,779	2,106.8
1890	107,488	103,620	3,868	2,678.9
1900	89,863	85,341	4,522	1,887.2
1910	71,531	66,856	4,675	1,430.1
1920	61,639	53,891	7,748	695.5
1930	74,954	59,802	15,152	394.7
1940	77,504	57,389	20,115	295.3
1950	117,629	77,008	40,621	189.6
1960	237,292	135,549	101,743	133.1
1970	431,583	226,733	204,850	110.7

Chinese American population in the United States by Regions, Divisions and States.

	1980 Total	1980 % Distribution	1970 Total	% Changes 1970–1980	1960 Total	% Changes 1960–1970
U.S. Total	806,027	100.0	435,062	85.3	237,292	83.3
Northeast	217,730	27.01	115,777	88.1	53,654	115.8
New England	32,969	4.09	18,113	82.0	8,527	112.4
Maine	484	.06	206	135.0	123	67.4
New Hampshire	790	.10	420	88.1	152	176.3
Vermont	271	.03	173	56.7	68	154.4
Massachusetts	25,015	3.10	14,012	78.5	6,745	107.7
Rhode Island	1,718	0.21	1,093	57.2	574	90.4
Connecticut	4,691	0.58	2,209	112.4	865	115.3
Mid-Atlantic	184,761	22.92	97,664	89.2	45,127	116.4
New York	148,104	18.37	81,378	82.0	37,573	116.6
New Jersey	23,366	2.90	9,233	153.1	3,813	142.1
Pennsylvania	13,291	1.65	7,053	88.4	3,741	88.5
North Central	72,905	9.04	39,343	85.3	17,863	120.2
East North Central	57,565	7.14	31,001	85.1	14,750	110.2
Ohio	9,911	1.23	5,305	86.8	2,507	131.5
Indiana	3,994	0.50	2,115	87.9	952	122.2
Illinois	28,590	3.55	14,474	97.5	7,047	105.4
Michigan	10,992	1.36	6,407	71.6	3,234	98.1
Wisconsin	4,097	0.51	2,700	51.7	1,010	167.3
West North Central	15,340	1.90	8,342	83.9	3,113	168.0
Minnesota	4,835	0.60	2,422	99.6	720	236.4
Iowa	2,110	0.26	993	112.5	423	134.8
Missouri	4,290	0.53	2,815	52.4	954	195.1
North Dakota	305	.04	165	84.9	100	65.0
South Dakota	269	.03	163	47.0	89	83.1
Nebraska	1,106	0.14	551	100.7	290	90.0
Kansas	2,425	0.30	1,233	96.7	537	129.4
South	90,616	11.24	34,284	164.3	16,605	106.5
South Atlantic	50,558	6.37	19,332	175.8	8,555	126.0
Delaware	1,004	0.12	559	79.6	191	192.7
Maryland	14,485	1.80	6,520	122.2	2,188	197.9
Dist. of Columbia	2,475	0.31	2,582	−4.2	2,632	−1.9

	1980 Total	1980 % Distribution	1970 Total	% Changes 1970-1980	1960 Total	% Changes 1960-1970
Virginia	9,360	1.16	2,805	233.7	1,135	147.1
West Virginia	881	0.11	373	136.2	138	170.3
North Carolina	3,170	0.39	1,255	152.6	404	210.6
South Carolina	1,388	0.17	521	166.4	158	229.7
Georgia	4,324	0.54	1,584	173.0	686	130.9
Florida	13,471	1.67	3,133	330.0	1,023	206.2
East South Central	7,565	0.94	4,235	78.6	2,074	104.2
Kentucky	1,318	0.16	558	136.2	288	93.8
Tennessee	2,909	0.36	1,610	80.7	487	230.8
Alabama	1,503	0.19	626	140.1	288	117.4
Mississippi	1,835	0.23	1,441	27.3	1,011	42.5
West South Central	32,493	4.03	10,717	203.2	5,977	79.3
Arkansas	1,275	0.16	743	71.3	676	9.9
Louisiana	3,298	0.41	1,340	146.1	731	83.3
Oklahoma	2,461	0.31	999	146.3	398	151.0
Texas	25,459	3.16	7,635	233.5	4,172	83.0
West	424,776	52.70	245,658	72.9	148,386	65.6
Mountain	19,509	2.42	9,245	110.0	5,966	55.0
Montana	349	0.04	289	20.8	240	20.4
Idaho	905	0.11	498	81.7	311	60.1
Wyoming	392	0.05	292	34.3	192	52.1
Colorado	3,897	0.48	1,489	161.7	724	105.4
New Mexico	1,441	0.18	563	156.0	362	55.5
Arizona	6,820	0.85	3,878	75.9	2,936	32.1
Utah	2,730	0.34	1,281	113.1	629	103.6
Nevada	2,978	0.37	955	211.8	572	66.9
Pacific	405,267	50.28	236,413	71.4	142,420	66.0
Washington	18,113	2.25	9,201	96.9	5,491	67.6
Oregon	8,033	1.00	4,814	66.9	2,995	60.8
California	322,340	39.99	170,131	89.5	95,600	78.1
Alaska	521	0.06	228	128.5	137	66.4
Hawaii	56,260	6.98	52,039	8.1	38,197	36.2

Source: U.S. Bureau of Census, *Race of the Population by States: 1980* (PC80-S1-3).
　U.S. Bureau of Census, *Subject Reports* (PC(2) 1C1960, PC (2) 1G 1970).

Compiled by K. L. Wang

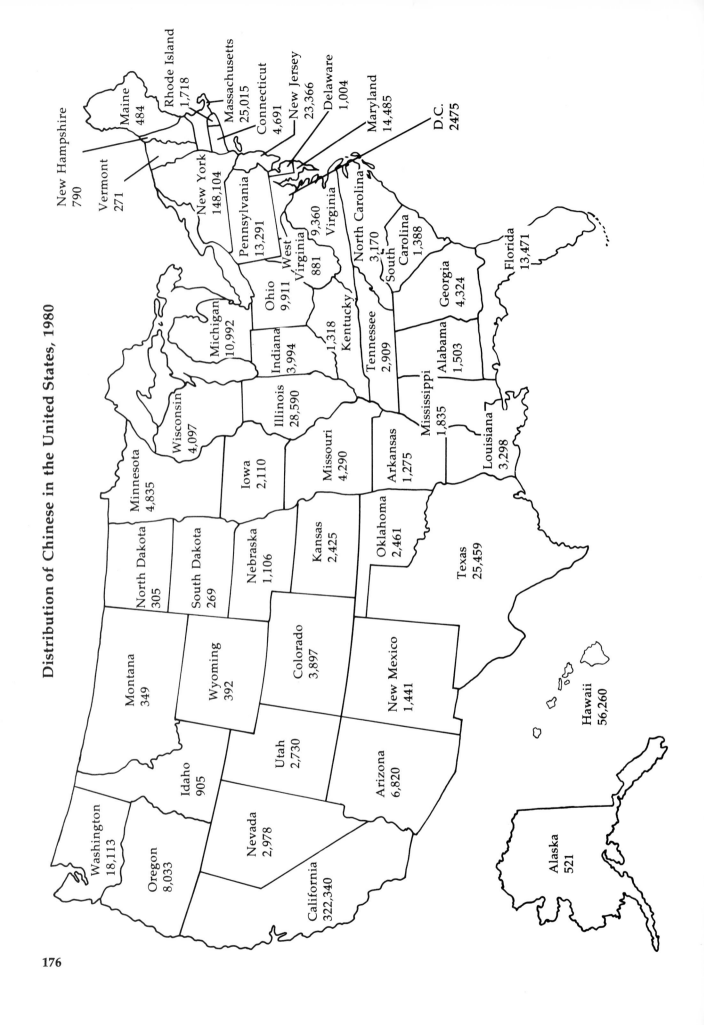

Distribution of Chinese in the United States, 1980

New Hampshire 790
Vermont 271
Maine 484
Rhode Island 1,718
Massachusetts 25,015
Connecticut 4,691
New Jersey 23,366
Delaware 1,004
Maryland 14,485
D.C. 2475
New York 148,104
Pennsylvania 13,291
West Virginia 881
Virginia 9,360
North Carolina 3,170
South Carolina 1,388
Georgia 4,324
Florida 13,471
Michigan 10,992
Ohio 9,911
Indiana 3,994
Kentucky 1,318
Tennessee 2,909
Alabama 1,503
Wisconsin 4,097
Illinois 28,590
Missouri 4,290
Arkansas 1,275
Mississippi 1,835
Louisiana 3,298
Minnesota 4,835
Iowa 2,110
Nebraska 1,106
Kansas 2,425
Oklahoma 2,461
Texas 25,459
North Dakota 305
South Dakota 269
Montana 349
Wyoming 392
Colorado 3,897
New Mexico 1,441
Idaho 905
Utah 2,730
Arizona 6,820
Hawaii 56,260
Washington 18,113
Oregon 8,033
Nevada 2,978
California 322,340
Alaska 521

176

Nativity of Chinese in the United States — 1900-1980

Year	Percentage of total	
	Native-born	Foreign-born
1900	10	90
1910	21	79
1920	30	70
1930	41	59
1940	52	48
1950	53	47
1960	61	39
1970	53	47
1980*	46	54

*Estimate

Source: U.S. Censuses, 1900–1970

The category of "Native-born" Chinese does not exclusively include those born in America. The Census Bureau includes in this category, for example, those born abroad with at least one parent who is an American citizen. Many Chinese claimed this derivative citizenship to immigrate to America. In actuality, then, the percentages of American-born Chinese are probably lower than they appear on the Census figures.

Indochinese Refugee Population Of Selected States by Rank as of June 30, 1981

Rank	State	Population Size
1.	California	173,955
2.	Texas	44,589
3.	Washington	23,336
4.	Pennsylvania	19,570
5.	Illinois	18,619
6.	Minnesota	16,738
7.	Oregon	15,189
8.	Virginia	15,030
9.	New York	14,331
10.	Louisiana	11,750
11.	Florida	9,304
12.	Massachusetts	8,890
13.	Michigan	8,862
14.	Colorado	8,499
15.	Iowa	7,841
	Other States	107,004
	Total:	503,507

Source: U.S. Department of Health and Human Services, Asian Refugee Program

Compiled by K. L. Wang

Notes

Unless otherwise noted, all interviews were conducted by the coauthors for use in this book.

Chapter 1

1. Thomas W. Chinn, ed., *A History of the Chinese in California: A Syllabus.* (San Francisco, 1969), p. 1 and Stan Steiner, *Fusang: The Chinese Who Built America.* (New York, 1979), pp. 3-4.
2. Marshall B. Davidson, "New York City and the China Trade Years, 1784-1860." *Seaport,* (Summer 1980), pp. 8-14.
3. Melvin Chang, *History of the Chinese in Hawaii.* (Honolulu, 1973), p. 2.
4. Albert Craig, John K. Fairbank and Edwin O. Reischauer, *East Asia: Tradition and Transformation.* (Boston, 1973), p. 450.
5. Among the earliest student arrivals was Yung Wing, one of three Chinese youths brought to America by returning missionary Rev. S. R. Brown. They reached New England in 1847. Yung Wing graduated from Yale College and became a Chinese government official who was instrumental in establishing American study opportunities for China's young people.
6. The term "coolie" was transliterated from the Chinese word *ku-li,* which means "bitter strength."
7. Chen Ji Ying, *Hua Yi Jin Zhou,* or *Overseas Chinese: The Splendid People.* (Taipei, 1964), p. 13.
8. Franklin Ng, "Asian-Americans and Pacific Islanders: A Neglected Aspect of the American Cultural Mosaic," in *American Ethnics and Minorities.* Joseph Collier, ed., (Los Alamitos, CA, 1978), p. 330.
9. Tin-Yuke Char, *The Sandalwood Mountains: Readings and Stories of the Early Chinese in Hawaii.* (Honolulu, 1975), p. 67.
10. Chen Ji Ying, p. 20.

Chapter 2

1. William Tung, *The Chinese in America: 1820-1973.* (Dobbs Ferry, NY, 1974), p. 88.
2. *Daily Evening Transcript,* February 27, 1868 as cited by Stuart Miller in *The Unwelcome Immigrant: The American Image of the Chinese: 1785-1882.* (Berkeley, 1969), p. 132.
3. Carey McWilliams, *Factories in the Field.* (Santa Barbara, CA, 1971), p. 23.
4. McWilliams, pp. 67-8.
5. McWilliams, pp. 71-2.
6. McWilliams, p. 60.
7. Jim and Lily Quock, Interview, San Francisco, 1979.
8. Richard Dillon, "China Camp: Cathay in Eldorado." *The Chinese in California Series,* (San Francisco, 1972).
9. Ping Chiu, *Chinese Labor in California: 1850-1880, An Economic Study.* (Madison, 1963), p. 120.
10. George Lee, Interview, San Francisco, 1979.
11. Mary Coolidge, *Chinese Immigration.* (New York, 1909), pp. 360-1.
12. Ping Chiu, pp. 89-93.
13. Doug and Art Chin, *Uphill: The Settlement and Diffusion of the Chinese in Seattle.* (Seattle, 1973), pp. 3-4.
14. John S. Hittell, *The Commerce and Industry of the Pacific Coast of North America.* (San Francisco, 1882), p. 372.
15. Edward Beattie, "China Joe," *The Alaska Sportsman,* (September, 1949), pp. 24-27.
16. John Kai, Interview, Tucson, 1979.
17. "Chinamen in the South; Organization of a Company in Arkansas to Promote the Immigration of Chinese Laborers," *Alta,* July 11, 1869, as cited by Gunther Barth, *Bitter Strength: A History of the Chinese in the United States, 1850-1870.* (Cambridge, 1964), p. 190.
18. Gunther Barth, pp. 189-190.
19. Barth, p. 196 and Berda Lum Chan, Interview, Houston, 1979.

20. Edward Wong and Mamie Wong Moy, Interview, Houston, 1979.
21. Robert Schmitt, *Demographic Statistics of Hawaii: 1778-1965.* (Honolulu, 1966), p. 41.
22. *Atlas of Hawaii.* (Honolulu, 1973), p. 99.
23. Report of the President, Bureau of Immigration (Honolulu, 1886), p. 5.

Chapter 3

1. Erasmus Doolittle, "Recollection of China." *Sketches by a Traveler,* (Boston, 1830), p. 253 cited by Stuart Miller, p. 29.
2. William H. Gilmas et al., eds., *The Journal and Miscellaneous Notebooks of Ralph Waldo Emerson.* (Cambridge, 1961), p. 244. cited by Miller, p. 16.
3. Miller, *The Unwelcome Immigrant,* p. 38-56.
4. Miller, pp. 57-80.
5. Miller, p. 61.
6. Samuel Goodrich, *A System of Universal Geography.* (Boston, 1833), pp. 905-6, cited by Miller, p. 94.
7. *Nile's National Register.* LXII. (1842), p. 99, cited by Miller, p. 110.
8. The "yellow peril" notion can be traced as far back as the thirteenth century when tales of Ghenghis Khan and his invading armies were told in Europe.
9. Stephen Williams, "The Chinese in the California Mines: 1848-1860." (San Francisco, 1971).
10. Williams.
11. Christopher H. Edson, *The Chinese in Eastern Oregon: 1860-1890.* (San Francisco, 1971), p. 41.
12. Elmer Clarence Sandmeyer, *The Anti-Chinese Movement in California.* (Chicago, 1973), p. 48.
13. Sandmeyer, p. 65.
14. Edson.
15. *The Times.* November 19, 1890 (London), cited by Roy T. Wortman, "Denver's Anti-Chinese Riot, 1880." *The Colorado Magazine,* (Fall, 1965), p. 283.
16. *Denver Times,* November 1, 1880 and *Rocky Mountain News,* October 30, 1880.
17. Edward J. M. Rhoads, "The Chinese in Texas." *Southwestern Historical Quarterly,* LXXXI (July, 1977), p. 10.
18. Edward C. Lyndon, *The Anti-Chinese Movement in the Hawaiian Kingdom: 1852-1886.* (San Francisco, 1975), pp. 46-7.
19. Paul Crane and Alfred Larson, "The Chinese Massacre," *Anti-Chinese Violence in North America.* Roger Daniels, ed. (New York, 1979), p. 48.
20. Roger Daniels, ed., *Anti-Chinese Violence in North America.* (New York, 1979), p. 48.
21. Daniels, pp. 912-915.
22. Other California towns where anti-Chinese action took place included Pasadena, Santa Barbara, Santa Cruz, San Jose, Oakland, Cloverdale, Redding, Anderson, Truckee, Lincoln, Sacramento, San Buenaventura, Napa, Gold Run, Sonoma, Vallejo, Placerville, Santa Rosa, Chico, Wheatland, Carson, Auburn, Nevada City, and Dixon. Sandmeyer, p. 97.

23. Lynwood Carranco, "Chinese Expulsion from Humboldt County." *Anti-Chinese Violence in North America.* Roger Daniels, ed., (New York, 1979), p. 334.
24. "The Chinese Experience in Arizona and New Mexico: 1870-1940," photo exhibition, The Arizona Historical Society and China Council of South Arizona, Tucson, 1979.
25. Chinn, p. 9.
26. Reverend Wilbur Choy, Interview, Seattle, 1979.
27. Letter from the United Chinese Society of Honolulu to Commissioner Keefe, dated April 1908, signed by C. K. Ai, Ching Shai, Chu Sem, Chang Chau, and Loo Joe.
28. John W. Foster, "The Chinese Boycott," *Atlantic Monthly.* XCVII (January, 1906), pp. 118-127.
29. See chapter four for further explanation of the expression "paper son."

Chapter 4

1. This poem by Ngott P. Chin was winner of a San Francisco contest sponsored by the *Chinese Times* and judged by the Angel Island Immigration Station Historical Advisory Committee.
2. Him Mark Lai, Genny Lim and Judy Yung, *Island: Poetry and History of Chinese Immigration on Angel Island, 1910-1940.* (San Francisco, 1980), p. 66.
3. Him Mark Lai, "Literature of Exclusion and Detention." *East West,* (February 25, 1976), p. 6.
4. Jim Quock, Interview, San Francisco, 1979.
5. Gene Eng, Interview, New York, 1979.
6. Locktin Eng, Interview, Seattle, 1979.
7. Naomi Jung, Interview by Ginger Chih for "Immigration of Chinese Women to the United States, 1900-1940." unpublished thesis, Sarah Lawrence College. (Bronxville, New York, 1977).
8. Kenneth Lim, Interview, Seattle, 1979.
9. Him Mark Lai and Philip Choy, *Outlines: History of the Chinese in America.* (San Francisco, 1971), p. 106.

Chapter 5

1. S. W. Kung, *Chinese in American Life: Some Aspects of Their History, Status, Problems and Contributions.* (Greenwich, CN, 1962), p. 101.
2. Lucie Cheng Hirata, "Free, Indentured, Enslaved: Chinese Prostitutes in Nineteenth Century America." *Signs: Journal of Women in Culture and Society,* V,1 (New York, 1979), p. 12.
3. Hirata, p. 18.
4. *Orientals and their Cultural Adjustment.* (Nashville, 1946), pp. 31-33.
5. Carol Green Wilson, *Chinatown Quest: One Hundred Years of Donaldina Cameron House.* (San Francisco, 1974) p. 35-43 and Doreen Der, Interview, Cameron House, San Francisco, 1979.

6. Dottie Mun, Interview, New York, 1979.

7. Tommy Jang, Interview, San Francisco, 1979.

8. Diane Mark, *The Chinese in Kula: Recollections of a Farming Community in Old Hawaii.* (Honolulu, 1975), pp. 12, 24.

9. Chih, p. 28.

10. Chih, p. 34.

11. Margaret Lowe, Interview by Ginger Chih, San Francisco, 1976.

12. Monetary gifts wrapped in red paper for good luck.

13. Vegetarian dish eaten during New Year's celebration.

14. Edith Wong, Interview by Ginger Chih, San Francisco, 1976.

15. Esther Don Tang, Interview, Tucson, 1979.

16. Mary Lee Chong, Interview by Diane Mark, Honolulu, 1973.

17. Harry Chew, Interview by Ginger Chih, San Francisco, 1976.

18. Paul Louie, Interview, Los Angeles, 1979.

19. Lily Quock, Interview, San Francisco, 1979.

20. Alice Fong Yu, Interview by Diane Mark, Piedmont, CA., 1972.

21. Jack Don, Interview, Tucson, 1979.

22. Fong Hing Sang, Interview, Tucson, 1979.

Chapter 6

1. Lyon Sharman, *Sun Yat Sen: His Life and Its Meaning: A Critical Biography.* (Palo Alto, 1934).

2. "Self Help: Jimmy Yen's Proven Aid for Developing Nations." Reprint from *The Reader's Digest,* October, 1961, p. 2.

3. Diane Mark, *The Chinese in Kula.* p. 32.

4. Him Mark Lai, Joe Huang and Don Wong, *The Chinese of America: 1785–1980.* (San Francisco, 1980), p. 67.

5. Open letter from Chang C. Kong, Honolulu, January 18, 1940.

6. Alice Fong Yu, Interview by Diane Mark, Piedmont, 1972.

7. Naomi Jung, Interview by Chih, 1977.

8. Mary Shem and Mamie Chu, Interview, Houston, 1979.

9. Edward and Emily Wong, Interview, Houston, 1979.

10. Mary Shem, Interview.

11. David Chin, Interview, New York, 1979.

12. Emilie Lau, Interview, Sacramento, 1979.

13. Hugh Liang, Interview, Washington, D.C., 1979.

14. Frank Chin, "James Wong Howe," in *Yardbird Reader, III.* (Berkeley, 1974), pp. 1–38.

15. Janet Chong, Shelley Mark, Edwin Kwok, May Eng, Wellington Lee, letter to *The Nation,* January 12, 1946.

16. Many Chinese were probably able to withstand the Depression a little better than the mass of Americans. This was due to the limited employment of Chinese in the large-scale industries, the mutual aid system of traditional organizations, and the economic concentration within Chinatowns, and within essential services. Substantial financial losses did occur among the Chinese as well, however, so their ability to cope must be regarded in relative terms.

17. "Chinese Women Protest Bill to Bar Their Race." *Dallas Morning News,* March 9, 1937 and "Alien Land Bill Heard." *The Light,* March 10, 1937 (Austin, TX).

18. Berda Lum Chan, Interview, Houston, 1979.

Chapter 7

1. Rose Hum Lee, "Chinese in the United States Today: The War Has Changed Their Lives." *Survey Graphic,* XXXI (October, 1942), p. 444.

2. William Der Bing, Interview, Houston, 1979.

3. Jack Don, Interview, Tucson, 1979.

4. Harold Lui, Interview, New York, 1979.

5. Liang Chi Shad, *The Changing Size and Changing Character of Chinese Immigration to the United States.* (Singapore, 1976), pp. 9–11.

6. Harold Lui, Interview.

7. Mary Shem, Interview.

8. Him Mark Lai, Interview, San Francisco, 1979.

9. Al Young, Interview, Seattle, 1979.

10. James T. Patterson, *America in the Twentieth Century.* (New York, 1976), p. 382.

11. Charles Chan, Interview, Houston, 1979.

12. Elsie Huang, Interview, Houston, 1979.

13. Shelley Mark, "Something to Fight For." *East Wind,* (Seattle, 1946).

14. *The Forgotten Minority: Asian Americans in New York City.* (November, 1977), p. 8.

15. Maurice Chuck, Interview, San Francisco, 1979.

16. Donald Tsai, Interview, Potomac, Maryland, 1979.

17. Donald Tsai, Interview.

18. Beng Ho, Interview, Houston, 1979.

19. Herbert King, Interview, Houston, 1979.

Chapter 8

1. "Success Story of One Minority Group in the United States" *U.S. News and World Report,* December 26, 1966, pp. 73, 76.

2. "Success Story . . ." *U.S. News and World Report.*

3. The national origins quota system upheld the Immigration Act of 1924 and the Walter-McCaran Act of 1952. The system based immigration limitations in proportion to the national origins of the United States population in 1920. If Chinese only composed one percent of the population, for example, then only one percent of the immigrants allowed entry into the United States could be of Chinese origin. Because the Chinese Exclusion laws had been in effect for two generations, the Chinese American population had been drastically reduced. Thus, the national origins quota clearly favored immigrants from Europe and discriminated against those from other areas of the world, such as Asia and the Pacific.

4. *The Forgotten Minority: Asians Americans in New York City.* p. 8.
5. *Manhattan Bridge Area Study: Chinatown.* (New York, 1979), pp. 16, 40.
6. "Sylvia Lee" is a pseudonym used at the interviewee's request.
7. Anthony Tam, "The Return of the Sweat Shop." *Neighborhood, The Journal for City Preservation,* (New York, 1978), pp. 35–39.
8. "Asian Americans; Facts and Figures,"*Bridge,* III, 4 (February, 1975), p. 36.
9. Pat Wong, Interview, New York, 1979.
10. Tom Tam, Interview, New York, 1979.
11. San Francisco Chinatown-North Beach Economic Opportunity Council Survey, 1967.
12. Tom Tam, Interview.
13. Richard Hessler, Michael Nolan, Benjamin Ogbru, Peter Kong-Ming New, "Intraethnic Diversity: Health Care of the Chinese Americans," in *Health and the Human Condition: Perspectives on Medical Anthropology,* Michael Logan and Edward Hunt, Jr., eds., (North Scituate, MA, 1978), pp. 348, 349, 354.
14. David Chin, Interview.
15. Mabel Jung, Interview, San Francisco, 1979.
16. George Woo, Interview, San Francisco, 1979.
17. Chinese Consolidated Benevolent Association, "Chinatown U.S.A. in Transition." (San Franscisco, October 1967), p. 2.
18. Peter Yu, "Youth Gangs." *Neighborhood,* p. 26.
19. Chinese Consolidated Benevolent Association, Press Release. (San Francisco, October 1967).

Chapter 9

1. Doreen Der, Interview.
2. Harold Lui, Interview.
3. Liz Young, Interview, New York, 1979.
4. Norman Nakamura, "The Nature of G. I. Racism," in *Roots: An Asian American Reader,* eds., Franklin Odo et al., (Los Angeles, 1971), p. 24.
5. Liz Young, interview.
6. Alex Hing, Interview, Oakland, 1979.
7. Alex Hing, Interview.
8. Alex Hing, Interview.
9. "I-Hotel." *San Francisco Journal,* August 10, 1977, p. 1.
10. George Lee, Interview, San Francisco, 1979.
11. Tom Tam and Liz Young, Interviews, 1979.
12. R. Takashi Yanagida, "The AAFEE Story." *Bridge,* III, 4 (February, 1975), pp. 47–51.
13. "New York Chinatown in An Uproar! 20,000 Protest Police Brutality." *Wei Min,* June–July, 1975, pp. 1, 4.

Chapter 10

1. Irvin Paik, "That Oriental Feeling: A Look at the Caricatures of the Asians as Sketched by American Movies," in *Roots,* pp. 30–32.

2. Judy Chu, "Anna May Wong," in *Counterpoint: Perspectives on Asian America,* Emma Gee et al., eds., (Los Angeles, 1976), p. 287.
3. Joe Finnigan, "Oriental and Eurasian Actors in Midst of Hollywood Boom." *Morning Telegraph.* April 18, 1961.
4. Paik, p. 34.
5. Beulah Quo, Interview by Irene Jue, Los Angeles, 1979.
6. Shih-Shan H. Ts'ai, "Chinese Immigration through Communist Eyes: An Introduction to the Historiography." in *The Asian American,* Norris Hundley, Jr., ed., (Santa Barbara, 1976), p. 56.
7. Him Mark Lai, "The Chinese Experience at Angel Island, part III." *East West,* February 25, 1976, p. 1.
8. Shawn Wong, "Longtime Californ.' " an introduction to *Calafia: The California Poetry,* (Berkeley, 1979), p. lxi.
9. Frank Chin, et al., eds., *Aiiieeeee! An Anthology of Asian American Writers.* (New York, 1975), p. 4.
10. *Aiiieeeee! An Anthology of Asian American Writers* was edited by Frank Chin, Jeffery Paul Chan, Lawson Fusao Inada and Shawn Wong and originally published by Howard University Press in 1975.
11. Shawn Wong, Interview, Seattle, 1979.
12. *New York Times* critic John Leonard called *Woman Warrior* "the best book I'd read in years" and *China Men* ". . . at the very least, the best book I've read in the four years since." John Leonard, "Books of the Times," in *New York Times.* June 3, 1960.
13. Susan Yim, "Frank Chin, Chinaman." *Honolulu Star Bulletin,* November 23, 1979, p. D–1.
14. Dora Fugh Lee, Interview, Bethesda, MD, 1981.
15. Susan Yim, "Real Life as the Artist Sees It." *Honolulu Star Bulletin,* February 20, 1980, p. C–1.
16. John Woo, Interview, New York, 1980.
17. "Charlie" Chin, Interview by James Yoshimoto and Diane Mark for *Gold Mountain D.C.,* November 1978, New York.

Chapter 11

1. President Jimmy Carter, Proclamation, 1979 Asian and Pacific American Heritage Week.
2. President Ronald Reagan, Proclamation, 1980 Asian and Pacific American Heritage Week.
3. Lemin Chin, Interview, New Jersey, 1981.
4. Stanley Sue, "Chinese American Mental Health," paper presented at Chinese American Studies Conference, San Francisco, October 1980, pp. 10–11.
5. Evelyn Lee, presentation on mental health services in *Civil Rights Issues of Asian and Pacific Americans: Myths and Realities.* (Washington, D.C., May 1979), p. 677.
6. Chalsa Loo and Connie Young Yu, "Chinatown: Recording Reality, Destroying Myths," presentation to the American Psychological Association Convention, Montreal, September 1, 1980.

7. Victorina Peralta, in *Civil Rights Issues,* p. 693.
8. Francis Hong, Interview, Los Angeles, 1979.
9. Poling Eng, Interview, New York, 1979.
10. Poling Eng, Interview.
11. William T. Liu and Alice K. Murata, "The Vietnam-ese in America: Refugees or Immigrants?" in *Bridge,*V, 3 (Fall, 1977), pp. 31–39.
12. William Chun Hoon, Interview by Irene Jue, Los Angeles, 1979.
13. Diane Wong, Interview, Seattle, 1979.
14. Maurice Chuck, Interview.

Sources Consulted

Interviewees and Resource Persons

Mary Au, Washington D.C.
Charles and Berda Chan, Houston
Marjorie Chan, Los Angeles
Vivien Chang, San Francisco
Chen Yu-Hsi, New York
Vincent Cheng, Pittsburg
Chi-Chang and Lucia Chih, San Francisco
"Charlie" Chin, New York
David Chin, New York
Lemin Chin, New Jersey
Lean Kuan Ching, Honolulu
Daniel K. E. Ching, Los Angeles
Carol Chong, Sacramento
Vera Chong, Honolulu
Christopher Chow, San Francisco
Philip Choy, San Francisco
Rev. Wilbur Choy, Seattle
Goldie Chu, New York
Mamie Chu, Houston
David Der, Hayward, CA
Doreen Der, San Francisco
William and Eleanor Der Bing, Houston
Anna Don, Tucson
Jack Don, Tucson
Gene Eng, New York
Locktin Eng, Seattle
Poling Eng, New York
Fong Hing Sang, Tucson
Larry Fong, Tucson
George Gee, Houston
Ted Gong, Orosi, CA
Alex Hing, San Francisco
Beng and Daisy Ho, Houston
Hanley Hoey, San Francisco
Francis Hong, Los Angeles
William Chun Hoon, Los Angeles
Dorothy Huang, Houston
Elsie Huang, Houston

Y. T. and Hazel Huang, Honolulu
Jackie Huey, New York
Connie Hui, San Francisco
Christina Hung, Houston
Tommy and Violet Jang, San Francisco
Harry Jew, San Francisco
Irene Jue, Los Angeles
Frank and Mabel Jung, San Francisco
Mary Jung, Los Angeles
Wing and Naomi Jung, San Francisco
John and Mamie Kai, Tucson
Suzanne Joe Kai and Herbert Kai, Tucson
Herbert and Peggy King, Houston
Yuri Kochiyama, New York
Clement Kong, Sacramento
Janet Kwai, San Francisco
Wilfred and Peggy Kwok, Houston
Gladys Kum, Honolulu
Him Mark Lai, San Francisco
Emilie Lau, Sacramento
Gordon Lau, San Francisco
Dora Fugh Lee, Bethesda, MD
George Lee, San Francisco
Shu-Wong Samuel Lee, Houston
Gilbert Leong, Los Angeles
Ken Lew, Houston
Hugh Liang, Washington D.C.
Kenneth and Ida Lim, Seattle
Wally Lim, San Francisco
Wing Yen Lim, Tucson
Ben-chieh Liu, Kansas City, MO
Katie Lo, San Francisco
Paul Louie, Los Angeles
Russ Lowe, San Francisco
Harold Lui, New York
Beverly Lum, Honolulu
Shirley Lum, Honolulu
Albert and Mae Mark, Seattle

Shelley Mark, Honolulu
Terese Mark, Seattle
Dottie Mun, New York
Franklin Ng, Fresno
Wong Shee Ong, San Francisco
Wei Chi Poon, Berkeley
Beulah Quo, Los Angeles
Jim and Lily Quock, San Francisco
Bob Santos, Seattle
Lanson Shum, Philadelphia
Mary Wong Shem, Houston
Theresa Sun, Los Angeles
Barbara Takei, Sacramento
Tom Tam, New York
Esther Don Tang, Tucson
Pam Tau, San Francisco
Donald and Sylvia Tsai, Potomac, MD
Pauline Tsui, Washington D.C.
Olia Wang, New York
Bonnie Wong, New York
Diane Wong, Seattle
Mary Ann Wong, Houston
Edward and Emily Wong, Houston
H. K. Wong, San Francisco
Martha Wong, Houston
Pat Wong, New York
Rita Wong, Seattle
Shawn Wong, Seattle
Stephanie and Truman Wong, San Francisco
Wong Shee Gong, Houston
George Woo, San Francisco
John Woo, New York
Wesley Woo, San Francisco
Rose Wu, San Antonio
Esther Yao, Houston
Amy Yee, Seattle
Benny Yee, Los Angeles
Dan Yee, Los Angeles
"T. J." Yee, Weehawken, NJ
Jim Yoshimoto, Chicago
Al Young, Seattle
Doug Young, Honolulu
Liz Young, New York
Connie Young Yu, San Francisco

Institutions

Alaska Historical Library
Arizona Historical Society
Asian American Legal Defense and Education Fund
Asian Women United, Inc.
Atlanta Historical Society
Basement Workshop
Bishop Museum
Bostonian Society
California Historical Society
California State Library, Sacramento
Cameron House

Carnegie Library of Pittsburg
Chicago Historical Society
Chinatown Health Clinic
Chinatown Planning Council
Chinatown Resource Development Center
Chinese Cultural Foundation
Chinese Historical Society
Chinese Newcomers Service
Colorado Historical Society
Denver Public Library
Hawaii Chinese History Center
Hawaii State Archives
Historical New Orleans Collection
Historical Society of Pennsylvania
Idaho State Historical Society
Institute of Texan Cultures
Inter*Im
Kansas City Public Library
Library of Congress
Minnesota Historical Society
Missouri Historical Society
Montana Historical Society
Museum of City of New York
National Archives
National Maritime Museum Association
Nebraska State Historical Society
Nevada Historical Society
Nevada State Historical Society
Nevada State Museum
New York Historical Society
New York Public Library
Northeastern Nevada Museum
Oregon Historical Society
Peabody Museum
Ping Yuen Tenants Association
Radcliff College
Research Reports
Seattle Historical Society
Smith College Women's History Archives
Southern Oregon Historical Society
Southern Pacific Transportation Company
State Historical Society of Wisconsin
State of Alabama, Department of Archives and History
University of California, Asian American Studies Library, Berkeley
University of California, Asian American Studies Library, Los Angeles
University of Washington, Suzzallo Library
Visual Communications
Washington State Historical Society
Wells Fargo Bank
Wing Luke Museum
Wyoming State Archives Museum

Books

Allen, Leonard, and Paul K. T. Sih, eds., *The Chinese in America.* St. John University Press: New York, 1976.

Barth, Gunther, *Bitter Strength: A History of the Chinese in the United States, 1850–1870.* Harvard University Press: Cambridge, MA, 1964.

Bastid, Marianne, Marie-Claire Bergere and Jean Chesneaux, *China from the Opium War to the 1911 Revolution.* Pantheon Books, Inc.: New York, 1976.

Chang, Melvin, *History of the Chinese in Hawaii.* Foundation for History and Humanities: Honolulu, 1973.

Char, Tin-Yuke, *The Sandalwood Mountains: Readings and Stories of the Early Chinese in Hawaii.* University Press of Hawaii: Honolulu, 1975.

Chen, Ji Ying, *Hua Yi Jin Zhou,* or *Overseas Chinese: The Splendid People.* Earth Publishing Co., Ltd.: Taipei, 1964. (Chinese language)

Chin, Art and Doug. *Uphill: The Settlement and Diffusion of the Chinese in Seattle.* Shorey Publishers: Seattle, 1973.

Chin, Leslie, *History of Chinese Americans in Baltimore.* The Greater Baltimore Chinese Americans Bicentennial Committee: Baltimore, 1976.

Chinese American Workers' Past and Present. Getting Together: San Francisco, 1970.

Chinn, Thomas W., H. Mark Lai and Philip Choy, eds., *A History of the Chinese in California: A Syllabus.* Chinese Historical Society of America: San Francisco, 1969.

Chiu, Ping, *Chinese Labor in California: 1850–1880.* University of Wisconsin: Madison, 1963.

Collier, Joseph, ed., *American Ethnics and Minorities.* Hwang Publishing Co., Los Alamitos, CA, 1978.

Coolidge, Mary Roberts, *Chinese Immigration.* Henry Holt and Co.: New York, 1909.

Craig, Albert, John K. Fairbank, and Edwin O. Reischauer, *East Asia: Tradition and Transformation.* Houghton Mifflin Company: Boston, 1973.

Daniels, Roger, ed., *Anti-Chinese Violence in North America.* Arno Press: New York, 1979.

Dicker, Laverne Mau, *The Chinese in San Francisco: A Pictorial History.* Dover Publications, Inc.: New York, 1979.

Dillon, Richard H., *The Hatchetmen: The Story of the Tong Wars in San Francisco's Chinatown.* Coward-McCann & Geoghegan: New York, 1962.

Edson, Christopher H., *The Chinese in Eastern Oregon: 1860–1890.* R and E Research Associates: San Francisco, 1971.

Fuchs, Lawrence H., *Hawaii Pono: A Social History.* Harcourt Brace Jovanovich, Inc.: New York, 1961.

Gee, Emma et al., eds., *Counterpoint: Perspectives on Asian America.* University of California Press: Los Angeles, 1976.

Genthe, Arnold, and Will Irwin, *Pictures of Old Chinatown.* Moffat, Yard and Co.: New York, 1908.

Glick, Carl, *Shake Hands with the Dragon.* McGraw-Hill Book Company: New York, 1941.

Hittell, John S., *The Commerce and Industry of the Pacific Coast of North America.* San Francisco: 1882.

Ho, Nelson Chia-Chi, *Portland's Chinatown: The History of an Urban Ethnic District.* Bureau of Planning: Portland, OR, 1978.

Hoexter, Corinne K., *From Canton to California: The Epic of Chinese Immigration.* Four Winds Press: New York, 1974.

Hom, Gloria Sun, *Chinese Argonauts: An Anthology of the Chinese Contributions to the Historical Development of Santa Clara County.* Foothill Community College: Foothill, CA, 1971.

Hsu, Francis L. K., *Americans and Chinese: Reflections on Two Cultures and Their People.* Doubleday and Co, Inc.: New York, 1970.

Hsu, Francis, *The Challenge of the American Dream: The Chinese in the United States.* Wadsworth Publishing Co., Inc.: Belmont, CA, 1971.

Jacobs, Paul and Saul Landau, *To Serve the Devil: Vol: II, Colonials and Sojourners.* Vintage Books: New York, 1971.

Kung, Shien Woo, *Chinese in American Life: Some Aspects of Their History, Status, Problems and Contributions.* Greenwood Press, Inc.: Westport, CN, reprint 1973.

Kuo, Chia-ling, *Social and Political Change in New York's Chinatown: The Role of Voluntary Associations.* Praeger Publishers, Inc.: New York, 1977.

Lai, Him Mark and Philip Choy, *Outlines: History of the Chinese in America.* Chinese American Studies Planning Group: San Francisco, 1971.

Lai, Him Mark, and Karl Lo, *Chinese Newspapers Published in North America, 1854–1975.* Association of Research Libraries: Washington D.C., 1976.

Lai, Him Mark, Genny Lim, and Judy Yung, *Island: Poetry and History of Chinese Immigrants on Angel Island, 1910–1940.* HOC DOI: San Francisco, 1980.

Lai, Him Mark, Joe Huang and Don Wong, *The Chinese in America, 1785–1980: An Illustrated History and Catalogue of the Exhibition.* Chinese Cultural Foundation: San Francisco, 1979.

Lan, Dean, *Prestige with Limitations: Realities of the Chinese American Elite.* R and E Research Associates: San Francisco, 1976.

Lee, Rose Hum, *The Chinese in the United States of America.* Hong Kong University Press: Hong Kong, 1960.

Lee, C. Y., *Days of the Tong Wars: California, 1847–1896.* Ballantine Books: New York, 1974.

Loewen, James W., *Mississippi Chinese: Between Black and White.* Harvard University Press: Cambridge, 1971.

Logan, Lorna E., *Ventures in Mission: The Cameron House Story.* Crawford Hobby Print Shop: San Francisco, 1971.

Lyndon, Edward C., *The Anti-Chinese Movement in the Hawaiian Kingdom: 1852–1886.* R and E Research Associates: San Francisco, 1977.

Mark, Diane, *The Chinese in Kula: Recollections of a Farming Community in Old Hawaii.* Hawaii Chinese History Center: Honolulu, 1975.

Martin, Mildred Crowl, *Chinatown's Angry Angel: The Story of Donaldina Cameron.* Pacific Books: Palo Alto, 1977.

McClellan, Robert, *The Heathen Chinese: A Study of American Attitudes Toward China: 1890–1905.* Ohio State University Press: Columbus, 1971.

McLeod, Alexander, *Pigtails and Gold Dust.* The Caxton Printers Ltd.: Caldwell, ID, 1948.

McWilliams, Carey, *Brothers Under the Skin.* Little, Brown and Co.: Boston, 1964.

McWilliams, Carey, *Factories in the Field.* Peregrin Publishers, Inc.: . Santa Barbara, CA, 1971.

Melendy, Howard Brett, *The Oriental Americans.* Hippocrene Books, Inc.: New York, 1972.

Miller, Stuart, *The Unwelcome Immigrant: The American Image of the Chinese, 1785–1822.* University of California Press, Los Angeles, 1969.

Nee, Victor and Brett, *Long Time Californ': A Documentary Study of an American Chinatown.* Houghton Mifflin Company: Boston, 1974.

Odo, Franklin et al., eds., *Roots: An Asian American Reader.* University of California Press: Los Angeles, 1971.

Odo, Franklin et al., *In Movement: A Pictorial History of Asian America.* Visual Communications/Asian American Studies Central, Inc.: Los Angeles, 1977.

Orientals and Their Cultural Adjustment. Fisk University: Nashville, 1946.

Patterson, James T., *America in the Twentieth Century.* Harcourt Brace Jovanovich, Inc.: New York, 1976.

Riggs, Fred W., *A Study of the Repeal of Chinese Exclusion.* Greenwood Press, Inc.: Westport, CN, reprint, 1972.

Sandmeyer, Elmer Clarence, *The Anti-Chinese Movement in California.* University of Illinois Press: Urbana, 1939.

Saxton, Alexander, *The Indispensable Enemy: Labor and the Anti-Chinese Movement in California.* University of California Press: Berkeley, 1971.

Schmitt, Robert, *Demographic Statistics of Hawaii: 1778–1965.* Honolulu, 1966.

Sen, I-Yao, *A Century of Chinese Exclusion Abroad.* Hong Kong: 1970. (Chinese language)

Shad, Liang Chi, *The Changing Size and Changing Character of Chinese Immigration to the United States.* Institute of Humanities and Social Sciences, Nanyang University: Singapore, 1976.

Sharman, Lyon, *Sun Yat-Sen, His Life and its Meaning: A Critical Biography.* Stanford University Press: Stanford, 1934.

Sparks, Theresa, *China Gold.* Academy Library Guild: Fresno, CA, 1954.

Steiner, Stan, *Fusang: The Chinese Who Built America.* Harper and Row Publishers, Inc.: New York, 1979.

Sue, Stanley, and Nathaniel Wagner, eds., *Asian Americans: Psychological Perspectives.* Science and Behavior Books, Inc.: Ben Lomond, CA, 1973.

Sue, Stanley, Nathaniel Wagner and Russell Endo., eds., *Asian Americans: Social and Psychological Perspectives.* Vol: II. Science and Behavior Books, Inc.: Ben Lomond, CA, 1980.

Sun, Zhen Tao, *Short History of Overseas Chinese in America.* Taiwan: 1962. (Chinese language).

Sung, Betty Lee, *Chinese American Manpower and Employment.* U.S. Department of Labor, Manpower Administration: Washington D.C., 1975.

Sung, Betty Lee, *Statistical Profile of the Chinese in the United States, 1970 Census.* U.S. Department of Labor: Washington D.C., 1975.

Sung, Betty Lee, *Mountain of Gold: The Story of the Chinese in America.* The Macmillan Company: New York, 1967.

Tung, William, *Chinese in America: 1820–1973.* Oceana Publications, Inc.: New York, 1974.

Wei Min She Labor Committee, *A Pictorial History of Chinese Working People in America.* United Front Press: San Francisco, 1974.

Williams, Stephen, *The Chinese in California Mines, 1848–1860.* R and E Research Associates: San Francisco, 1971.

Wilson, Carole Green, *Chinatown Quest: One Hundred Years of Donaldina Cameron House.* California Historical Society: San Francisco, 1974.

Wong, Eugene Franklin, *On Visual Media Racism: Asians in the American Motion Pictures,* Arno Press: New York, 1979.

Wong, James, *Aspirations and Frustrations of the Chinese Youth in the San Francisco Bay Area: Aspirations Upon the Societal Scheme.* R and E Research Associates: San Francisco, 1977.

Wong Sam and Associates, *An English-Chinese Phrase Book.* Cubery and Co.: San Francisco, 1875.

Wu, Cheng-Tsu, ed., *Chink! Evidence of Anti-Chinese Prejudice Pervading our Country.* New American Library: New York, 1972.

Wu, Yuan-li, *The Economic Condition of Chinese Americans.* Pacific Asian American Mental Health Research Center: Chicago, 1980.

Zee-Cheng, Robert, *Development and Contributions of a Silent Minority: The Chinese in the Greater Kansas City Area.* Chinese in the Greater Kansas Area: Kansas City, 1975.

Novels, Poetry, Autobiographies and Anthologies

Asian American Women, Stanford University Asian American Students, Palo Alto, 1976.

Asian Women, Asian Women's Journal Staff, Berkeley, 1971.

Asian Writers Project, *Sojourner IV.* Berkeley Unified School District: Berkeley, 1974.

Berssenbrugge, Mei-mei, *Random Possession.* Ishmael Reed Books: New York, 1979.

Chang, Diana, *A Passion for Life.* Random House, Inc.: New York, 1961.

Chang, Diana, *The Frontiers of Love.* Random House., Inc.: New York, 1956.

Char, Tin-Yuke, *The Bamboo Path: Life and Writings of a Chinese in Hawaii.* Hawaii Chinese History Center: Honolulu, 1977.

Chiang, Fay, *In the City of Contradictions.* Sunbury Press: New York, 1979.

Chiang, Fay; Helen Wong Huie; Jason Hwang; Richard Oyama; and Susan Yung, *American Born and Foreign.* Sunbury Press, New York, 1979.

Chin, Frank, et al., eds., *AIIIEEEEE! An Anthology of Asian American Writers.* Doubleday and Co.,: New York, 1975, originally published by Howard University Press, 1975.

Chin, Frank, "Confessions of the Chinatown Cowboy," *Bulletin of Concerned Asian Scholars,* IV 3 (Fall, 1972), 58–70.

Chock, Eric; Darrell Lum; Gail Miyasaki; Dave Robb; Frank Stewart; and Kathy Uchida, eds., *Talk Story: An Anthology of Hawaii's Local Writers.* Petronium Press: Honolulu, 1978.

Chu, Louis, *Eat a Bowl of Tea.* University of Washington Press: Seattle, 1979; originally pub. by Lyle Stewart: New York, 1961.

Harvey, Nick., ed., *Ting: The Caldron: Chinese Art and Identity in San Francisco.* Glide Urban Center: San Francisco, 1970.

Hsu, Kai-yu and Helen Palubinskas, *Asian American Authors.* Houghton Mifflin Co.: Boston, 1972.

Huie, Kin, *Reminiscences.* San Yu Press: New York, 1932.

Kingston, Maxine Hong, *The Woman Warrior: Memoirs of a Girlhood Among Ghosts.* Alfred A. Knopf, Inc.: New York, 1976.

Kingston, Maxine Hong, *China Men.* Alfred A. Knopf, Inc.: New York, 1980.

Lee, Ching Yang, *Flower Drum Song.* Farrar, Straus & Girious, Inc.: New York, 1957.

Leong, George, *A Lone Bamboo Doesn't Come from Jackson St.,* Isthmus Press: San Francisco, 1977.

Leong, Monfoon, *Number One Son.* East/West Publishing Co.: San Francisco, 1975.

Li, Ling Ai, *Life is For a Long Time.* Hastings House: New York, 1972.

Lin, Yutang, *Chinatown Family.* The John Day Co.: New York, 1948.

Ordinary Women: An Anthology of Poetry by New York City Women. Ordinary Women Books: New York, 1979.

Reed, Ishmael, proj. dir., *Calafia: The California Poetry.* Yardbird Books: Berkeley, 1979.

Telemaque, Eleanor Wong, *It's Crazy to Stay Chinese in Minnesota.* Thomas Nelson, Inc.: New York, 1978.

Ward, David Hsin-Fu, *Asian American Heritage: An Anthology of Prose and Poetry.* Washington Square Press: New York, 1974.

Wong, Jade Snow, *Fifth Chinese Daughter.* Harper and Row Publishers, Inc.: New York, 1945.

Wong, Nellie, *Dreams in Harrison Railroad Park.* Kelsey St. Press: 1977.

Wong, Shawn, *Homebase.* I Reed Books: New York, 1979.

Wong, Shawn and Frank Chin, eds., *Yardbird Reader.* Vo. III. Yardbird Publishing, Inc.: Berkeley, 1974.

Yellow Pearl. Basement Workshop, Inc.: New York, 1972.

Yep, Lawrence, *Child of the Owl.* Harper and Row Publishers, Inc.: New York, 1972.

Yep, Lawrence, *Dragonwings.* Harper and Row Publishers, Inc.: New York, 1976.

Young, Alida E., *Land of the Iron Dragon.* Doubleday Publishing Company: New York, 1978.

Young, Nancy Foon and Judy R. Parrish, eds., *MONTAGE: An Ethnic History of Women in Hawaii.* General Assistance Center for the Pacific: Honolulu, 1977.

Yung, Wing, *My Life in China and America.* Henry Holt & Co.: New York, 1908.

Articles

"Alien Land Bill Heard." *The Light,* March 10, 1937 (Austin, TX).

"America's Chinatowns Feel Shock Waves." *U.S. News and World Report,* March 5, 1979.

Asbury, Herbert, "Doyer Street." *The American Mercury,* VII, 30 (June, 1926).

Beattie, Edward, "China Joe." *Alaska Sportsman,* September 1949.

Buck, Rinker, "The New Sweatshops: A Penny for Your Collar." *New York Magazine,* January 29, 1979.

Chan, Doug, "Asian Americans Leave the Seventies: A Decade Round Up, "*The San Francisco Journal,* January 2, 1980.

Chan, Kit Mui L., "The Chinese Americans in the Mississippi Delta." *Journal of Mississippi History,* XXXV, I (1973).

"Chinatown Seeks Solution to Troubles with Police." *Chinatown News,* I., May 24, 1975.

"Chinese Women Protest Bill to Bar their Race." *Dallas Morning News,* March 9, 1937.

Chu, George, "Chinatowns in the Delta: The Chinese in the Sacramento/San Joaquin Delta." *California Historical Society Quarterly,* XLV (1960).

Cleveland, David, "Choo San Goh's Dynamic Challenge to Dance," *Dancemagazine,* July, 1980.

Davidson, Marshall B., "New York City and the China Trade Years, 1784–1860." *Seaport,* (Summer 1980).

Dillon, Richard H. "China Camp: Cathay in Eldorado." *The Chinese in California Series,* Book Club of California: San Francisco, 1972.

Finnigan, Joe, "Oriental and Eurasian Actors in Midst of Hollywood Boom." *Morning Telegraph,* April 18, 1961.

Foster, John, "The Chinese Boycott." *Atlantic Monthly,* January, 1906.

George, Brian T., "The State Department and Sun Yat Sen: American Policy and the Revolution Disintegration of China, 1920–1924." *Pacific Historical Review,* XLVI, (August, 1977).

Hall, John Philip, "The Knights of St. Crispin in Massachusetts, 1869–1878," *Journal of Economic History,* XVII, (June 1958).

Haynor, Norman S., and Charles Reynolds, "Chinese Family Life in America." *American Sociological Review,* II, 5, (October, 1937).

Heywood, Herbert, "China in New England." *New England Magazine,* XXVII, June, 1903.

Hibben, John Grier, "The Chinese Student in America." *North American Review,* (January, 1912).

Hill, Herbert, "Anti-Oriental Agitation and the Rise of Working Class Racism." *Society*, January/February, 1973.

Hirata, Lucie Cheng, "Free, Indentured, Enslaved: Chinese Prostitutes in Nineteenth Century America." *Signs: Journal of Women in Culture and Society*, V, I, (Autumn, 1979).

Hoy, William, "Native Festivals of the California Chinese." *Western Folklore*, VIII, July, 1948.

Jacobson, Mark, "New York's Other Mafia." *The Village Voice*, January 31, 1977.

Jacobson, Mark, "Nicky Louie's Mean Streets: Tongs Strike Back in Chinatown." *The Village Voice*, February 7, 1977.

Jones, Idwall, "Cathay on the Coast." *The American Mercury*, VII, 32, August 1926.

Karlin, Jules Alexander, "The Anti-Chinese Outbreak in Tacoma, 1885." *Pacific Historical Review*, XXIII, (August 1954).

Kwoh, Beulah Ong, "The Occupational Status of American-born Chinese Male College Graduates." *American Journal of Sociology*, LIII, 3, (November, 1947).

Larson, Robert, "Was America the Wonderful Land of Fusang?" *American Heritage* XVII, 3, April, 1966.

Lee, Rose Hum, "Chinese in the United States Today: The War Has Changed Their Lives."*Survey Graphic*, XXXI (October, 1942).

Lee, Rose Hum, "Social Institutions of a Rocky Mountain Chinatown." *Social Forces*, XXVII, (October, 1948).

Lee, Rose Hum, "Stranded Chinese Students in the United States." *Phylon*, XIX, 2, (Summer, 1958).

Lindsey, David, "Cathay Comes to El Dorado." *American History Illustrated*, July, 1975.

Mark, Shelley, "Something to Fight For." *East Wind*, Seattle, 1946.

Mason, William, "The Chinese in Los Angeles." *Los Angeles County Museum of Natural History Quarterly*, VI, 2, Fall, 1967.

Milloy, Ross, "Vietnam Fallout in a Texas Town." *The New York Times Magazine*, April 6, 1980.

Murphey, Rhoads, "Boston's Chinatown," *Economic Geography*, XXVIII, (July, 1952).

Neustadt, David, "They Also Serve: Waitering, A Changing Union and Chinatown Struggles." *The Village Voice*, May, 18, 1980.

O'Brien, Robert, "Status of Chinese in the Mississippi Delta." *Social Forces*, XIX (March, 1941).

Olmstead, Roger, "The Chinese Must Go." *California Historical Quarterly*, L, 3, September 1971.

Ourada, Patricia, "The Chinese in Colorado." *Colorado Magazine*, XXIX, 4, April, 1952.

Owens, Kenneth, "Pierce City Incident, 1885-1886." *Idaho Yesterday*, Fall, 1959.

Quinn, Larry, "Chink Chink Chinaman: Beginning of Nativism in Montana." *Pacific Northwest Quarterly*, LVII, 2, April, 1967.

Raushenbush, Winifred, "The Great Walls of Chinatown," *The Survey*, LVI, 3, May 1, 1926.

Rhoads, Edward J. M., "The Chinese in Texas." *Southwestern Historical Quarterly*, LXXXI, 1, July, 1977.

Runner, George T., "Chinese Influence in the Development of the Western United States." *The Annals of the American Academy*, (November 30, 1930).

"Self Help: Jimmy Yen's Proven Aid for Developing Nations." reprint from *The Reader's Digest*, October, 1961.

Spier, Robert, "Food Habits of Nineteenth Century California Chinese," *California Historical Society Quarterly*, XXVII, March and June, 1958.

"Success Story of One Minority Group in the United States." *U.S. News and World Report*, December 26, 1966.

Tipton, Gary P., "Men Out of China: Origins of the Chinese Colony in Phoenix." *Journal of American History*, (Autumn, 1977).

Watson, Douglas, "Did the Chinese Discover America?" *California Historical Quarterly*, XIV, March, 1935.

Wey, Nancy, "Fiddletown's Chinese Past." *California Living Magazine*, July, 29, 1979.

Wolfe, Tom, "The New Yellow Peril." *Esquire*, LXXIII, 6, December, 1969.

Wortman, Roy, "Denver's Anti-Chinese Riot, 1880." *The Colorado Magazine*, XLII, Fall, 1965.

Yee, Min, "Chinatown in Crisis." *Newsweek*. February 23, 1970.

Yuan, D. Y., "Chinatown and Beyond: The Chinese Population in Metropolitan New York." *Phylon*, (Winter, 1966).

Journals, Newspapers and Periodicals

Amerasia Journal, Los Angeles
Asian American Review, Berkeley
Bridge Magazine, New York
Bulletin of Concerned Asian Scholars, Special Issue on Asian Americans IV, 3 (1972)
California Historical Society Quarterly, Special Issue, Chinese in California, LVII, 1. (Spring, 1978).
East West
Getting Together
Honolulu Star Bulletin
International Examiner
Journal of Social Issues, Special Asian American Edition
Neighborhood: The Journal for City Preservation, Special Issue on Chinatown I, 3 (December, 1978).
The San Francisco Journal
Wei Min Bao

Dissertations, Papers, Proceedings, Reports

BeDunnah, Gary R., "A History of the Chinese in Nevada, 1855-1904." Unpublished dissertation, University of Nevada, 1966.

Chih, Ginger, "Immigration of Chinese Women into the United States, 1900–1940." Unpublished thesis, Sarah Lawrence College, 1977.

Chin, James Wilbur, "Problems of Assimilation and Cultural Pluralism Among Chinese-Americans in San Francisco: An Exploratory Study." Unpublished dissertation, University of the Pacific, 1965.

Chinatown Report, Chinatown Study Group, New York, 1969.

Civil Rights Issues of Asian and Pacific Americans: Myths and Realities. United States Commission on Civil Rights, 1979.

Courtney, William, "San Francisco's Anti-Chinese Ordinances; 1850–1900." Unpublished dissertation, University of San Francisco, 1956.

The Life, Influence and Role of the Chinese in the United States, 1776–1960. Proceeding Papers of the National Conference on Chinese Americans held at the University of San Francisco, July 1975. Chinese Historical Society, San Francisco, 1976.

Loo, Chalsa, and Connie Young Yu, *Chinatown: Recording Reality: Destroying Myths.* Chinatown Housing and Health Research Project, Santa Cruz, CA, 1980.

Lott, Juanita Tamayo, and Canta Pian, *Beyond Stereotypes and Statistics: Emergence of Asian and Pacific American Women.* Organization of Pan Asian Women: Washington D.C., 1979.

Manhattan Bridge Area Study, *Chinatown.* New York City Planning Commission: 1979.

Mei, June Y., "The Social Structure of San Francisco Chinatown, 1848–1906." Asian American Labor History Conference. University of California, Los Angeles, 1978.

New York State Advisory Committee, *The Forgotten Minority: Asian Americans in New York City.* Government Printing Office, Washington D.C., 1977.

Nicholson, John, "The Chinese in Nineteenth Century Arizona: Some Aspects of Anglo-Chinese Relations, a Preliminary Study," paper presented to the Western History Association, Santa Fe, Oct. 1971.

Ohnuki, Emiko, "The Detroit Chinese: A Study of Socio-Cultural Changes in the Detroit Chinese Community from 1872–1963." Unpublished dissertation. University of Wisconsin, 1964.

Rapkin, Chester, "Chinatown Urban Renewal Workshop: Current Status of Two of America's Chinatowns, New York/Hawaii." National Association of Housing and Redevelopment, 1971.

A Study of Selected Socio-Economic Characteristics of Ethnic Minorities Based on the 1970 Census; Vol: II, *Asian Americans.* Urban Associates, Inc. for U.S. Department of Health, Education and Welfare: Government Printing Office, Washington, D.C., 1971. Canta Pian, author.

Wong, Arthur, Y., with Laureen Wong and Nani Mark, "Historical Analysis and Economic Outlook of Chinese in Hawaii." Hawaii Chinese History Center, 1974.

Index